PRACTICAL Manual

PHYSICAL EDUCATION

CBSE Class XI

Author
Priyanshu Pal

Name...

Class......................... Section......................... Roll No.......................

School...

Arihant Prakashan (School Division Series)

Arihant Prakashan (School Division Series)

卐 Administrative & Production Offices

Regd. Office
'Ramchhaya' 4577/15, Agarwal Road, Darya Ganj, New Delhi -110002
Tele: 011- 47630600, 43518550; Fax: 011- 23280316

Head Office
Kalindi, TP Nagar, Meerut (UP) - 250002, Tel: 0121-7156203, 7156204

卐 Sales & Support Offices
Agra, Ahmedabad, Bengaluru, Bareilly, Chennai, Delhi, Guwahati, Hyderabad, Jaipur, Jhansi, Kolkata, Lucknow, Nagpur & Pune

卐 **Price :** ₹375.00

卐 **PO No. :** TXT-29-T071331-6-26

Published by Arihant Publications (India) Ltd.

For further information about the books from Arihant, log on to **www.arihantbooks.com** or email to **info@arihantbooks.com**

Follow us on

Contents

PHYSICAL FITNESS TESTS

TEAM GAMES

TEAM GAMES (CWSN)

Syllabus

GUIDELINES FOR INTERNAL ASSESSMENT
(PROJECTS)

PRACTICAL	(Max. Marks 30)
Physical Fitness Test: SAI Khelo India Test, Brockport Physical Fitness Test (BPFT)*	6 Marks
Proficiency in Games and Sports (Skill of any one IOA recognized Sport/Game of Choice)**	7 Marks
Yogic Practices	7 Marks
Record File ***	5 Marks
Viva Voce (Health/ Games & Sports/ Yoga)	5 Marks

*Test for CWSN (any 4 items out of 27 items. One item from each component: Aerobic Function, Body Composition, Muscular strength & Endurance, Range of Motion or Flexibility)

**CWSN (Children With Special Needs – Divyang): Bocce/Boccia , Sitting Volleyball, Wheelchair Basketball, Unified Badminton, Unified Basketball, Unified Football, Blind Cricket, Goalball, Floorball, Wheelchair Races and Throws, or any other Sport/Game of choice.

**Children with Special Needs can also opt any one Sport/Game from the list as alternative to Yogic Practices. However, the Sport/Game must be different from Test - 'Proficiency in Games and Sports'

Record File shall include:

Practical-1: Fitness tests administration. (SAI Khelo India Test)

Practical-2: Procedure for Asanas, Benefits & Contraindication for any two Asanas for each lifestyle disease.

Practical-3: Anyone one IOA recognized Sport/Game of choice. Labelled diagram of Field & Equipment. Also, mention its Rules, Terminologies & Skills.

INDEX

S.No.	Name of the Activity/Project	Page No.	Date	Remarks

INDEX

S.No.	Name of the Activity/Project	Page No.	Date	Remarks

INDEX

S.No.	Name of the Activity/Project	Page No.	Date	Remarks

PRACTICAL Manual

PHYSICAL EDUCATION

CERTIFICATE

This is to certify that Activities &
Projects recorded in this Practical Notebook
have been performed by ____________________
(Student's name)

of ________ of ______________________________
(class/section) (school name)

during academic session ____________________

....

Examiner's Signature | Principal's Signature (with school stamp) | Teacher's Signature

Physical Fitness Test : Sai Khelo India Test

Physical fitness refers to a general state of health and well-being and more specifically an individual's ability of participating in specific physical tasks, which require high level of effort. It is achieved through correct nutrition, moderate-vigorous physical exercise & activity and sufficient rest.

SAI (Sports Authority of India) Khelo India Fitness Test measures the ability and physical fitness of the children of age group 5-8 years and age group 9-18+ years.

Age Group: 5-8 Years/ Classes 1 to 3

Designed for Classes 1-3, this test calls for the children to acquire Fundamental Movement Skills (FMS), which provide the base for many physical activities including dancing, running and playing games. In most sports, Locomotor, Manipulative and Body Management abilities are of key importance and lead to success.

Following are the abilities of children in Classes 1-3 which need to be measured and tracked. These are important for controlling the body in various situations

- Body Composition (BMI)
- Balance (Flamingo Balance)
- Coordination (Plate Tapping)

Age Group: 9-18+ Years / Classes 4 to 12

Students of Classes 4-12 are required to have an overall physical fitness. The following components are to be considered in Physical Health and Fitness Profile.

- Body Composition (BMI)
- Strength
  - (a) Abdominal (Partial Curl-up)
  - (b) Muscular Endurance (Push Ups for Boys, Modified Push Ups for Girls)
- Flexibility (Sit and Reach Test)
- Cardiovascular Endurance (600 Meter Run/Walk)
- Speed (50 mt. Dash)

Test Description

The following are the Khelo India Fitness Tests which can be done in school

Body Composition (BMI)

Body Composition is tested by the BMI. It refers primarily to the distribution of muscle and fat in the body. Body size such as height, lengths and girths are also grouped under this category.

Body Mass index or BMI can be calculated by dividing the weight of a person (in kilograms) by the square of their height (in meters).

Higher BMI indicates higher fat content in a body. Thus,

$$BMI = W/H^2$$

where, W = body weight in kilograms and H = height in meters

Equipment Required

- Flat and clean surface
- Weighing Machine
- Stadiometer/Measuring Tape pasted on a wall

Procedure

Measuring Height Accurately

- Remove obstacles like the participant's shoes and hair ornaments that can interfere with the measurement.
- Take the height measurement against a flat surface such as a wall with no molding.
- Have the participant stand with their feet flat, together and back against the wall. Check to see that their legs are straight, arms are at sides and shoulders are level.
- Make the participant look straight ahead and ensure that the line of sight is parallel with the floor.
- Take the measurement while the participant stands with head, shoulders, buttocks and heels touching the flat surface (wall). Depending on the overall body shape of the participant, all points may not touch the wall.
- Use a flat headpiece to form a right-angle with the wall and lower the headpiece until, it firmly touches the crown of the head.
- Make sure the measurer's eyes are at the same level as the headpiece.
- Lightly mark where the bottom of the headpiece meets the wall.
- Then, using a metal tape, measure from the base on the floor to the marked measurement on the wall to get the correct height measurement.
- Accurately record the height to the nearest 0.1 centimeter.

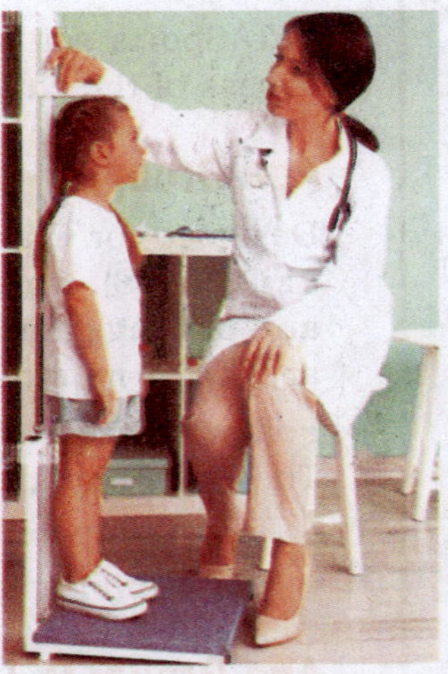

Measuring Height

Measuring Weight Accurately

- Use a digital scale. Place the scale on firm flooring such as tile or wood rather than carpet.
- Ask the participant to remove any bulky clothing, their shoes and any heavy object that they might be carrying.
- Have the participant stand with both feet in the center of the scale.
- Record the weight to the nearest decimal fraction e.g. 30.6 kilograms.

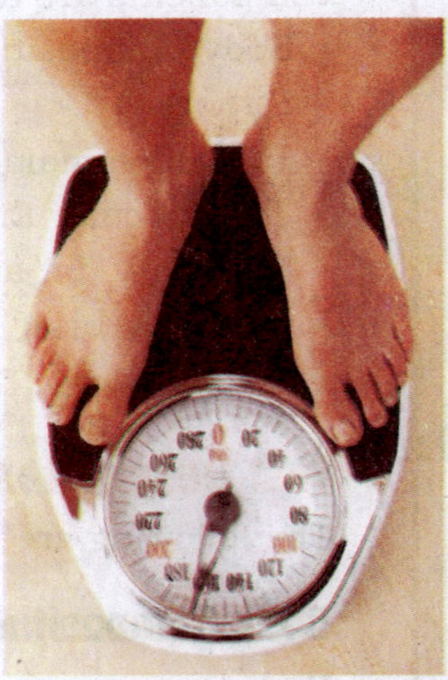

Measuring Weight

Scoring

A higher score typically indicates increased levels of body fat. Height will be recorded in centimeters (cm) and millimeters (mm). Weight will be recorded in kilograms (kg) and grams (g).

Use the table given below to determine your BMI category.

Category	Range
Underweight	Below 18.5
Healthy	18.5 - 24.9
Overweight	25.0 - 29.9
Obesity	30.0 and above

Plate Tapping Test (Class 1 to 3/Age group 5-8 years)

It measures the speed and the coordination of limb movement of children.

Equipment Required

- Table (adjustable height)
- Rectangle (30 x 20 cm)
- 2 yellow discs (20 cm diameter)
- Stopwatch

Procedure

- The table height should be adjusted so that the subject is standing comfortably in front of the discs. The two yellow discs are placed with their centers 60 cm apart on the table. The rectangle is placed between both discs.
- The non-preferred hand is placed on the rectangle. The subject moves the preferred hand back and forth between the discs over the hand in the middle as quickly as possible.
- This action is repeated for 25 full cycles (50 taps).

Plate Tapping Test

Scoring

- The time taken to complete 25 cycles is recorded.

Evaluation can be done by examiner by using a norms table as given below

	Excellent	Good	Average	Fair	Poor	Bad
Boys (Tapping Timing in sec.)	15	20	25	30	35	40
Girls (Tapping Timing in sec.)	15	20	25	30	35	40

Administrative Suggestions

- Participants should be encouraged to stand in a balanced posture with their feet apart to match the shoulder width.
- If the participant can maintain a constant pace, results are usually better.

Flamingo Balance Test (Class 1 to 3)

It measures a person's ability to balance successfully on a single leg. This test assesses the strength of the leg, pelvic and trunk muscle as well as static balance.

Equipment Required

- Non- slippery even surface
- Can be done on just standing on beam.
- Stopwatch

Procedure

- Stand on a beam and maintain balance by holding the instructor's hand (if required).
- While balancing on the preferred leg, the free leg is flexed at the knee and the foot of this leg held close to the buttocks.
- Start the watch as the instructor lets go of the participant/subject.
- Pause the stopwatch each time the subject loses balance.
- Resume over, again timing until they lose balance. Count the number of falls in 60 seconds of balancing.

Flamingo Balance Test

Scoring

- The total number of falls or loss of balance in 60 seconds of balancing is recorded.
- If there are more than 15 falls in the first 30 seconds, the test is terminated.

To evaluate the performance of participants, examiner can create own norms as given below

	Excellent	Good	Average	Fair	Poor	Bad
Boys Falls in 60 seconds (No.)	No fall	1 to 2 falls	3 to 5 falls	6 to 9 falls	10 to 12 falls	13 above
Girls Falls in 60 seconds (No.)	No fall	1 to 2 falls	3 to 5 falls	6 to 9 falls	10 to 12 falls	13 above

Administrative Suggestion

- Participants should be encouraged to focus their eyes on a stationary object straight ahead.

Strength

(a) Abdominal: Partial Curl Up (30 seconds) (Class 4 to 12/Age group 9-10 years)

It measures abdominal muscular strength and endurance of the abdominals and hip flexors, which are important in back support and core stability.

Equipment Required

- Flat clean cushioned surface with two parallel strips (6 inches apart)
- Stopwatch
- Recording sheets
- Pen

Procedure

- The participant lies on a cushioned, flat, clean surface with their knees flexed at 90 degrees, with hands straight on the sides (palms facing downwards) closer to the ground, parallel to the body.
- The participant raises the trunk in a smooth motion, keeping the arms in position, curling up the desired amount (at least 6 inches above/along the ground towards the parallel strip).
- The trunk is lowered back to the floor, so that the shoulder blades or upper back touch the floor.

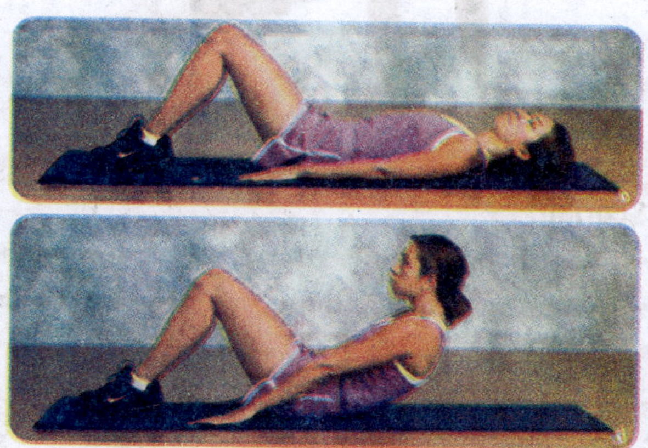

Partial Curl Up

Scoring

- Record the maximum number of curl ups in a certain time period of 30 seconds.

It can be evaluated by using the norms table. Examiner can also create own norms for evaluation like given below

	Excellent	Good	Average	Fair	Poor	Bad
Boys Partial Curl-ups (No.)	25	20	15	10	5	0
Girls Partial Curl-ups (No.)	20	15	10	5	3	0

Administrative Suggestions

- Participants should be encouraged to keep normal breathing rate.
- Results are usually better if the participant can maintain constant pace during the activity.

(b) Muscular Endurance : Push Ups (Boys)/Modified Push Ups (Girls) (For 9 to 18 years Age group)

- It measures upper body strength, endurance and trunk stability.

Equipment Required

- Flat clean cushioned surface or gym mat

Procedure

- Have the participant lie on a mat/cushioned surface with their body and legs in a straight, feet slightly apart, their arms at shoulder width apart, extended and at a right angle to the body. Only their hands and toes should touch the floor.
- Keeping the back and knees straight, the participant lowers the body to a predetermined point, to touch some other object or until there is a 90-degree angle at the elbows, then returns back to the starting position with the arms extended.
- This action is repeated and the test continues until exhaustion or until they can do no more in rhythm or have reached the target number of push-ups.

- **For Girls** Push-up technique is with their knees touching the ground instead of toes.

Push Ups (Boys)

Push Ups (Girls)

Scoring

- Record the number of correctly completed push ups.
- Evaluation can be done by examiner by using a norms table as given below

	Excellent	Good	Average	Fair	Poor	Bad
Boys Push-ups (No.)	50	40	30	20	10	0
Girls Push-ups (No.)	40	30	20	10	5	0

Administrative Suggestions

- Participants should be encouraged to keep the back straight.
- Results are usually better if the participant can maintain constant pace during the activity.

Flexibility : Sit and Reach (For 9 to 18 years Age group)

It measures the flexibility of the lower back and hamstring muscles. A good level of flexibility of the hamstrings and lower back is advocated as it plays a key role in health related fitness.

Equipment Required

- Sit and Reach box with dimensions 12″ x 12″ (sides), 12″ x 10″ (front and back), 12″ x 21″ (top), inscribe the top panel with cm/mm gradations.
- It is crucial that the vertical plane against which the participant's feet will be placed is exactly at the 23 cm mark.
- Flat clean cushioned surface or gym mat.

Procedure

- This test involves sitting on the floor with legs stretched out straight ahead. Participants should remove their shoes. The soles of the feet are placed flat against the Sit and Reach box. Both knees should be locked and pressed flat to the floor - the tester may assist by holding them down.
- With the palms facing downwards and the hands on top of each other, the subject reaches forward along the measuring line as far as possible.
- Ensure that the hands remain at the same level, not one reaching further forward than the other. After some practice reaches, the subject reaches out and holds that position for one-two seconds while the distance is recorded. Make sure that there are no jerky movements.

Sit and Reach

Scoring

- The score is recorded (difference between initial position and final position), in cm and mm, as the distance reached by the hand.

To evaluate the performance of participants examiner can create own norms as given below

	Excellent	Good	Average	Fair	Poor	Bad
Boys Sit and Reach (centimeters)	+20 cm	+15 cm	+10 cm	0 cm	-10 cm	-15 cm
Girls Sit and Reach (centimeters)	+20 cm	+15 cm	+10 cm	0 cm	-10 cm	-15 cm

Administrative Suggestions

- Proper warm-up and static stretching of the lower back and posterior thighs is integral.
- A partner placing his/her hands lightly across knees can prevent the flexing of knees.
- Keep the hands over each other (fish pose). Besides, in order to prevent the test apparatus from sliding away from the participants during the test, it should be placed against a wall or a similar immovable object.
- The test trial is repeated if
  - (i) The hands reach out unevenly or
  - (ii) The knees are flexed at the time of doing the test.

Cardiovascular Endurance: 600 Mtr Run/Walk

It measures cardiovascular fitness or cardiovascular endurance.

Equipment Required

- Stopwatch
- Whistle
- Marker cone
- Lime powder
- Measuring Tape, 200 or 400 mts with 1.22 mt (minimum 1 mt) width preferably on a flat and even playground with a marking of starting and finish line.

Procedure

- Participants are instructed to run 600 mts as fast as possible.
- The participants begin on signal 'Ready, Start'. As they cross the finish line, elapsed time should be announced to them.
- Walking is permitted but the objective is to cover the distance in the shortest possible time.

Scoring

- Time taken for completion (Run or walk) in min, sec.
- To evaluate the timing of participants examiner can create own norms for evaluation as given below

	Excellent	Good	Average	Fair	Poor	Bad
Boys Timing (min & sec.)	1:45 m/s	2:00 m/s	2:15 m/s	2:30 m/s	2:45 m/s	3:00 m/s
Girls Timing (min & sec.)	2:00 m/s	2:15 m/s	2:30 m/s	2:45 m/s	3:00 m/s	3:15 m/s

Administrative Suggestions

- Participants should be encouraged to practice running with emphasis placed on the concept of pace.
- Results are usually better if the participant can maintain constant pace during most of the run and perhaps use a strong closing effort.

50 Mtr Dash (Standing Start) (For 9 to 18 years Age Group)

It measures acceleration and speed.

Equipment Required

- Measuring tape or marked track
- Cone markers
- Stopwatch
- Flat and clear surface of at least 60 meters

Procedure

- Participants should be instructed to do a thorough warm up, including some practice starts and acceleration.
- Start from a stationary position, with one foot in front of the other. The front foot must be on or behind the starting line. This starting position should be static (dead start).
- The test administrator should provide hints for maximising speed (such as keeping low, driving hard with the arms and legs) and encourage to continue running hard through the finish line.

Scoring

The timing of the participants can be compared for evaluation. Examiner can also create own norms for evaluation as given below

	Excellent	Good	Average	Fair	Poor	Bad
Boys Timing (sec.& milli sec.)	6.5 (sec.)	7.5 (sec.)	8.5 (sec.)	9.5 (sec.)	10.5 (sec.)	11.5 (sec.)
Girls Timing (sec.& milli sec.)	8.0 (sec.)	9.0 (sec.)	10.5 (sec.)	11.5 (sec.)	12.5 (sec.)	13.5 (sec.)

Administrative Suggestions

- Participants should be encouraged to practice running with emphasis placed on the concept of pace.
- Results are usually better if the participant can maintain constant pace during most of the run and perhaps use a strong closing effort.

Do's and Dont's

Preparing for Assessments

To participate in Physical Fitness Assessments, some good preparation can go a long way.

1. It is recommended that the assessments are done twice a year (for Term I and Term II in each academic year). The minimum gap between tests should be 4 months.
2. Find out what is required. Most fitness tests will require a combination of evaluations to assess speed, endurance/stamina, strength, flexibility and body composition. Read about these tests and plan for the same.
3. Determine the current abilities. Pretend you are taking their test today and perform each exercise. Note how close they came to the goal and how much further they need to go.
4. Calculate the time you have to prepare. You need adequate time to prepare for the test.

5. Participants must pace themselves. Maintaining a constant tempo is crucial for completing long and repetitive exercises, like Curl-ups, Push-ups and 600 mt run/walk. If you work too fast at the beginning of the exercise, you may become fatigued quickly. It is more effective to maintain a steady pace throughout.
6. Participants should be encouraged to practice for few weeks with emphasis placed on the concept of pace. Results are usually better if the participant can maintain consistency in performance during this practice period.

Before a Test

Get Appropriate Clothing

1. Participant to wear comfortable clothes with sports shoes.
   (a) In case shoes are not available, he/she can run bare-feet. He/she needs to take precaution so that the foot doesn't get hurt with pointed objects in the playing fields.
   (b) Avoid leather shoes.
2. Get clothes that are comfortable to wear and run or bend (e.g. T-shirt and comfortable fitting trousers/half pants).
3. Wearing socks that will keep the feet dry.

Safety Measures

1. If you plan to do for a group of people, decide date/time when you want to do the test.
2. Ensure that the play field is flat and clear from stones/pointed objects that may injure children.
3. Ensure that the equipment required for the tests are available at the place where you want to do the tests.
4. Have a First Aid Box.

Medical

No participant with known medical problems are allowed to take part in the test.

Test	Resource Required
Body Composition (BMI)	1 test administrator, 1 recorder
Coordination (Plate Tapping Test)	1 test administrator, 1 recorder
Balance (Flamingo Balance Test)	1 test administrator, 1 recorder
Flexibility (Sit and Reach Test)	1 test administrator, 1 recorder
Strength-Core (Partial Curl-up)	1 test administrator, 1 recorder
Muscular Endurance (Push Ups for Boys, Modified Push Ups for Girls)	1 test administrator, 1 recorder
Cardiovascular Endurance (600 Mtr. Run/Walk)	1 person at start, 1 person for each lane at finish
Speed (50 Mtr. Dash)	1 person at start, 1 person for each lane at finish

Additional Volunteers: 1 per 20 participants, if you are doing for a larger group.

List of Equipments

Test	Equipment
Body Composition (BMI)	Height Measuring Tape, Weight Machine, Even and non-slippery hard surface
Strength Abdominal (Partial Curl-up)	Stopwatch, Gym/Yoga Mat, Marking Tape (for 6 inches parallel strips)
Muscular Endurance (Push Ups for Boys, Modified Push Ups for Girls)	Gym/Yoga Mat
Flexibility (Sit and Reach Test)	Sit and Reach Box (dimensions: 12′′ ×12′′ (sides) 12′′ ×10′′ (front and back) 12′′ ×21′′ (top). Inscribe the top panel with centimeter/mm gradations), Gym/Yoga Mat
Cardiovascular Endurance (600 mtr. Run/Walk)	200 or 400 mtr. with 1.22 mt (minimum 1 mt) width track marking of starting and finish line, Stopwatch (1 per lane)
Speed (50 mtr. Dash)	Stopwatch (1 per lane), cone markers, Marked track of at least 60 meters with 1.22 mt (minimum 1 mt) lane with starting and finish line
Coordination (Plate Tapping)	Table (adjustable height), 2 yellow discs (20 cm diameter), Rectangle (30×20 cm), Stopwatch
Balance (Flamingo Balance Test)	Stopwatch, beam locally procured of a standard brick shape and height

Test Conduct Procedure

1. Briefing to the participants:

a. Instruct for warm-up to avoid injury.

b. Test Demonstration: Provide demonstration of test procedure.

2. Steps:

a. Arrange the participants in the desired groups.

b. Tester reaches to the desired station.

c. Equipment to be placed at the station.

Viva-Voce

Q.1 What does BMI stand for?

Ans. BMI stands for Body Mass Index.

Q.2 Name any two components of physical fitness for children aged 5–8 years.

Ans. Coordination, Balance

Q.3 Which test measures speed and coordination of limb movement in young children?

Ans. Plate Tapping Test measures limb movement speed in young children.

Q.4 What is used to measure height during BMI assessment?

Ans. Stadiometer/Measuring Tape is used to measure height during BMI assessment.

Q.5 What does the Flamingo Balance Test assess?

Ans. The Flamingo Balance Test assesses Static balance.

Q.6 Which muscle group is tested by the Partial Curl-up?

Ans. The partial Curl-up tests the Abdominals muscle group.

Q.7 What is the main equipment needed for Sit and Reach Test?

Ans. The main equipment needed for the sit and Reach Test is a Sit and Reach Box.

Q.8 Which test measures cardiovascular endurance in students?

Ans. 600 Meter Run/Walk measures cardiovascular endurance in students.

Q.9 What is the standard duration for the Partial Curl-up test?

Ans. The standard duration for the partial Curl-up test is 30 seconds.

Q.10 How is weight recorded during the BMI test?

Ans. During the BMI, the weight is recorded kilograms (kg).

Q.11 What is the main objective of the 50 Meter Dash?

Ans. The main objective of the 50 Meter Dash is to measure speed and acceleration.

Q.12 Which test is performed differently for boys and girls in the 9–18 age group?

Ans. The Push-up/Modified Push-up test is performed differently for boys and girls.

Q.13 What is the minimum gap recommended between two fitness assessments?

Ans. A minimum gap of 4 months is recommended between two fitness assessments.

Q.14 What should participants avoid during the Sit and Reach Test?

Ans. During the sit and Reach test, participants should avoid Flexing knees.

Q.15 Which test is terminated if a participant loses balance more than 15 times in 30 seconds?

Ans. Flamingo Balance Test is terminated if a participant loses balance more than 15 times in 30 seconds.

Test 2

Brockport Physical Fitness Test (BPFT)

The Brockport Physical Fitness Test (BPFT) was developed by Dr. Joseph Winnick and Dr. Francis Short from the college at Brockport. It is a criterion-referenced tool for measuring health-related fitness. This means that the test scores are compared to established standard linked to good health. The approach use health aspects related to physical activity to set these standards which helps evaluate how well someone's fitness meets these health benchmarks.

Project Target

Between 1993 and 1998, the US Department of Education's Office of Special Education and Rehabilitative Services funded 'Project Target', a research study designed to develop a health-related, criterion-referenced physical fitness test for youngsters aged 10 to 17 with disabilities.

The project was entitled 'Project Target:

Criterion- Referenced Physical Fitness Standards for Adolescents with Disabilities'. It was centered at the State University of New York, College at Brockport.

Target Group

The Brockport Physical Fitness Test is designed for both able-bodied youngsters and those with disabilities such as mental retardation, spinal cord injuries cerebral palsy, blindness, congenital anomalies and amputation.

Tests

The BPFT includes 27 different test items that can be customised for nearly all students. The tests includes a mix of traditional fitness tests and tests specifically modified for youngsters with disabilities. These test items fall under three components of physical fitness.

- Aerobic functioning
- Body composition
- Musculoskeletal functioning

Aerobic Functioning

Aerobic functioning is a term that encompasses both aerobic capacity (maximum oxygen uptake) and aerobic behaviour (the ability to perform aerobic activity at specified levels of intensity and duration.

The tests for aerobic functioning are

- **Target Aerobic Movement Test** It tests the ability to sustain a moderate intensity of (any) physical activity by maintaining a heart rate between 70 and 85 percent of maximal predicted heart rate for 15 minutes.
- **One-mile Run/Walk** In this activity, the participant has to run or walk as fast as possible over a one-mile distance.

- **PACER Test (20 m or 15 m)** It is a maximal aerobic fitness test where participants run 20 m shuttles at increasing speeds. This is a modified version for vision impaired children.

Body Composition

Body composition provides an indication of the degree of leanness/fatness of the body.

The tests for body composition are

- **Skinfold Measures** This test estimates the percentage of body fat by measuring skinfold, thickness at specific parts in the body. Skinfold measurements are generally taken as specific sites on the right side of the body. These specific sites are triceps, subscapular and calf.
  - (a) *Triceps Skinfold* It is measured vertically on back of arm midway top shoulder point and elbow.
  - (b) *Calf Skinfold* It is measured inside of the right lower leg at the greatest calf girth.
  - (c) *Subscapular Skinfold* It is measured at the inferior angle of the right scapula.

  Calipers are used to measure the thickness of the skin at the triceps, subscapular and calf measurement sites.

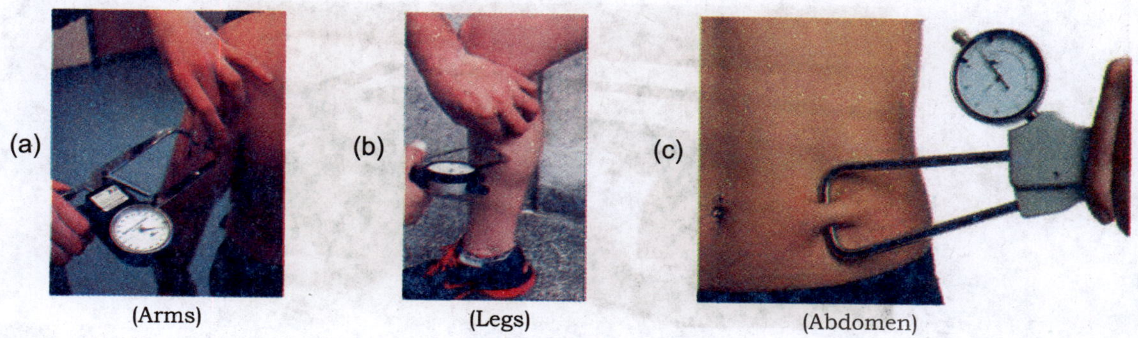

(a) (Arms) (b) (Legs) (c) (Abdomen)

Skinfold Measures

- **Body Mass Index** It is calculated by taking a person's weight and dividing it by their height squared.

$$\text{Body Mass Index} = \frac{\text{Weight (in kg)}}{\text{Height (in m}^2\text{)}}$$

Modified Body Mass Index (BMI) Measurement Guidelines

- *Height Measurement with Prosthetics/Braces* Measure the height of participants wearing prosthetic devices or braces while they are wearing these items.
- *Supine Height Measurement* Participants who cannot support their body weight in a standing position can lie on a mat while their body length is measured with a tape measure.
- *Height Measurement for Participants with Cerebral Palsy* For participants with cerebral palsy who cannot stand erect, measure body segments using a tape measure (i.e. floor to knee, knee to hip, hip to head) and sum these segments to determine the total body length for BMI calculation.
- *Weight Measurement with Prosthetics/Braces* Measure the weight of participants with prosthetic devices or braces either by removing these items or by subtracting their weight.
- *Weight Measurement for Wheelchair Users* For participants using a wheelchair, determine their weight by either taking them out of the wheelchair or weighing them in the wheelchair and then subtracting the wheelchair's weight.

- *Weight Measurement for Participants with Amputations or Congenital Anomalies* When weighing participants with amputations or congenital anomalies, take care when comparing with others or calculating BMI. For participants with leg amputations, adjust the weight as follows
  - Below-knee amputation: Add 1/8 of the body weight.
  - Above-knee amputation: Add 1/9 of the body weight.
  - Hip amputation: Add 1/6 of the body weight.
- *Bioelectrical Impedance Analysis* It measures the resistance of body tissues to the flow of a small electrical signal and from that the proportion of body fat is calculated.

Musculoskeletal Functioning

Musculoskeletal functioning is a component that combines measures of muscular strength, muscular endurance and flexibility/range of motion.

Strength/Endurance exercises and tests for musculoskeletal functioning are

- *Trunk Lift* While lying face down, lift the upper body off the floor as high as you can using the muscles of the back. This test is designed to measure trunk extension, strength and flexibility.

Trunk Lift

- *Grip Strength* A measure of hand and arm strength, using the dominant hand to grip a dynamometer with as much force as possible.

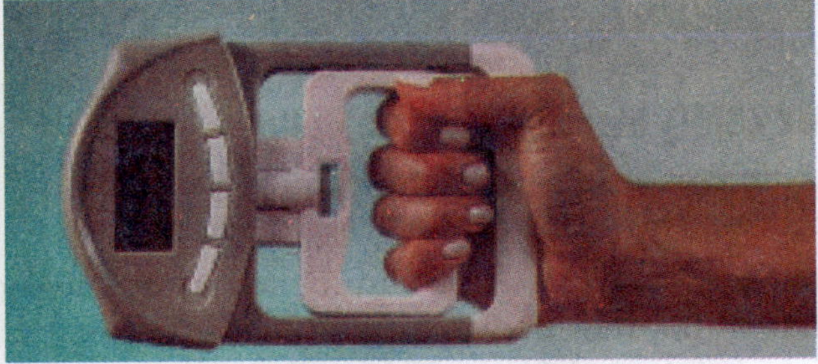

Grip Strength

- *Bench Press* Perform as many bench presses as possible using a 35lb (15.9kg) barbell. This test is designed to measure upper extremity, strength and endurance.

Bench Press

- ***Isometric Push-up*** Hold a raised push-up position for upto 40 seconds. This test is designed to measure upper body strength and endurance.

Isometric Push-up

- ***Push-up*** Complete as many push-ups as possible at a rate of 1 push-up every 3 seconds.
- ***Seated Push-up*** Extend the arms and raise the body out of a chair and hold this position for as long as possible.
- ***Dumbbell Press*** Lift a 15lb (6.8kg) dumbbell as many times as possible at a specific cadence while sitting on a chair.

Dumbbell Press

- ***Reverse Curl*** A measure of hand, wrist and arm strength. While sitting on a chair, the subject must perform one repetition of bringing a 1lb (0.5kg) dumbbell from the thigh to the flexed-arm position, holding it there for 2 seconds, then returning it to the thigh in a controlled manner.

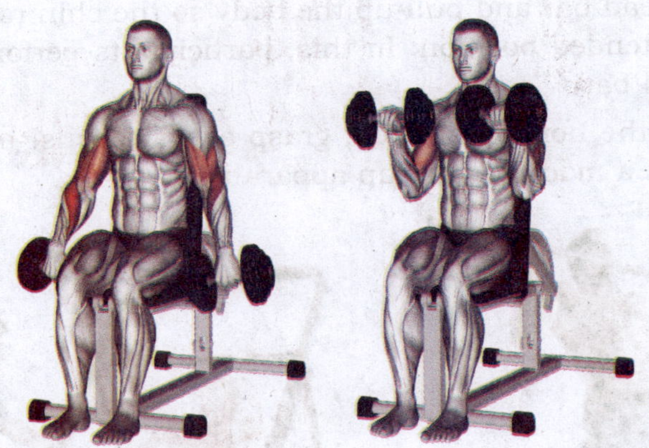

Reverse Curl

- ***Push/ Walk (40m)*** Walk or push a wheelchair at a comfortable speed for 40 min, with a 5 min start zone. It is not a race, participants are encouraged to travel at the speed they usually use for mobility. To pass, they must cover the 40 meters distance in less than 60 seconds while keeping the heart rate below 120 bpm (walkers) or 114 bpm (wheelchair users).

- ***Wheelchair Ramp** Test* A test of upper-body strength and endurance, in which participants attempt to push their wheelchairs up a standard wheelchair ramp. The ramp must be at least 8 feet (2.4 meters) long, at a gradient of 8.3%.
- ***Curl-Up*** Complete upto 75 curl-ups at a rate of 1 every 3 seconds. The hands slide 4-5 inches along the ground for a complete repetition.
- ***Curl-Up (modified)*** The curl-up test, though with the hands resting on the thighs rather than by the side.
- ***Extended Arm Hang*** Hanging from an overhead bar with straight arms for upto 40 seconds.
- ***Flexed Arm Hang*** The flexed arm hang test measures upper body strength and endurance, timing how long someone can remain with the chin above a horizontal bar.

Curl-Up

Curl-Up (Modified)

Extended Arm Hang

Flexed Arm Hang

- ***Pull-Up*** Grasp an overhead bar and pull-up the body so the chin raises above the bar, then return to arms fully extended position. In this, participants perform as many pull-ups as possible using overhead bar.
- ***Pull-Up (modified)*** With the horizontal body, grasp a bar set just out of reach and pull-up towards the bar. It uses a modified pull up apparatus.

Pull-up

Pull-up (Modified)

Flexibility tests for musculoskeletal functioning are

- **Back-Saver Sit and Reach** It is performed with one leg bent. It is designed to measure the flexibility of the left and the right legs, separately.
- **Shoulder Stretch** Touch the fingertips together behind the back by reaching over the shoulder and down the back with one arm and across the back with the other arm. It measure upper body flexibility.

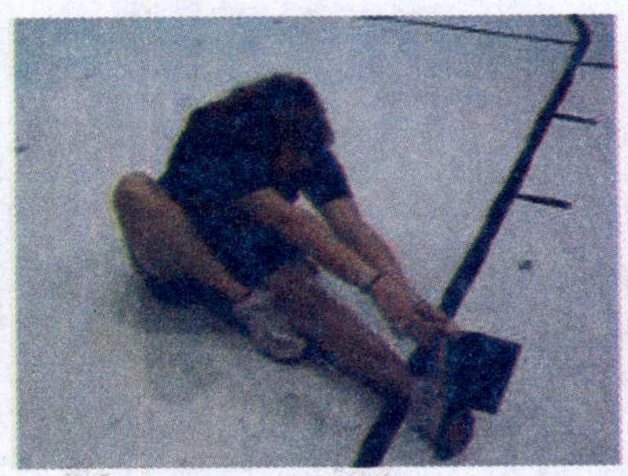

Back-Saver Sit and Reach

Shoulder Stretch

- **Apley Scratch Test (modified)** Attempt to reach overhead with one hand and touch the top of the opposite shoulder blade. This test is designed to measure the upper body flexibility.
- **Thomas Test (modified)** It requires the subject to sit at the very edge of a bench, then roll back onto the bench while pulling both knees to the chest. Measures hip flexibility.

Thomas Test (Modified)

- **Target Stretch Test** It is a screening instrument used to estimate movement extent in a joint. It includes a series of test mentioned below

(i) Wrist extension
(ii) Elbow extension
(iii) Shoulder extension
(iv) Shoulder abduction
(v) Shoulder external rotation
(vi) Forearm supination
(vii) Forearm pronation
(viii) Knee extension

General Recommendations for Administering BPFT

Although the BPFT includes 27 test items, testers generally administer only 4 to 6 items to a particular individual. The following list provides general recommendations for administering the BPFT

- Practice administering test items and be confident of mastery in administering them before taking formal measurements.
- Develop forms for selecting test items and recording scores or use materials developed as part of the Brockport Physical Fitness Test.
- Describe the test to participants and explain what it is intended to assess.
- Ensure that individuals being tested dress appropriately, exercise clothing and sneakers (where appropriate) are recommended.
- Plan and provide general and specific warmups, as appropriate.
- Provide cool-down activities after testing. This is especially important after aerobic-functioning test items.
- Provide a positive testing atmosphere. Encourage individuals being tested to try their best and continually provide positive reinforcement for effort.
- Compare participants' performances with criterion-referenced standards rather than with other individual's performance.
- Administer not more than half of the items on a particular day. If fatigue appears to be influencing performance, provide longer rest intervals between test items.
- Administer aerobic-functioning tests in last.
- Administer running items on a surface that is flat and hard.
- Give participants who are blind, the opportunity to become clearly oriented to a test station or testing area. This is particularly important for tests that involve running.
- Provide careful demonstrations for participants with hearing impairment. Give instructions in writing or manually (e.g. signing, finger spelling). Use hand signals to start and stop activities.
- Administer the following test items individually to one participant at a time- Target Aerobic Movement Test (TAMT), percent body fat, skinfolds, extended-arm hang, flexed-arm hang, modified pull-up, pull-up, dominant grip strength, bench press, curl-up, modified curl-up, 40 meter push/walk, reverse curl, seated push-up, trunk lift, wheelchair ramp test and most flexibility or range of motion test items (except shoulder stretch).
- The PACER, one-mile run/walk and shoulder stretch may be administered to small groups of subjects at once. However, it may be necessary or appropriate to provide partners for assistance.
- The following items can be administered to groups of two or three- dumbbell press, isometric push-up and push-up. For the dumbbell press, provide spotters.

Equipments Required For Conducting BPFT

Relatively inexpensive materials are required for conducting the BPFT such as a stopwatch, ruler, grip dynamometer, 35lb barbell, seated push-up blocks, 11lb weight, ramp, curl-up strip, pull-up bars, skinfold caliper, height-weight scale, sit and reach apparatus, heat range monitor, 15lb dumbbell and calibrated tapes.

Safety Guidelines and Precautions

The test items used in the BPFT, including both traditional and non-traditional exercises, are similar to those found in other fitness assessments. Although the BPFT is considered safe, one must recognise that accidents are possible. Use the following guidelines and precautions when administering test items

- Personnel who administers the test should be qualified and knowledgeable about physical fitness testing and disability.
- Maximise the safety of all youngsters. Professionals using this test should follow the policies of their school or agency regarding medical information, records and clearance for activity. Any other professional can only administer this test after getting an approval from a physician who is aware of the health status of the individual taking the test.
- Avoid administering tests under conditions of unusually high or low temperature or humidity, or when windy. Youngsters with spinal cord injury may be especially prone to problems with thermo-regulation including overheating.
- Ensure that individuals being tested clearly understand test instructions. Provide opportunities for students to practice test items.
- Terminate the test item if the individual being tested experiences dizziness, pain or disorientation.
- Avoid comparing participants' performances with each other.
- Spot youngsters where necessary and appropriate.
- Incorporate warm-up and cool-down periods as appropriate for test items.

General Brockport Physical Fitness Test Form

This form identifies all test items on the Brockport Physical Fitness Test (BPFT). It can be used as a resource for developing a fitness test for a particular student, recording results and matching results to fitness zones. The BPFT typically includes four to seven test items: one for aerobic functioning, one for body composition and at least two for musculoskeletal functioning.

Student name: .... Sex: ...... M ...... F .... Age (yr): ....

Height : .... Weight: .... Date: ....

Classification: .... Subclassification: ....

Aerobic Functioning

Test item	Units of Measure	Test Scores	Adapted Fitness Zone (if applicable)	Healthy Fitness Zone
Aerobic Capacity				
Mile run or walk	min/sec			
20 m (laps)	#			
15 m (laps)	#			
Aerobic Behaviour				
TAMT	P/F		None	

Body Composition

Test Item	Units of Measure	Test Scores	Adapted Fitness Zone (if applicable)	Healthy Fitness Zone
Percent body fat	%		No AFZ for body composition	
Triceps	(mm)			
Triceps + subscapular	(mm)			
Triceps + calf	(mm)			
Body mass index				

Musculoskeletal Functioning

Test Item	Units of Measure	Test Scores	Adapted Fitness Zone (if applicable)	Healthy Fitness Zone
Strength and Endurance				
Reverse curl	#			
40 m push/walk	P/F			
Ramp test	feet			
Push-ups	#			
Seated push-ups	#			
Pull-ups	#			
Modified pull-ups	#			
Dumbbell press	#			
Bench press	#			
Grip strength	kg.			
Isometric push-ups	sec.			
Extended arm hang	sec.			
Flexed arm hang	sec.			
Curl-ups	#			
Modified curl-ups	#			
Flexibility or Range of Motion				
Trunk lift	#			
Shoulder stretch, right	P/F			
Shoulder stretch, left	P/F			
Back-saver sit-and-reach, right	in.			
Back-saver sit-and-reach, left	in.			

Test Item	Units of Measure	Test Scores	Adapted Fitness Zone (if applicable)	Healthy Fitness Zone
Modified thomas test	0-3			
Modified apley test	0-3			
Target stretch test	0-2			
Wrist extension, right	0-2			
Wrist extension, left	0-2			
Elbow extension, right	0-2			
Elbow extension, left	0-2			
Shoulder extension, right	0-2			
Shoulder extension, left	0-2			
Shoulder abduction, right	0-2			
Shoulder abduction, left	0-2			
Shoulder external rotation, right	0-2			
Shoulder external rotation, left	0-2			
Forearm supination, right	0-2			
Forearm supination, left	0-2			
Forearm pronation, right	0-2			
Forearm pronation, left	0-2			
Knee extension, right	0-2			
Knee extension, left	0-2			

Interpretation : ....

Needs : ....

Viva-Voce

Q.1 What is the full form of BPFT and who developed it?

Ans. BPFT means Brockport Physical Fitness Test, it was developed by Dr. Joseph Winnick and Dr. Francis Short.

Q.2 What is the purpose of the Brockport Physical Fitness Test?

Ans. To measure health-related fitness using criterion-referenced standards linked to good health.

Q.3 Who are the target participants of the BPFT?

Ans. Able-bodied youth and those with disabilities such as cerebral palsy, spinal cord injury, mental retardation, blindness, amputation, and congenital anomalies.

Q.4 Name the three main components tested in the BPFT.

Ans. Aerobic functioning, Body composition, Musculoskeletal functioning.

Q.5 What is the PACER test and who is it modified for?

Ans. PACER test is a maximal aerobic fitness test involving 20m shuttles at increasing speeds. It is modified for vision-impaired children.

Q.6 What are the sites used for skinfold measurement in body composition assessment?

Ans. The sites used for skinfold measurement in body composition are Triceps, Subscapular and Calf.

Q.7 How is weight adjusted for participants with leg amputations during BMI measurement?

Ans.
- Below-knee : Add 1/8 of body weight
- Above-knee : Add 1/9 of body weight
- Hip amputation : Add 1/6 of body weight

Q.8 What does musculoskeletal functioning assess in the BPFT?

Ans. It assesses muscular strength, muscular endurance, and flexibility/range of motion.

Q.9 Which test in BPFT evaluates trunk extension strength and flexibility?

Ans. Trunk Lift test evaluates trunk extension strength and flexibility.

Q.10 What device is used in the Grip Strength test?

Ans. The device used in the Grip strength test is Dynamometer.

Q.11 Name one flexibility test in BPFT that evaluates flexibility of each leg separately.

Ans. Back-Saver Sit and Reach

Q.12 Which test measures upper body strength by hanging with the chin above a bar?

Ans. Flexed Arm Hang test measures upper body strength by hanging with the chin above a bar.

Q.13 What is the recommended number of BPFT items to be administered per individual?

Ans. The recommended number of BPFT items to be administered per individual is 4 to 6 items.

Q.14 Why should aerobic-functioning tests be administered last during BPFT?

Ans. Aerobic - functioning test should be administered last during BPFT to prevent fatigue from affecting performance in other tests.

Q.15 What safety guideline is important before administering the BPFT to students with disabilities?

Ans. An important safety guideline is Medical clearance and understanding of health status by a physician.

Game 1

Cricket

History

The origin of cricket can be traced back to Tudor era in the early 16th century England. During the 18th century, the game of cricket went through several developments. The first official match was played between Kent and Middlesex in 1719 and the first rules for the game were framed in the year 1744. The world's first cricket club was formed in Hambledon in the 1760s and the world-famous Marylebone Cricket Club (MCC) was founded in 1787.

In 1788, the MCC published its first revision of the laws and became the guardian of cricket's regulations. Imperial Cricket Conference was formed in the year 1909 by representatives from Australia, England and South Africa. It was renamed as International Cricket Conference in 1965 and later named as International Cricket Council (ICC) in 1989. The first Indian Cricket Club was named as Orient Club Mumbai, which was founded in 1848. Cricket is played in three formats namely, Test Match (started from 1877), One Day (started from 1971) and Twenty-20 (started from 2005).

Measurements and Specifications

(i) Players in a Team = 11 + 5 (extra) = 16
(ii) Number of Umpires = 2 + 1 (Third Umpire)
(iii) Weight of Cricket Ball = 5.5 Ounce (156 gm)/4.75 ounces for junior cricket
(iv) Circumference of the Ball = 9 inches (22.5 cm)
(v) Colour of Ball = Red/White/Pink
(vi) Length of Bat = 38 inches (96.5 cm)
(vii) Widest Part of Bat = 4.25 inches (10.8 cm)
(viii) Bat Thickness (depth) = 2.64 inches (16.7 cm)
(ix) Bat Edges = 1.56 inches (4.0 cm)
(x) Breadth of Pitch = 10 Feet (3.05 m)
(xi) Shape of Ground = Elliptical
(xii) Distance between Stumps = 66 Feet (22 Yards or 20.12 m)
(xiii) Height of Stumps = 28 inches (71.1 cm)
(xiv) Breadth of Stumps = 9 inches (22.8 cm)
(xv) Size of Bails = 4.5 inches (11 cm)
(xvi) Inner Circle from Wickets = 30 Yards (27.4 m)
(xvii) Outer Circle from Wickets = 75 Yards (68.5 m)
(xviii) No. of scorers = 2
(xiv) Time for changing every innings = 10 min. (For Twenty-20 and Test matches), 30-45 min. (For Oneday)
(xx) Player changing time = 2 min.

(xxi) Formats of cricket = Test match, One Day and Twenty 20

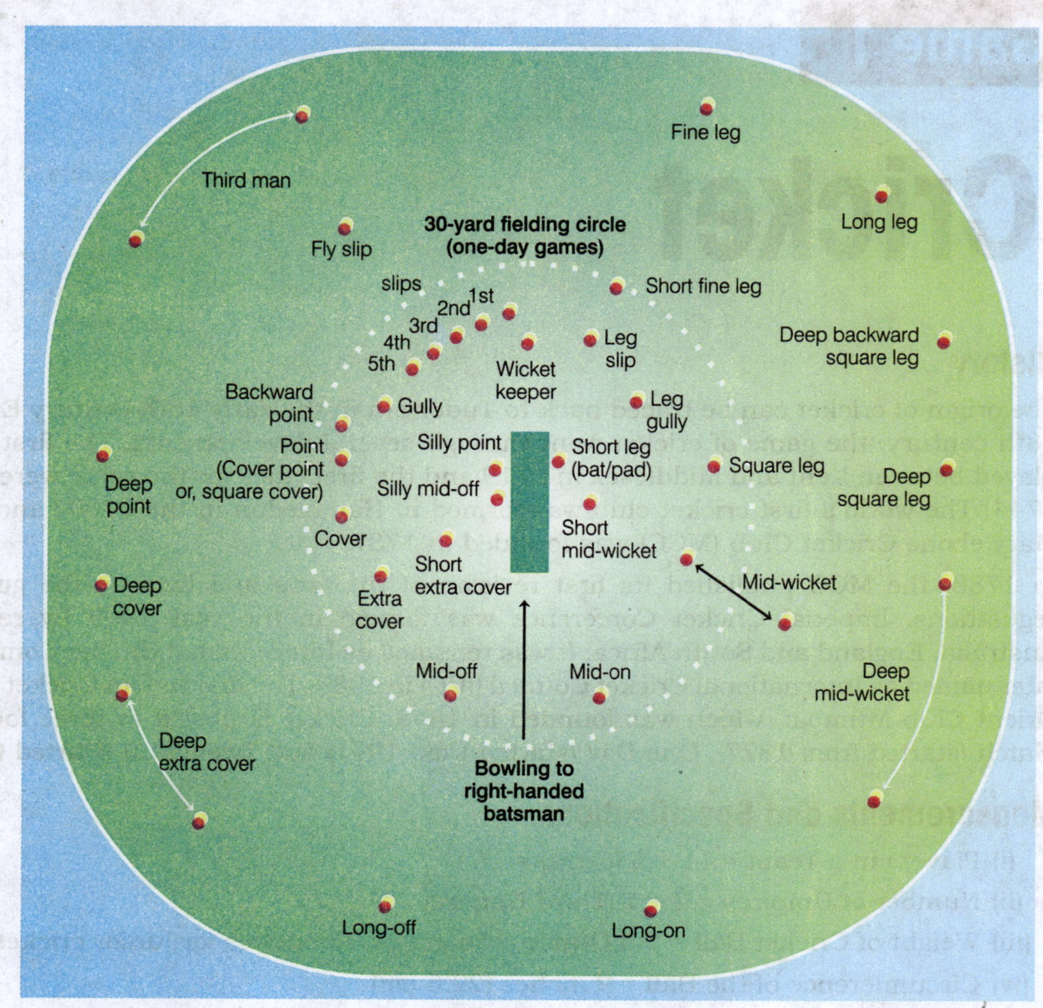

Cricket Ground with Fielding Position

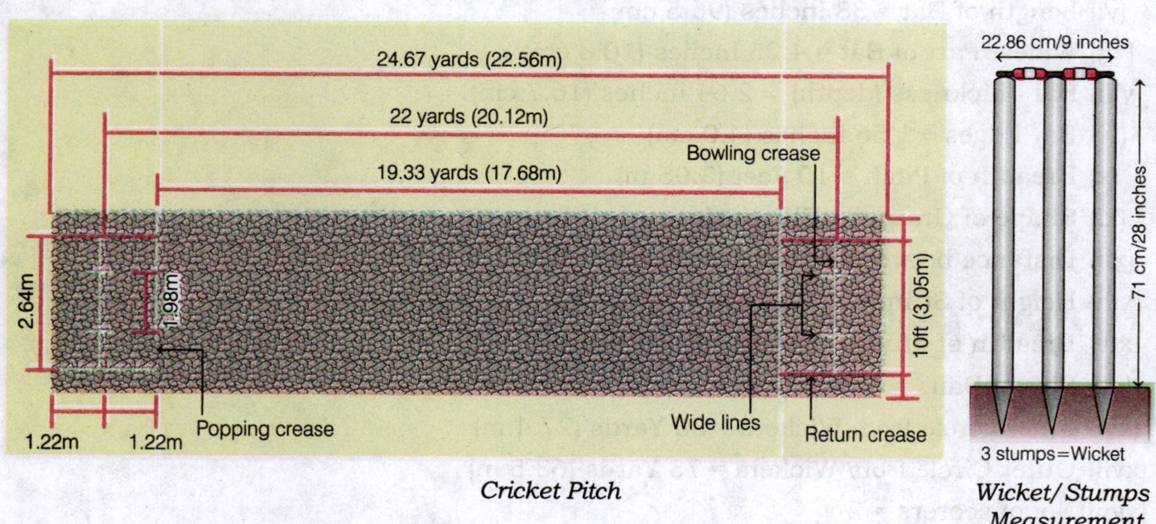

Cricket Pitch

Wicket/ Stumps Measurement

Terminology

Arm Ball	A ball bowled by a slow bowler which has no spin on it and so does not turn as expected, but stays on a straight line.
Asking Rate	The runs required per over for a team to win the match.
Ball	Red ball is used for first-class (Test match) and most club cricket and white ball is used for one-day and Twenty-20 matches. Now-a-days, pink ball is also used for day-night test matches.
Ball Tampering	The illegal act of changing the condition of the ball by artificial means, usualy scuffing the surface, picking or lifting the seam of the ball, or applying substances other than sweat or saliva.
Bat-Pad	A fielding position close to the batsman designed to catch balls which pop-up off the bat, often via the batsman's pads.
Batter	Another word for batsman.
Beamer	A ball that does not bounce and passes the batsman at or about head height.
Bend your Back	The term used to signify the extra effort put in by a fast bowler to obtain some assistance from a flat pitch.
Bouncer	A short-pitched ball which passes the batsman at chest or head height.
Boundary	The perimeter of a cricket field, or the act of the batsman scoring a four or a six.
Box	An abdominal protector worn by batsmen and wicketkeepers.
Bump Ball	A ball which is played off the bat almost instantly into the ground and is caught by a fielder.
Bye	A run scored when the batsman does not touch the ball with either his bat or body.
Carry your Bat	An opening batsman who remains not out till the end of innings.
Chinaman	A ball bowled by a left-arm slow bowler that turns into the right-hand batsman, in effect a left-arm leg-spinner.
Chucker	A term used for a bowler who throws the ball. It is considered as an illegal bowling action.
Closing the Face	When the batsmen turns the face of the bat inwards and, in doing so, hits the ball to the leg side.
Corridor of Uncertainty	A term which describes an area just outside the batsman's off stump where he is unsure whether he has to leave or play the ball.
Cross Bat	A cross-batted shot is where the batsman holds his bat horizontally when striking the ball. Hooks, pulls and cuts are examples of cross-batted shots.
Dead Ball	This term was first used in the year 1798. A ball from which no run can be scored or wicket can be taken.
Declaration	When the batting side ends their innings before all of their players are out.
Drifter/ Floater	A delivery bowled by an off-spinner which curves away from a right-hander, and then carries straight on instead of turning.

Duck	When a batsman is dismissed without scoring any runs.
Duckworth Lewis	Two mathematicians, Frank Duckworth and Tony Lewis, devised a system in order to decide one-day cricket matches when rain interrupts the play.
Economy Rate	The average number of runs a bowler concedes per over.
Extras	These are the runs not scored by batsmen but still adds up to the total score. There are four common extras - byes, leg byes, wide and no-balls. In Australia these are known as sundries.
Featherbed	A pitch which is batsmen-friendly.
Full Toss	A ball that reaches the batsmen without any bounce. When it is above waist height, it is called a beamer.
Googly	It is a leg-spinner's delivery that turns into the right-hander and away from the left-hander.
Half Volley	A ball that is the perfect length for driving, fuller than a good length but not a full-toss.
Handled the Ball	If a batsman deliberately touches the ball with his hands, he can be given out.
Hawk-Eye	A tracking technology which helps to explain the intricacies of the sport, Hawk-Eye is helpful in judging LBWs.
Hit the Ball Twice	If a batsman deliberately strikes the ball twice to gain runs, he can be given out.
Hit the Deck	The bowler's ability to deliver the ball from height and extract extra bounce from the pitch.
Inside-Out Shot	A stroke where the batsman moves towards the leg side and hits a ball around leg stump into the off-side.
Leading Edge	When the batsman mishit the ball and edges it forward in the opposite direction to which he was attempting to play.
Leg-Bye	When the ball deflects off the pad and the batsmen run. A shot must be offered to the ball. Leg-byes do not count against the bowler.
Leg-Break/ Spin	When the ball pitches and turns from leg to off for a right-handed batsman.
Leg-Cutter	A ball which cuts and moves away from the right-handed batsman towards the offside.
Maiden	An over where no runs are scored excluding byes or leg-byes.
Middle	To hit the ball from the meat of the bat, "to middle it" is to connect really well. Middle is also the centre of the field.
Minefield	The pitch is in such a state of disrepair that it is almost impossible to play "proper" shots as the ball is popping up everywhere.
Nervous Nineties	The psychological pressure on the batsman knowing he is approaching a century.
No-Ball	An illegitimate delivery, usually when the bowler has overstepped on the front crease.

Occupy the Crease	When a batsman stays at the wicket but scores slowly, often with the intention of playing out for a draw.
Off-Break/ Spin	A ball turning into the right-hander from off to leg.
Off the Mark	When the batsman scores his first run.
Off-Side	The side of the pitch which is to batsman's right (if right-handed), or left (if left-handed).
Out	There are ten possible ways of being out: bowled, caught, hit wicket, LBW, stumped, timed out, handled the ball, obstruction, hit the ball twice, and run out.
Outside Edge	When the ball hits the edge of the bat which is furthest away from his body.
Out-Swing	When the ball swings away from the batsman towards the slips.
Pair	When a batsman scores Zero run in both innings.
Pinch-Hitters	Lower-order batsmen promoted in the line-up to try and hit up a few quick runs.
Play On	When a batsman hits the ball but it goes on to hit the stumps and he is bowled.
Plumb	When the batsman is clearly LBW, he is said to be plumb in front.
Ring Field	A standard fielding arrangement, with men positioned in a circle all around the batsman saving each single.
Run-Rate	It is of particular importance in a one-day game. This is the average number of runs scored per over, and is used as a guide to a team's progress.
Runner	A player who is called upon by a batsman who might otherwise need to retire hurt.
Sledging	The act of verbally abusing or unsettling a batsman, in an attempt to make him lose concentration and give his wicket away.
Standing Back / Standing Up	It is place where a wicket-keeper positions himself for a particular bowler. He stands back for fast bowlers, and stands up for spinners.
Stonewall	To protect one's wicket at all costs.
Strike Rate	The number of runs a batsman scores per 100 balls; the number of deliveries a bowler needs to take his wickets.
Swing	A ball that curves through the air, as opposed to off the seam.
Tailender	Players who come in towards the end of an innings, generally at number 8, 9, 10 and 11.
Twelfth Man	A substitute fielder (and drinks waiter) for the chosen eleven. If called upon to play, he is permitted to field wherever he is needed, but can neither bat nor bowl.
Walk (To)	The improbable act of a batsman giving himself out, without waiting for an umpire's decision.
Yorker	A ball bowled (a delivery) that hits the cricket pitch around the batsman's feet.

Cricket Equipments

Cricket Equipments

Latest/General Rules

1. Each captain shall nominate 11 players plus a maximum of 4 substitute fielders in writing to the ICC Match Referee before the toss. The ICC Match Referee shall not be from the same country as of the participating teams.
2. The bowling crease, which is the back edge of the crease marking, is the line that marks the end of the pitch. It shall be 8 ft 8 in/2.64 m in length.
3. The popping crease, which is the back edge of the crease marking, shall be in front of and parallel to the bowling crease and shall be 4 ft/1.22 m from it. The popping crease shall be marked to a minimum of 9.33 yards/7.68 m on either side of the imaginary line joining the centres of the two middle stumps.
4. During the match, no umpire shall be replaced, although this can be done in exceptional circumstances such as injury or sickness of the umpire.
5. In a game of cricket, a batsman can be declared out by a number of ways. *They are*
   - Bowled
   - Caught
   - Leg before Wicket
   - Stumped
   - Hit Wicket
   - Handled Ball
   - Timed Out
   - Hit Ball Twice
   - Obstruction
   - Run-out
   - Mankading Out
   - Returning the Ball
   - Out on No-ball
6. *In following situations, batsman is not given out*
   - No Appeal, No Out
   - If Bails don't Fall then Not-Out
7. **Rules for Test Match** Test match is played across five consecutive days and has four innings. Each team bats and bowls twice. A standard day of test cricket consist of three sessions of two hours each, with 40 minutes break for lunch and 20 minutes break for tea. In test match, 90 overs are bowled in day which are divided as 30 overs per session.

8. **Rules for One-day Match** One-day matches take about 8 hours, each inning lasting about 4 hours (240 minutes) and there is an official break of 45 minutes interval between two innings. Two drink breaks are permitted in each inning which is usually 1 hour 10 minutes apart. Each team faces a fixed number of 50 overs. Each bowler is restricted to bowl a maximum of 10 overs. In the first 10 overs of an innings, the fielding team should have only 2 fielders outside the 30-yard circle. It is known as powerplay. Between 11 to 40 overs, few fielders are allowed to field outside the 30-yards circle. In final 10 overs, five fielders are allowed to field outside the 30-yard circle.
9. **Rules for T-20 Match** Teams have a single innings each restricted to a maximum of 20 overs. Game is completed in about three hours, each inning lasting around 90 minutes with an official break of 10 minutes between the innings. If a bowler delivers a no-ball by overstepping the crease, 1 run is awarded to opposite team and next delivery is designated as a 'free hit'. During the first 6 overs, a maximum of two fielders can be outside the 30-yard circle. This is known as powerplay. After the first 6 overs, a maximum five fielders can be outside the fielding circle. At anytime, not more than five fielders can be on the leg side. The fielding/bowling team should start their 20th over within 75 minutes of the start of the match, otherwise the batting side is credited an extra 6 runs for every over bowled after 75 minutes.

Umpires

Umpires in cricket play a crucial role in ensuring the game is conducted fairly and according to the rules. Here are the key aspects of their role

Roles and Responsibilities

- *Decision Making* Umpires make decisions on various aspects of the game, including dismissals (like LBW, run-outs, stumping), no-balls, wides, boundaries, and other on-field events.
- *Enforcing Rules* Ensuring that the Laws of Cricket and the playing conditions are followed by all players and team officials.
- *Managing Conduct* Overseeing the conduct of players and maintaining discipline on the field, including issuing warnings or penalties for breaches of conduct.

Types of Umpires

- *On-field Umpires* Two umpires on the field; one stands behind the stumps at the bowler's end (known as the main umpire), and the other stands at square leg (known as the leg umpire).
- *Third Umpire* Also known as the TV umpire, who uses video evidence to assist the on-field umpires in making decisions, particularly for run-outs, stumpings, and boundary calls.
- *Fourth Umpire* Assists with various duties off the field, such as bringing on new balls, checking the condition of the pitch, and stepping in if an on-field umpire is unable to continue.

Key Duties

- *Checking Equipment* Ensuring that players' equipment, such as bats, gloves, and protective gear, comply with the rules.
- *Timing* Keeping track of the game's timing, including intervals, drinks break, and the duration of each session.
- *Overseeing the Toss* Conducting the toss and ensuring it is done correctly.
- *Counting Deliveries* Keeping count of the number of balls bowled in each over.
- *Communicating Decisions* Clearly signaling and communicating decisions to players, scorers, and spectators.

Umpire Hand Signals

Fundamental Skills and Techniques

Batting

It is a skill that involves a combination of techniques and strategies to score runs and defend the wicket.

Types of Shots

- *Block* The forward defensive shot. The principle of a forward defensive stroke is to block the ball rather than to score runs.
- *Cut* A shot played off a short-pitched ball on the off-side near to 90 degrees from the wicket.
- *Drive* A straight-batted shot, played by swinging the bat vertically through the line of the ball. A drive can be a cover drive, straight drive, on drive or square drive.
- *Hook* A horizontal bat shot against a rising ball.
- *Leg Glance* A stroke played to flick the ball.
- *Pull* A cross-batted shot played to a ball around waist height by swinging the bat horizontally towards mid-wicket or square leg.
- *Sweep* A cross-batted shot played to a low bouncing ball, usually from a slow bowler, by kneeling on one knee and sweeping it to the leg.
- *Reverse Sweep* A reverse sweep is a cross-batted sweep shot played in the opposite direction to the standard sweep, thus instead of sweeping the ball to the leg side, it is swept to the off-side.

- *Slog* A powerful pull shot played over mid-wicket, usually hit in the air in an attempt to score a six.

Batting Skills

Bowling

It is a skill that involves delivering the ball to the batsman with the aim of getting them out or restricting their ability to score runs. Here are the fundamental components of bowling

- *Grip and Action* Holding the ball correctly and having a consistent bowling action to deliver accurate and varied balls.
- *Line and Length* Bowling the ball in the right areas to challenge the batsman, targeting good lengths and lines.
- *Variation* Using different types of deliveries, like fast, swing, spin, yorkers, and bouncers to keep the batsman guessing.

Fielding

- It is a skill that involves preventing the batsmen from scoring runs and attempting to get them out. Here are the key components of fielding
- *Catching* Techniques for catching the ball, both in the air and on the ground.
- *Throwing* Accurate and powerful throwing to return the ball quickly to the wicketkeeper or bowler.
- *Ground Fielding* Stopping the ball efficiently and quickly to prevent runs.

Catching

Throwing

Ground Fielding

Wicket-keeping

- It is a specialised fielding position that requires a unique set of skills and attributes. The wicket-keeper plays a crucial role in the field, both in catching the ball and in effecting dismissals. Here are the key components of wicket-keeping
- **Stance and Positioning** Being in the right stance and position to catch or stump the ball effectively.
- **Glove Work** Skillful use of gloves to catch and stump, requiring quick reflexes and coordination.
- **Anticipation and Movement** Reading the game and moving swiftly to react to balls coming from the bowler or fielder.

Popular Cricket Tournaments

International

- ICC Cricket World Cup
- ICC Champions Trophy
- T20 World Cup
- Ashes Series
- Champions League Twenty-20
- NatWest Series
- Border-Gavaskar Trophy
- Asia Cup
- Commonwealth Bank Series

National

- Duleep Trophy
- Vijay Hazare Trophy
- Deodhar Trophy
- Ranji Trophy
- Irani Cup
- Syed Mushtaq Ali Trophy
- Indian Premier League

Popular Venues

India

- Eden Gardens, Kolkata
- Wankhede Stadium, Mumbai
- M. Chinnaswamy Stadium, Bangalore
- Feroz Shah Kotla (Arun Jaitley Stadium), Delhi
- M. A. Chidambaram Stadium, Chennai
- Narendra Modi Stadium, Ahmedabad

Australia

- Melbourne Cricket Ground (MCG), Melbourne
- Sydney Cricket Ground (SCG), Sydney

England

- Lord's Cricket Ground, London
- The Oval, London

New Zealand

- Eden Park, Auckland
- Basin Reserve, Wellington

United Arab Emirates (UAE)

- Dubai International Cricket Stadium, Dubai, UAE
- Sharjah Cricket Stadium, Sharjah, UAE
- Sheikh Zayed Stadium, Abu Dhabi, UAE

Popular Cricket Awardees

Arjuna Awardees

- 1961 Saleem Durani
- 1964 Mansur Ali Khan Pataudi
- 1965 Vijay Manjrekar
- 1966 Chandu Borde
- 1967 Ajit Wadekar
- 1968 E.A.S. Prasanna
- 1969 Bishan Singh Bedi
- 1970 Dilip Sardesai
- 1971 Srinivasaraghavan Venkataraghavan
- 1972 Eknath Solkar
- 1972 B.S. Chandrashekhar
- 1974 Anjan Bhattacharjee
- 1975 Sunil Gavaskar
- 1976 Shanta Rangaswamy
- 1977-78 Gundappa Vishwanath
- 1979–80 Kapil Dev Nikhanj
- 1980–81 Chetan Chauhan
- 1980–81 Syed Kirmani
- 1981 Dilip Vengsarkar
- 1982 Mohinder Amarnath
- 1983 Diana Edulji
- 1984 Ravi Shastri
- 1985 Shubhangi Kulkarni
- 1986 Mohammad Azharuddin
- 1986 Sandhya Agarwal
- 1989 Madan Lal
- 1993 Manoj Prabhakar
- 1993 Kiran More
- 1994 Sachin Tendulkar
- 1995 Anil Kumble

- 1996 Javagal Srinath
- 1998 Sourav Ganguly
- 1998 Nayan Mongia
- 2001 VVS Laxman
- 2003 Harbhajan Singh
- 2005 Anju Jain
- 2009 Gautam Gambhir
- 2011 Zaheer Khan
- 2013 Virat Kohli
- 2015 Rohit Sharma
- 2017 Cheteshwar Pujara
- 2018 Smriti Mandhana
- 2019 Ravindra Jadeja
- 2020 Ishant Sharma
- 2023 Mohammed Shami
- 1997 Ajay Jadeja
- 1998 Rahul Dravid
- 2000 Venkatesh Prasad
- 2002 Virender Sehwag
- 2003 Mithali Raj
- 2006 Anjum Chopra
- 2010 Jhulan Goswami
- 2012 Yuvraj Singh
- 2014 Ravichandran Ashwin
- 2016 Ajinkya Rahane
- 2017 Harmanpreet Kaur
- 2019 Poonam Yadav
- 2020 Depti Sharma
- 2021 Shikhar Dhawan

Dronacharya Awardees

- 1986 Desh Prem Azad
- 1990 Ramakant Achrekar
- 2016 Rajkumar Sharma
- 2019 Sanjay Bharadwaj
- 2022 Dinesh Jawahar Lad
- 1987 Gurcharan Singh
- 2004 Sunita Sharma
- 2018 Tarak Sinha
- 2021 Sarkar Talwar

Rajiv Gandhi (Major Dhyan Chand) Khel Ratna Awardees

- 1997 Sachin Tendulkar
- 2018 Virat Kohli
- 2021 Mithali Raj
- 2007 Mahendra Singh Dhoni
- 2020 Rohit Sharma

Padma Shree Awardees

- 2010 Ramakant Achrekar (Cricket coach)
- 2010 Virender Sehwag (Indian cricketer)
- 2011 VVS Laxman (Test match specialist)
- 2012 Ravi Chaturvedi (Author of 23 books on cricket and commentator)
- 2012 Jhulan Goswami (All round cricketer)
- 2014 Anjum Chopra (Indian woman cricketer)
- 2014 Yuvraj Singh (Indian cricketer)
- 2015 Mithali Raj (Captain of Indian women's cricket team)
- 2016 Sushil Doshi (First cricket commentator in Hindi)
- 2017 Virat Kohli (Indian cricketer)
- 2017 Shekhar Naik (Captain of India national blind cricket team)
- 2019 Gautam Gambhir (Indian cricketer)
- 2020 Zaheer Khan
- 2023 Gurucharan Singh (Former Indian Cricketer and Coach)
- 2025 Ravichandran Ashwin

Winners of the CEAT Cricket Rating

- 1995–96 Brian Lara
- 1997–98 Sanath Jayasuriya
- 1999–2000 Sourav Ganguly
- 2001–02 Muttiah Muralitharan
- 2003–04 Brian Lara
- 1996–97 Venkatesh Prasad
- 1998–99 Jacques Kallis
- 2000–01 Muttiah Muralitharan
- 2002–03 Ricky Ponting
- 2004–05 Jacques Kallis

- 2005–06 Ricky Ponting
- 2007–08 Mahela Jayawardene
- 2009–10 Shane Watson
- 2011–12 Virat Kohli
- 2014–15 Kumar Sangakkara
- 2016–17 Ravichandran Ashwin
- 2018–19 Virat Kohli
- 2020-21 Not Awarded
- 2022–23 Shubman Gill
- 2006–07 Muttiah Muralitharan
- 2008–09 Gautam Gambhir
- 2010–11 Jonathan Trott
- 2013–14 Virat Kohli
- 2015–16 Joe Root
- 2017–18 Virat Kohli
- 2019–20 Rohit Sharma
- 2021-22 Not Awarded
- 2023–24 Rohit Sharma

Viva-Voce

Q.1 Where did cricket originate and in which era?

Ans. Tudor-era England, early 16th century.

Q.2 When was the first official cricket match played and between which teams?

Ans. The first official cricket match was played in 1719, between Kent and Middlesex.

Q.3 Who founded the Marylebone Cricket Club (MCC) and in which year?

Ans. MCC was founded by Thomas Lord in 1787.

Q.4 What is the global governing body of cricket called today?

Ans. Today, the global governing body of cricket is called International Cricket Council (ICC).

Q.5 Name the three main formats of international cricket.

Ans. Test, One Day International (ODI), Twenty-20 (T20).

Q.6 How many players are there in a cricket team, including substitutes?

Ans. 16 (11 players + 5 substitutes).

Q.7 What is the standard weight of a senior cricket ball?

Ans. The standard weight of a senior cricket ball is 156 grams (5.5 ounce).

Q.8 What is the length of a cricket pitch?

Ans. The length of a cricket pitch is 22 yards (20.12 meters).

Q.9 How many stumps are there at each end of the pitch?

Ans. Three.

Q.10 What is a "duck" in cricket?

Ans. Getting out without scoring a run.

Q.11 What is a "maiden over"?

Ans. An over in which no runs are scored excluding byes or leg-byes.

Q.12 What is a "googly"?

Ans. A deceptive delivery bowled by a leg-spinner that turns the opposite way.

Q.13 What is the maximum number of overs a bowler can bowl in a One Day International?

Ans. A bowler can bowl a maximum of 10 overs in a One Day International.

Q.14 What is the size of the boundary from the centre of the pitch in international cricket?

Ans. In Internatinal Cricket, the maximum boundary length is 75 yards (68.5 meters) from the centre of the pitch.

Q.15 Name one way a batsman can be given out.

Ans. Bowled.

Q.16 What is the main duty of the third umpire?

Ans. The third umpire's main duty is to use video replays for close calls.

Q.17 What is a "powerplay" in limited overs cricket?

Ans. A powerplay in limited-over cricket is a period with fielding restrictions.

Q.18 Name one popular international cricket tournament.

Ans. ICC Cricket World Cup.

Q.19 Who was the first Indian to win the Rajiv Gandhi Khel Ratna Award in cricket?

Ans. Sachin Tendulkar was the first Indian who win the Rajiv Gandhi Khel Ratna Award in cricket.

Q.20 Name a famous cricket stadium in India.

Ans. Eden Gardens, Kolkata.

Game 2

Handball

Handball is a team sport in which two teams of seven players each (six outfield players and a goalkeeper) pass a ball using their hands with the aim of throwing it into the goal of the team. A standard match consists of two periods of 30 minutes, and the team that scores more goals wins.

History

Handball was introduced in Germany by famous Gymnast, Konrad Koch in 19th century and was modified by Frederik Knudsen in 1911 (Denmark). The International Amateur Handball Federation was founded in 1928 during the Amsterdam Olympics.

Men's field Handball was played at the 1936 Olympic Games in Berlin. However, handball remained suspended from Olympics until 1970s.

The sport re-emerged as team handball in the 1972 Summer Olympics in Munich for men. Women's team handball was added at the 1976 Olympics in Montreal. On 11th July, 1946, the International Handball Federation (IHF) was formed at the initiative and invitation of Denmark and Sweden.

In India, the game was started in 1970. Handball Federation of India, founded in 1955, is the national body that regulates the selection and training of handball players in India.

Measurements and Specifications

(i) Dimensions of the playing field = 40 m × 20 m
(ii) Height of the goals post = 2 m
(iii) Width of the goal post = 3 m
(iv) Width of the goal lines between goal posts = 8 cm
(v) Length of 7 m line = 1 m
(vi) Length of the 4 m line = 15 cm
(vii) Total number of players = 12 (6 on court players, 1 goalkeeper and 5 substitutes).
(viii) Ball (for men): weight between 425 and 475 gm, circumference between 58 and 60 cm.
(ix) Ball (for women): weight between 325 and 375 gm, circumference between 54 and 56 cm.
(x) Duration of match = 2 halves of 30 minutes each with a 10 minutes break in between.
(xi) Number of officials = 5 (2 Referees, 1 Scorer, 1 Time-keeper, 1 Recorder)
(xii) In case of tie = 2 halves of 5 minutes each with 1 minute break in between.
(xiii) Ball Weight (female 8-14 years and male 8- 12 years) = 290 to 330 gm, circumference between 50 to 52 cm
(xiv) Shooting Circle: Inner shooting circle = 6 m
Outer circle/free throw line = 9 m
(xv) Penalty Point = 7 m
(xvi) Free Zone area = 3 m all around the playing field.

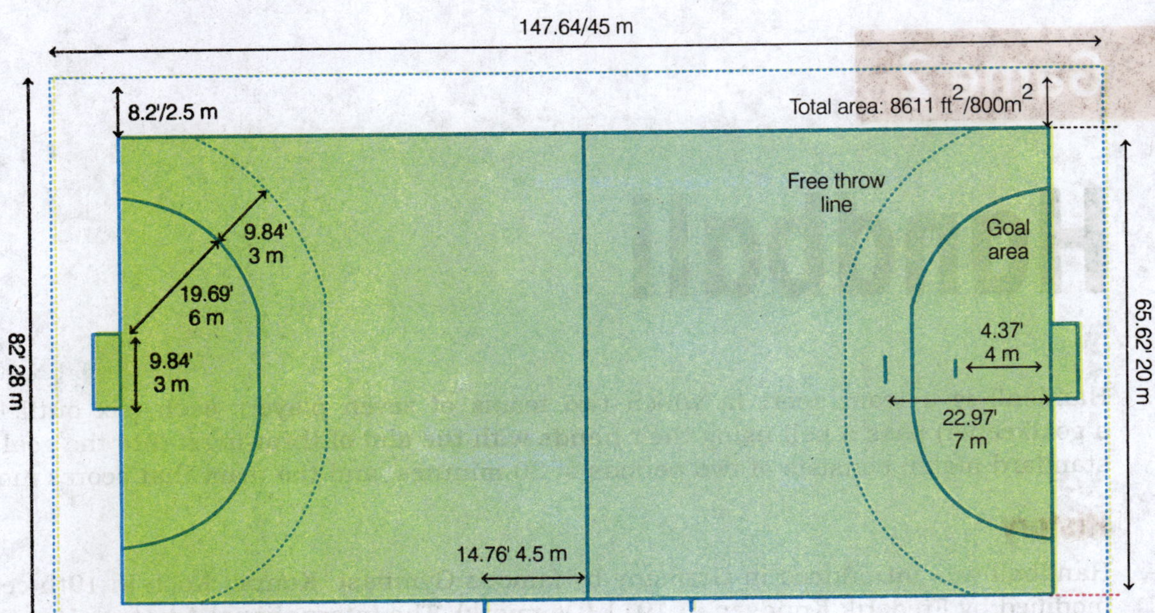

Handball Court

Terminology

Corner Throw	This is awarded when the ball is played over his/her own goal line by a defending player (except the goalkeeper) on either side of the goal. The game is restarted by a throw from the corner of the court by one of the attacking players. The player must place one foot on the corner and throw the ball by using one of his hands.
Court Player	A member of the team playing on the court except the goalkeeper.
Double Dribble	This is receiving the ball, bouncing it, then holding the ball and bouncing it again. This is against the rules.
Fault	A fault is illegally served ball.
Free-Throw	It is allowed to the opposition team while other team does a foul during the game. The ball is thrown from a line 9 mts away from the goal.
Goal	A goal is scored when the ball has hit the curtain between the tape marks and under the top tape marking. A ball that hits the tape does not count as a goal.
Goal Area	The arc around goalpost at 6 m distance is called goal line and the area enclosed by this arc is called *goal area.* It is restricted for all players except goalkeeper.
Goalkeeper/Goalie	A player who defends the goal while opposition attempts to score goals. Only the goalie or goal keeper is permitted to play inside the goal area.
Goal Throw	This is awarded when the ball rebounds off the goalkeeper over the endline or is thrown over the endline by the attacking team. The goalie needs to make the throw inside the goal area in order to restart the game.

7 Metre Throw This is awarded when a foul destroys a clear chance to score. The thrower steps with one foot behind the 7 m line with only the defending goalkeeper between him and the goal. The goalkeeper must keep a distance of 3 m, which is marked by a short tick on the floor. All players must be outside the free-throw line when the throw is taken. The player taking the throw has 3 seconds to shoot after the referee's whistle. Any player may take the 7 m throw.

Passive Play It is illegal to keep the ball in a team's possession without making a recognisable attempt to attack and try to score. In other words, a team cannot stall the game. In this case, a free-throw is awarded to the other team.

Penalty Throw This is awarded to the offensive team when an offensive player is prevented from making a clear goal-scoring chance by a foul made by a defensive player. The player taking the penalty throw is required to make a direct attempt to score a goal from the penalty throw line.

Referee Throw This is awarded when the ball touches anything above the court or after a simultaneous infringement of the rules. The referee throws the ball vertically between two opposing players, who may grab the ball or tap it to a teammate. All other players must be 3 m away from the throw. The referee throw is always taken at centre court.

Throw-in This is awarded when the ball goes out of bounds on the sideline or when the ball is last touched by a defensive player (excluding the goalkeeper) and goes out of bounds over the endline. The throw-in is taken from the spot where the ball crossed the sideline or if it crossed the endline, from the nearest corner. The thrower must place one foot on the sideline to execute the throw. All opposing players must stay 3 m away from the ball.

Throw-off It takes place from the centre of the court. The thrower must touch the middle line with one foot. The remaining offensive players stay in their court and defending players keep a 3 m distance from the thrower.

Line-Cut During attempt for goal if a player cuts or crosses the goal line, this is a violation.

Shuffling It is again a strategic move during attack when man-to-man check by defenders is done. In this, player moves or changes his position to break the defence of defenders.

Safety Zone It is an area around the handball court 3 metres on all sides of the court.

Tie-Rule If there is tie in regular time then extra-time of 5 min of two halves is given. If tie still exists, then five penalty throws are taken alternatively by each team to break the tie.

Yellow Card It is warning against player who is not playing under rules. Warning is given when he pulls of hits the ball from opponents, blocks opponent with arms or legs, restrains, holds, passes, runs or jumps into opponent, endangers opponent.

Red Card It means disqualification of a player who is repeatedly committing obstruction in spite of warning. He is not allowed to play further.

Latest/General Rules

1. A handball game is played between 2 teams of 12 players each.
2. The game consists of 2 halves of 30 minutes period for men and 25 minutes for women, with a 10 minutes half-time break.
3. The object of the game is to score more goals than the opposing team and to prevent them from goaling in your court.
4. A player is allowed to run with the ball for 3 steps or to hold the ball for 3 seconds. Using the outstretched arms or legs to obstruct, push, hold, trip or hit is not allowed.
5. A player is not allowed to endanger an opponent with the ball, pull, hit or punch the ball out of the hands of an opponent, contact the ball below the knee or dive on the floor for a rolling or stationary ball.
6. The referee gives only one warning (showing a Yellow Card) to a player for rule violations and a total of three to a team.
7. A disqualification (referee showing a Red Card) is the equivalent of three 2-minutes suspensions. A disqualified player must leave the court and bench, but the team can replace the player after the 2-minutes suspension expires. An exclusion (meaning expulsion) is given for assault. The excluded player's team continues short of one player for the rest of the game.
8. The game starts with a throw-off from centre line by team that win the toss or after the goal scored by opponent.
9. Only the goalkeeper is allowed inside the goal area.
10. A player in possession of the ball shall not take more than 3 steps while holding the ball; player should not hold the ball without dribble for more than 3 seconds.

Duties of the Game

Duties of Referee He is responsible for fair play in the match. He is the final authority on the rules and regulations from the start to the end of the match. Referee performs toss before the start of the match. He has the final say on every decision of the match.

Duties of Scorer He takes notes of all the proceedings of the match in a chronological order, alongwith the points gained, time and substitutions made. He makes a record of all the fouls made by each player of each team. Scorer maintains a score sheet with all the details of each player.

Duties of Timekeeper He notifies and assists the referee regarding the time issues of the game. He is responsible for notifying referee about the time at which each part of the match has to begin. This needs to be done atleast three minutes before the actual start of the game. He shall start timeout watch for charged timeout. The timekeeper also keeps record of the various times and situations when the match was paused and resumed.

Fundamental Skills and Techniques

Some fundamental skills and techniques required for handball are as follows

1. **Catching the Ball** Accurate catching is very important and ensures a fast, smooth and efficient game. Catching the ball with two hands is the best method.
2. **Passing** This is one of the basic technical elements. A pass must be accurate (so that the player to whom the ball is passed has no problem when catching the ball), fast and tactically useful. A pass should be directed to that player whose position may endanger the opponents.

There are various techniques to make a pass

(i) *Bounce Pass* Ball is bounced approximately three feet in front of the receiver.

(ii) *Hook Pass* It is a jump shot pass where a player simply releases the ball to his teammate while making a jump in the air.

(iii) *Chest Pass* It is a frequent pass of the ball performed with the fingers of two hands. Ball is held close to the chest while making such a pass.

3. **Shooting** Making an attempt to goal is called *shooting.* While shooting, the muscles of the lower and upper limbs, pelvic region and trunk are actively engaged. Scoring a goal requires the use of few special tricks. *Three of such special tricks are*

   (i) *Dive Shot* In this, the player makes a dive towards the goal with the ball in his/her hands. He/She should release the ball at the last possible moment during a dive.

   (ii) *Jump-Throw* In this, the shooter runs a short distance (maximum of three steps) and jumps to throw the ball at the goal. It is an effective technique specially when there are one or two players of the opposing team who may be chasing the ball nearby.

   (iii) *Fall-away Throw* This throw is mainly used for throws over goalpost from the wings (at the edge of the goal area). The shooter jumps up, followed by a twist in the air to attain a horizontal position and then throws the ball.

Jump Throw

Fall-away Throw

Throw Dribbling

4. **Dribbling** Dribbling or bouncing on the ground is performed by the combined action of the elbow and wrist joints. The angle of the bounced ball depends on the speed that the player is moving at.
5. **Three-for-Two Rule** It is a strategic move in which two defenders come close and restrain the opponent to throw the ball.
6. **Fake** Pretend you're going to do something (like shoot or pass) to trick the defender or goalie, then quickly do something different.
7. **Screen** Stand in a way that blocks the defender's view or path, making it easier for a teammate to get the ball or score.
8. **Underhand Shot** Shoot the ball with a low, sweeping motion from below your waist, often to catch the goalie off guard.
9. **Lob Shot** Shoot the ball high so it goes over the goalie's head into the net, useful when the goalie is out of position.

10. **Goalkeeper's Technique** Playing as a goalkeeper requires a lot of physical and mental effort. A goalkeeper must be very fit, bold and self-controlled. His actions are not only limited to defending the goal. The basic stance of a goalkeeper is arms raised to the side with his legs apart.

Goalkeeper's Technique

Popular Tournaments

International

- Olympic Games
- Open National Championship (USA)
- SAARC Handball Championship
- Flanders Handball Trophy (Europe)
- Asian Games
- Commonwealth Games
- World Youth Cup
- International Handball Federation Cup

National

- HFI Men's National Handball Championship, HFI Women's National Handball Championship, Ashok Memorial Tournament
- NIS Indoor Stadium (Patiala and Gandhi Nagar), Indira Gandhi Stadium (New Delhi), PAP campus ground (Jalandhar), Sports Complex (Bengaluru), Tata Sports Complex (Tata Nagar)

Popular Handball Awardees

Arjuna Awards

- 1978 Manjit Singh
- 1990 Surjeet Singh
- 1997 R. Lubhaya
- 1984 Roshan Lal
- 1994 Malkit Singh
- 1999 Anjesh Kumar

Popular International Players

- Ivano Balic (Croatia)
- Nikola Karabatic (France)
- Arpad Sterbik (Spain)
- Eduarda Amorim (Brazil)

Viva-Voce

Q.1 Who introduced Handball in Germany during the 19th century?

Ans. Handball was introduced in Genmany during the 19th century by Konrad Koch.

Q.2 In which year was Handball introduced in India?

Ans. Handball was introduced in India in 1970.

Q.3 How many players are allowed on the handball court from each team at a time?

Ans. 7 players are allowed on the handball court from each team at a time.

Q.4 What is the total number of players in a handball team including substitutes?

Ans. 12 players (7 are on the court and 5 are substitutes)

Q.5 What are the dimensions of a standard handball court?

Ans. The dimensions of a standard handball court is 40 meters × 20 meters

Q.6 How long is each half in a men's handball match?

Ans. In a men's handball match, each half is 30 minutes long.

Q.7 From what distance is a 7-metre throw taken?

Ans. A 7- meters throw is taken from a distance of 7 meters.

Q.8 Which type of shot is performed by jumping and shooting over defenders?

Ans. The type of shot performed by jumping and shooting over defenders is a Jump Throw.

Q.9 Name the foul where a player dribbles, stops, and then dribbles again.

Ans. Double Dribble.

Q.10 Which official is responsible for maintaining the score sheet?

Ans. Scorer is responsible for maintaining the score sheet.

Q.11 What card is shown for a warning in handball?

Ans. For warning in handball, yellow card is shown.

Q.12 Which zone is restricted only to the goalkeeper?

Ans. Goal area is restricted only to the goalkeeper.

Q.13 Which international player belongs to France?

Ans. Nikola Karabatic belongs to France.

Q.14 What is the weight of the handball used in women's category?

Ans. The weight of the hand ball used in women's category is 325–375 grams

Q.15 Name any one popular national handball tournament in India.

Ans. HFI Men's National Handball Championship.

Game 3

Tennis

History

Modern Tennis has its roots in 12th century Northern France, where ball was struck with the palm of the hand and it was known as 'jen de paume' which evolved into Tennis. Later in the 16th century, the rackets came into use and the game was known as Tennis. The term Tennis came from the old French word 'tenez' which meant 'hold'.

In 1872, world's first Tennis club was founded in England. The world's oldest Tennis Tournament, the Wimbledon Championship was first played in 1877 in London. Then the US Open, the French Open and the Australian Open started. These four became the most prestigious events in Tennis known as Grand Slam.

The All India Tennis Association (AITA) was established in 1920 to oversee and promote tennis in India. The organisation played a key role in organising national championships and developing tennis infrastructure across the country. AITA also facilitated India's involvement in international competitions, including the Davis Cup, where India has been a consistent participant since 1921.

The International Tennis Federation (ITF) is the sport's global governing body. It establishes specifications for equipments, court dimensions and surfaces, certifies officials and umpires and maintains the rules.

Measurements and Specifications

- Length of the court (Singles and Doubles) = 23.77 m (78 feet)
- Breadth for Singles= 8.23 m (27 feet)
- Breadth for Doubles = 10.97 m (36 feet)
- Height of the posts = 1.07 m (3 feet 6 inches)
- Diameter of the posts= 15 cm (6 inches)
- Height of the net from the centre = 0.91 m (3 feet)
- Width of the strap = 5 cm (2 inches)
- Service line distance from centre line and parallel to it = 6.40 m (21 feet)
- Width of the serivce court for Singles = 4.11 m (13 feet 6 inches)
- Width of the service court for Doubles = 5.50 m (18 feet)
- Width of all court service line = 5 cm (2 inches)
- Distance of posts away from side lines = 0.91 m (3 feet)
- Distance between base line and service line = 5.49 m (18 feet)
- Band covering = 5 to 6.3 cm
- Diameter of the cord or metal = 0.8 cm

- Diameter of Tennis Ball = 2.57 –2.70 inches (6.5 – 6.85 cm)
- Weight of Tennis Ball = 56 – 59.4 gm
- Colour of Ball = White or yellow
- Length of Rocket = 32 inches
- Width of Frame =12.5 inches
- Breadth of string = 29.21 cm
- Length of string = 39.37 cm

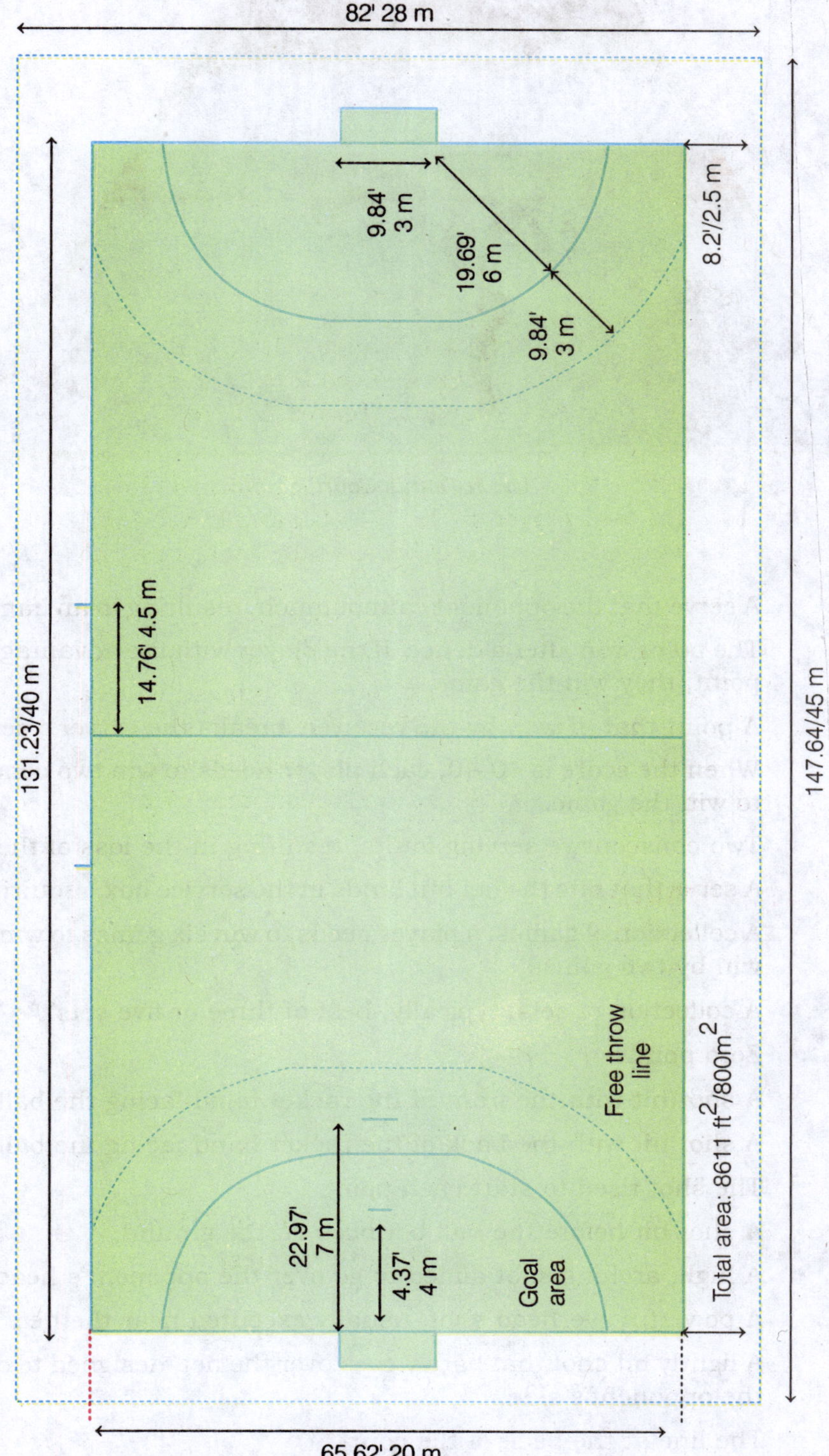

Layout of Lawn Tennis Court

Tennis Court

Tennis is played on a rectangular flat surface, usually made of grass, clay or hard material. A net is stretched across the full width of the court, parallel with the baselines, dividing it into two equal ends.

Lawn Tennis Court

Terminology

Ace	A serve that the opponent cannot touch, resulting in an immediate point.
Advantage	The point won after a deuce. If the player with the advantage wins the next point, they win the game.
Break Point	A point that, if won by the receiver, breaks the server's serve.
Deuce	When the score is 40-40, each player needs to win two consecutive points to win the game.
Double Fault	Two consecutive serving faults, resulting in the loss of the point.
Let	A serve that hits the net but lands in the service box, requiring a re-serve.
Set	A collection of games; a player needs to win six games to win a set but must win by two games.
Match	A collection of sets; typically, best of three or five sets.
Love	Zero points
Forehand	A shot hit with the front of the racket hand facing the ball.
Backhand	A shot hit with the back of the racket hand facing the ball.
Serve	The shot used to start each point.
Volley	A shot hit before the ball bounces on the ground.
Lob	A high, arching shot aimed to go over the opponent's head.
Smash	A powerful overhead shot, usually executed near the net.
Drop Shot	A lightly hit shot that barely goes over the net, designed to drop quickly on the opponent's side.
Baseline	The line at the back of the court.
Service Box	The area where a serve must land.
Net	The barrier dividing the two halves of the court.

Rally	A sequence of back-and-forth shots between players.
Tiebreak	A special game played to decide a set when the score is 6-6, with the first player to 7 points (must win by 2) winning the set.
Foot Fault	A violation where the server steps over the baseline before hitting the ball.
Topspin	A shot with topspin that causes the ball to dip quickly and bounce higher.
Backspin (Slice)	A shot with backspin that causes the ball to stay low and float.
Lob	A high, arching shot designed to go over the opponent and land deep in their court.
Inside-Out Shot	A shot where the player hits the ball from the inside of their stance to the opposite side of the court.
Inside-In Shot	A shot where the player hits the ball from the inside of their stance to the same side of the court.

General Rules

(i) *Serve* The server stands behind the base line, between the centre mark and the alley lane. The server cannot step on and over any lines while serving. The server must toss the ball upward and hit it over the net into the box diagonally across from him. The server gets two chances to make a good serve.

(ii) *Return and Rally* The served receiver has to return the ball after one bounce. He must hit the ball over the net and it has to land within the alley lines and the base line. In the same way, the game continues. The ball remains in play until it bounces twice before being hit, is hit out, or fails to go over the net.

(iii) *Let* A service is a let if the ball touches the net, band or strap but is good service, if it touches the receiver before hitting the ground and if the receiver is not ready when the service is delivered.

(iv) *Change of Sides* The player will change the sides at the end of 1st, 3rd and every subsequent alternate game of each set unless the total number of games in each set is in even number.

(v) *Penalties* There are certain penalties while playing Tennis. These are as follows

Touching opponent's ground, carrying the ball or catching it in the racket. Hitting the ball two times before it has crossed the net, if the ball hits or touches anything (clothes) or throwing the racket or verbal abuse.

(vi) *Officials* Only professional tournaments are officiated. One official watches the lines to call whether the ball is in or not. The senior umpire has the power to overrule all other judges. There is also a match referee who sits in the stands and watches.

(vii) *Scoring* In tennis, scoring begins with points, where players compete to reach 4 points to win a game. The points are counted as 15, 30, 40, and "game", but to win a game, a player must be ahead by at least two points. If both players reach 40 points, it's called "deuce," and the game continues until one player wins two consecutive points, first gaining "advantage" and then the game. A set is won by the first player to win six games with a two-game lead; if the score ties at 6-6, a tiebreaker is usually played. A match consists of several sets, and the player who wins the majority of the sets wins the match.

(viii) *Winning* A point is won when a player successfully hits the ball into the opponent's court in a way that they can't return it, or when the opponent makes an error like hitting the ball out of bounds, into the net, or failing to return the ball before it bounces twice. Points can also be won if the opponent double faults during their serve. These points accumulate to win games, sets and ultimately the match.

Fundamental Skills

The fundamental Tennis skills and techniques are as follows

(i) **Tennis Serves** There are several types of serves, like, topspin, topspin-slice, flat, slice and many others. Most importantly the serve must be developed as a primary weapon, while achieving pin-point accuracy and depth.

Tennis Serves

(ii) **The Grips** The grip is very vital for making a stroke. There are three basic grips—Eastern, Western and Continental, used to execute the forehand strokes and drives.

(iii) **Strokes** Hitting the Tennis ball with a Tennis racket is called a Tennis stroke. Few of the important strokes include–Tennis Forehand Strokes, Tennis Backhand Strokes, Tennis Lob, Smash, Tennis Volley, etc.

Popular International Tournaments

1. Davis Cup (Men)
2. Olympic Tennis Championship
3. US Open
4. Asian Tennis Championship
5. Hopman Cup (Men/Women)
6. ATP World Tour Finals
7. Miami Open
8. Madrid Open
9. Italian Open
10. Sony-Ericsson Open
11. Australian Open
12. UNICEF Open

Popular Venues

1. Wimbledon - London, England
2. Roland Garros - Paris, France
3. Arthur Ashe Stadium - New York City, USA
4. Rod Laver Arena - Melbourne, Australia
5. Indian Wells Tennis Garden - Indian Wells, California, USA
6. Madrid Arena - Madrid, Spain

Popular Tennis Awardees

Arjuna Awardees

- 1990 Leander Paes
- 1995 Mahesh Bhupathi
- 1996 Gaurav Natekar
- 1997 Asif Ismail
- 2000 Akhtar Ali
- 2001 Sandeep Kirtane
- 2004 Sania Mirza
- 2011 Somdev Devvarman
- 2016 Shri Rohan Bopanna
- 2020 Divij Sharan
- 2021 Ankita Rana

Rajiv Ghandhi (Major Dhyan Chand) **Khel Ratna Awardees**

- 1997 Leander Paes
- 2015 Sania Mirza

Dhyan Chand Awardees

- 2014 Zeeshan Ali
- 2015 Shiv Prakash Mishra
- 2019 Nitten Kirrtane
- 2020 Nandan P. Bal

Padma Shri Awardees

- 2024 Rohan Bopanna

Popular Tennis Players

India

1. Vijay Amritraj
2. Anand Amritraj
3. Ramanathan Krishnan
4. Ramesh Krishnan
5. Leander Paes
6. Mahesh Bhupathi
7. Sania Mirza
8. Somdev Devvarman

International

Male	Female
Bjorn Borg (Sweden)	Billy Jean King (USA)
John McEnroe (USA)	Steffi Graf (Germany)
Pete Sampras (USA)	Martina Navratilova (Czech Republic and USA)

Male	Female
Boris Becker (Germany)	
Rafeal Nadal (Spain)	Monica Seles (Serbia)
Rogar Federer (Switzerland)	Serena Williams (USA)

Viva-Voce

Q.1 Tennis derived from which ancient French game?

Ans. Tennis is derived from an ancient French game called Jeu de paume.

Q.2 What is the meaning of the word "tenez" in French?

Ans. The French word 'tenez' means Hold or take heed.

Q.3 When was the All India Tennis Association (AITA) formed?

Ans. All India Tennis Association (AITA) formed in 1920.

Q.4 What is the name of the first grand Slam tournament ever held?

Ans. The first grand slam tournament ever held was "The Wimbledon Championship" which was first played in 1877.

Q.5 Which organization governs Tennis worldwide?

Ans. International Tennis Federation (ITF) governs Tennis Worldwide.

Q.6 What is the length of a standard tennis court?

Ans. The length of a standard tennis court is 23.77 m.

Q.7 What is the height of the net at the centre in tennis?

Ans. The height of the net at the centre in tennis is 0.91 m.

Q.8 What is the official diameter range of a tennis ball?

Ans. The official diameter range of a tennis ball is 6.5 to 6.85 cm.

Q.9 What is the maximum length of a tennis racket?

Ans. The maximum length of a tennis racket is 32 inches.

Q.10 What is the term for a score of zero in Tennis?

Ans. The term for a score of zero in Tennis is Love.

Q.11 What is a "let" in tennis?

Ans. A serve that hits the net but lands in service box, requiring a re-serve.

Q.12 What do you call a score of 40–40?

Ans. A score of 40-40 in tennis is called Deuce.

Q.13 Name one Indian tennis player who won the Arjuna Award in 2004.

Ans. Sania Mirza.

Q.14 Which Indian tennis player won a Khel Ratna in 1997?

Ans. The Khel Ratna Award in 1997 was given to tennis player Leander Paes.

Q.15 What is the most prestigious tennis stadium in London?

Ans. Wimbledon is the most prestigious tennis stadium in London.

Game 4

Athletics

(Track and Field)

History

The term Athletics is derived from the Greek word **Athlos** which means **'contest'**. In ancient Greece, "athletics" was known as "track and field".

Track and field are mostly an individual sport with around 30 different events. These events are divided into 'Track Events' (Sprints, Middle distance, Long distance, Hurdle, Relay, Steeplechase and Obstacle races), and 'Field Event' (Jumping and Throwing). People first practiced a simple form of these events in Egypt over 4,000 years ago. The first organised athletics competition took place in 776 BC in Olympia, Greece.

The first modern Olympic games was held in **1896** in Athens, Greece. It was consisted mainly of track and field events.

In **1912**, the International Amateur Athletic Federation (IAAF) was established and it became the international governing body for athletics. In **1928** Amsterdam Olympic games the track and field events were opened for female athletes for the first time. Athletic Federation of India (AFI) then Amateur Athletics Federation of India was formed in 1946 at the initiative of Maharaja Yadavindra Singh and Prof. Guru Dutt Sondhi.

In **1960**, the major athletics competitions for disabled athletes were first introduced in Summer Para Olympics. From the **1960s**, athletics gained more exposure through television coverage. In the late **1970s**, the amateur status of the sport began to be displaced by growing professionalism.

In **1982**, the IAAF abandoned amateurism and later changed its name to International Association of Athletics Federations.

Types Of Events

Mainly, there are two types of events in Athletics: Track events and Field events.

Track Events

In these events, the athletes compete against time or clock. A variety of running events are held on the track. *These are as follows*

(i) *Sprint Races* 100 m, 200 m, 400 m

(ii) *Middle Distance Races* 800 m, 1500 m

(iii) *Long Distance Races* 3000 m, 5000 m, 10000 m

(iv) *Marathon Race* (42.195 km), 20 km walk, 50 km walk

(v) *Hurdle Races* 100 m (women), 110 m (men), 400 m (women/men)

(vi) *Relay Races* 4 × 100 m, 4 × 400 m

(vii) *Steeplechase Races* 3000 m (m/w)

Field Events

Field events are classified into two types, which are as follows

(i) *Throwing Events* Shot put, discus throw, hammer throw, javelin throw.

(ii) *Jumping Events* Long jump, high jump, triple jump, pole vault.

Decathlon and Heptathlon Events

Decathlon Events (M) 100 m sprint, long jump, shot put, high jump, 400 m sprint, 110 m hurdles, discus throw, pole vault, javelin throw and 1500 m run.

Decathlon Events (M)

Heptathlon Events (W) 100 m hurdles, high jump, shot put, 200 m sprint, long jump, javelin throw and 800 m run.

Heptathlon Events (W)

The Standard Track

In athletics, a proper track is the most essential thing. A standard track (400 m) consists of 2 straight paths and 2 curves (making one circle). The straight paths of the track should be in parallel to each other and the curves connecting them.

The straight paths of a standard track may be from 70 to 90 m, but in international competitions, straight path of 84 m is preferred. All lines over the track are marked 5 cm thick.

Standard track (400 m) = 2 straight + 2 curves = 2 straight + circumference of circle ($2\pi R$)

In standard track, a straight path is 84 m.

$\therefore$ 2 straight = 84 + 84 = 168 m

$\therefore$ Circumference of circle ($2\pi R$) = 400−168 = 232 m

$$\text{Radius } (R) = \frac{232}{2\pi} = \frac{232}{2 \times 3.14} = 36.90 \text{ m}$$

This is known as Running Radius (RR).

$\therefore$ Running Radius (RR) = 36.90 m

The track is marked 30 cm inside the running radius to avoid fouls.

$\therefore$ Marking Radius (MR) = 36.90−0.30 = 36.60 m

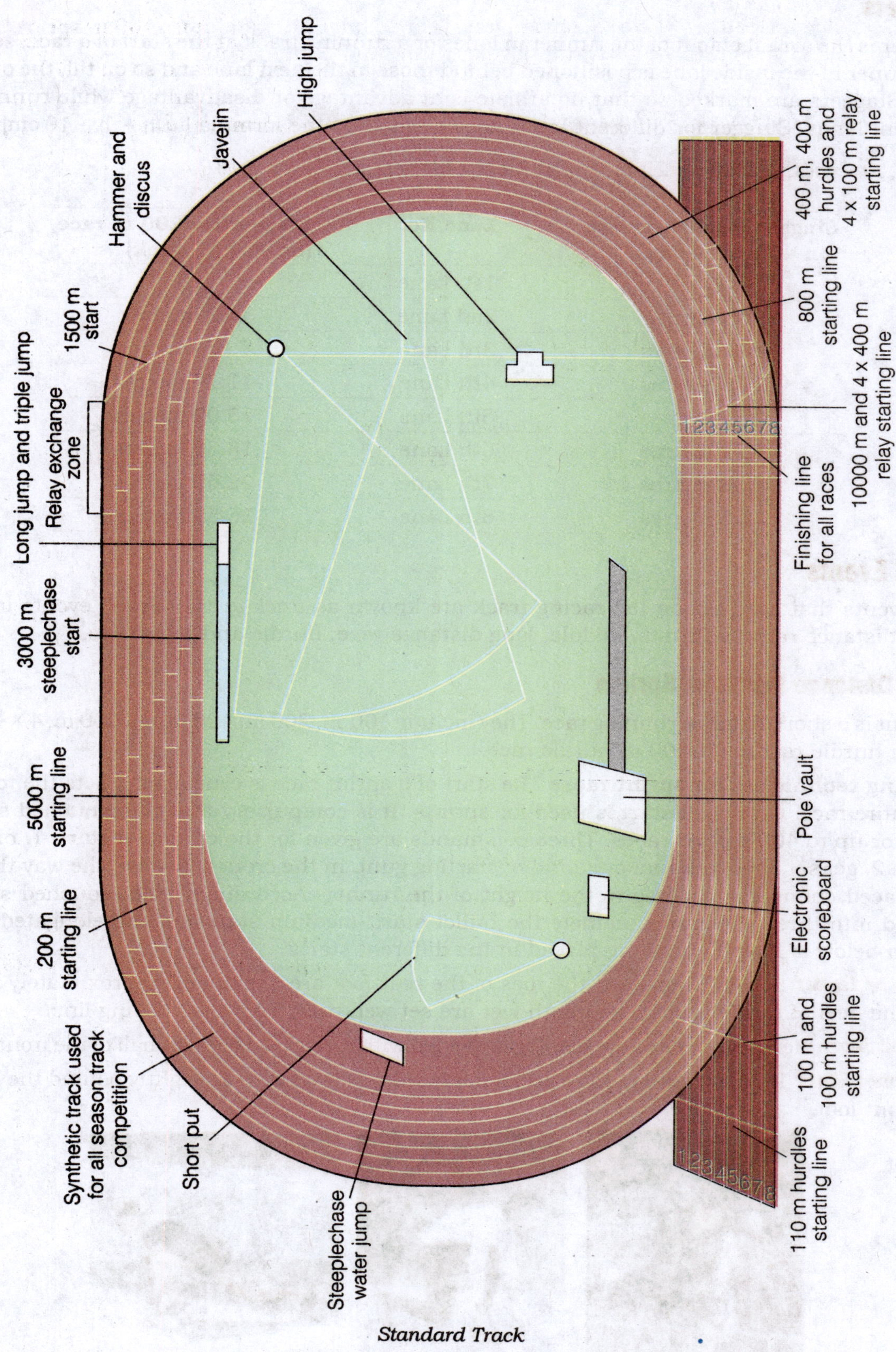

Standard Track

Staggers

Stagger is the arrangement of the runner in lanes or a running track at the start of a race, so that, the runner in the inside lane is positioned behind those in the next lane and so on till, the outside lane. Staggers are marked so that no athlete is at advantage or disadvantage while running in different lanes. Stagger for different lanes is calculated by the formula $[w(n-1) - 10 \text{ cm}] \times 2\pi$ where, w = width of lane 1.22 m, n = number of lanes, $\pi = \frac{22}{7}$ or 3.14

Stagger for 400 m race (on 400 m track)	Lane No.	Stagger for 200 m race (on 400 m track)
0	1st Lane	0
7.04 metres	2nd Lane	3.52 metres
14.71 metres	3rd Lane	7.35 metres
22.38 metres	4th Lane	11.19 metres
30.05 metres	5th Lane	15.02 metres
37.72 metres	6th Lane	18.86 metres
45.38 metres	7th Lane	22.69 metres
53.05 metres	8th Lane	26.52 metres

Track Events

The events that are held on the racing track are known as *track events*. Track events include short distance race or sprints, middle, long distance race, hurdle and relay race.

Short Distance Races or Sprints

A sprint is a short distance running race. They include 100 m, 200 m, 400 m, 4 × 100 m, 4 × 400 m, 110 m hurdle races and 100 m hurdle race.

Starting techniques for sprint races The start of a sprint race is crucial as it sets the tone for the entire race. Crouched start is used for sprints. It is compulsory that the crouched start is used for up to 400 metres races. Three commands are given for the crouched start: 1. on your marks 2. get set 3. go (a signal or sound of starting gun). In the crouched start, the way the legs are placed changes according to the height of the runner. Accordingly, the crouched start is divided into three categories, namely the bullet start, medium start and the elongated start. Shown below is how the legs are placed in the different starts.

Bunch or Bullet Start In this start, the toes of the rear foot are positioned approximately in line with the heel of the front foot, and both feet are set well back from the starting line.

Medium Start Here, the knee of the rear leg is aligned with a point in the front half of the front foot.

Elongated Start In this position, the knee of the rear leg is level with or slightly behind the heel of the front foot.

Bunch or Bullet Start

Medium Start

Elongated Start

Finishing Techniques used in Sprint Races

Athletes uses the following three techniques in finishing races

(i) *Run through technique* In this type of finish, the athlete maintains full speed and crosses the finish line without slowing down or adjusting their stride.

(ii) *Drop finish technique or lunge* In this type of finish, the athlete bends both arms backward and tries to touch the tape on the finish line with their chest when they are just one step away.

(iii) *Shoulder shrugging technique* In this type of finish, the athlete turns their chest sideways and shrugs their opposite shoulder into the tape at the very last moment.

Middle Distance Races

The most common middle distance track events are the 800 m and 1500 m. These races require different skills and tactics to win. *The following steps are followed in middle distance races*

(i) *Standing Start* In middle-distance races, athletes use a standing start because a crouched start isn't helpful. The starter only says "on your marks" without giving a "set" signal. At this point, runners take their positions behind the starting line. Their front leg should be slightly bent, and they should lean forward a bit. Elbows should be bent, and arms relaxed. Runners should focus on the sound of the starting gun.

(ii) *Starting of the Race* At the starting signal, athletes push off powerfully, accelerate smoothly, and then settle into a steady pace to conserve energy.

(iii) *Running Technique* Runners should lean slightly forward, keep their torso relaxed, and swing their arms naturally with bent elbows. Stride smoothly with a consistent cadence, breathe deeply and rhythmically, and start at a steady pace. Focus on form, pace, and breathing to maintain endurance and efficiency.

(iv) *Finishing the Race* For the finish, sprint hard, maintain good form, and lean slightly forward as you cross the line. Focus on the finish line, push through fatigue, and use all your remaining energy.

Long Distance Races

There are three common long distance running events in track and field competitions: 3000 m, 5000 m, 10000 m, Cross Country (20 km) and Marathon (50 km).

Hurdle Races

A hurdle race is one, in which obstacles are placed at intervals along the track that the runners must jump over on their way to the finishing line. Typical hurdle races are 100 m (for women), 110 m (for men) and 400 m (for men and women).

There are 10 hurdles in each lane, set out in accordance with the following table

Hurdle Distances

Race Distance	Hurdle Height	Distance of 1st Hurdle from Start	Distance Between Hurdles	Distance of last Hurdle from Finish Line
Men's 110 m	1.067 m $\left(3\frac{1}{2}\text{ ft}\right)$	13.72 m	9.14 m	14.02 m
Men's 400 m	0.91 m (3 ft)	45 m	35 m	40 m
Women's 100 m	0.84 m $\left(2\frac{3}{4}\text{ ft}\right)$	13 m	8.50 m	10.50 m
Women's 400 m	0.84 m $\left(2\frac{3}{4}\text{ ft}\right)$	45 m	35 m	40 m

Relay Races

In relay races, teams of runners compete against each other. Typically, a team is made of 4 runners of the same sex. The first runner starts with the baton and runs, handing-off to the second runner at the first exchange point. Similarly, the second passes to the third, the third to the fourth. The fourth runner runs the final and completes the finish line. There is usually a designated area where athletes must exchange the baton. Common relay races are the 4 × 100 m and the 4 × 400 m.

Field Events

Generally, there are two types of field events : Throwing events and Jumping events.

Throwing Events

There are four major throwing events in the Olympic games. They are shot put, discus throw, javelin throw and hammer throw.

1. Shot Put

The shot put is a track and field event involving throwing a heavy spherical object as far as possible. It is a throwing event, where a metallic ball is pushed from a throwing circle. The ball used in the game is also called as *shot.*

To qualify, competitors make 3 throws each and best 8 throwers make 3 more attempts. When there are 8 competitors or fewer, they are allowed to take 6 throws each.

Measurements and Specifications

Shot Weight	*Men*	: 7.26 kg (16 lbs)
	Women	: 4 kg (8.8 lbs)
Shot Diameter	*Men*	: 110-130 mm
	Women	: 95-110 mm
Throwing Circle	*Diameter*	: 2.135 meters (7 feet)
Surface	Typically made of concrete or a similar material	
Angle of Sector	34.92 degrees	
Stop board *(trig)*	*Width*	: 1.22 meters (4 feet)
	Height	: 10 cm (4 inches)

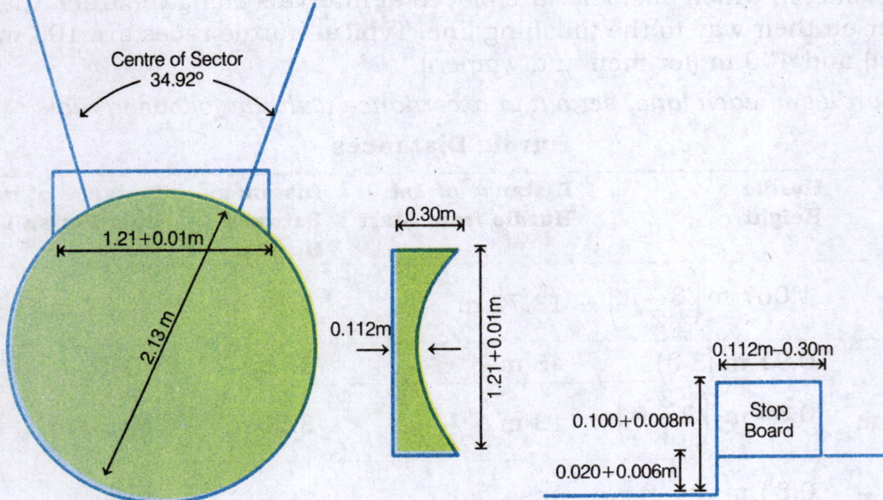

Short Put Circle and Stop Board

Techniques

O'Brien Style (Glide Technique)

1. *Starting Phase* Begin with a low crouch, then push off with the rear foot, lifting it from the back of the circle.
2. *Glide Phase* Glide smoothly across the circle, moving from the rear foot leaving the circle to landing the foot in the centre.
3. *Transition Phase* Transition from the rear foot landing in the centre of the circle to the front foot planting in the power position.
4. *Delivery Phase* Once in the power position, use your legs and torso to deliver the shot, extending your arm as the shot is pushed out.
5. *Recovery Phase* Maintain balance and ensure you remain within the circle after releasing the shot.

Rotational Technique (Spin Technique)

1. *Starting Phase* Begin with a low stance and rotate on the ball of your foot, starting the spin from the back of the circle.
2. *Glide Phase* Spin around the circle, using rotational momentum as you transition from the rear foot to the centre.
3. *Transition Phase* Move from the rear foot landing in the centre to the front foot grounding, completing the spin to face the throw direction.
4. *Delivery Phase* Use the spin momentum and leg drive to deliver the shot, pushing it out with maximum force as you extend your arm.
5. *Recovery Phase* Balance yourself and ensure you stay within the circle after the shot has been released.

2. Discus Throw

The discus throw is a track and field event in which an athlete throws a heavy disc called a discus in an attempt to mark a farther distance than their competitors. Discus is circular-shaped, made up of wood or metal fitted with circular rim of metal on edge. Discus requires fast, accelerated rotations from the back to the front of the circle and the skills used must be executed accurately.

Measurements and Specifications

Discus Weight	*Men*	:	2 kg (4.4 lbs)
	Women	:	1 kg (2.2 lbs)
Discus Diameter	*Men*	:	219-229 mm (8.6-9 inches)
	Women	:	180-210 mm (7.1-8.3 inches)
Throwing Circle	*Diameter*	:	2.5 meters (8.2 feet)
Angle of Sector	34.92 degrees		
Throwing Area	The discus must land within a sector marked by lines extending from the centre of the throwing circle.		

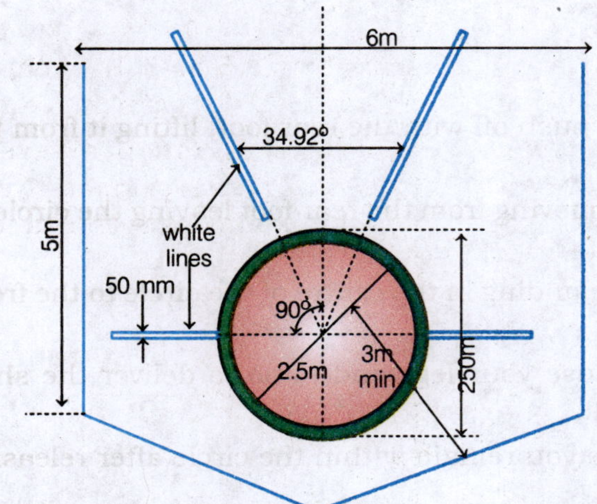

Discus Throw Measurements

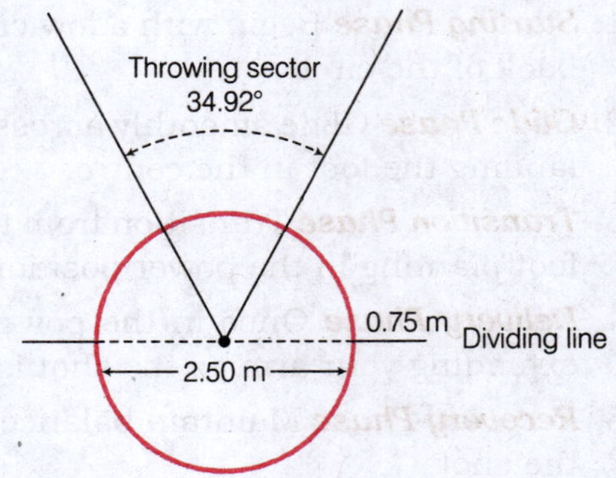

Layout of Discus Throw Sector

Techniques

1. *Starting Position* Stand with feet shoulder-width apart, holding the discus with your palm up.
2. *Wind-Up* Rotate your body, shifting weight to the rear leg, and use your non-throwing arm for balance.
3. *Rotation* Spin on your rear foot, keeping low and balanced as you turn your body.
4. *Release* Face the throw direction, flick the wrist to propel the discus, and extend your arm fully.
5. *Recovery* Maintain balance and stay within the circle after the throw.

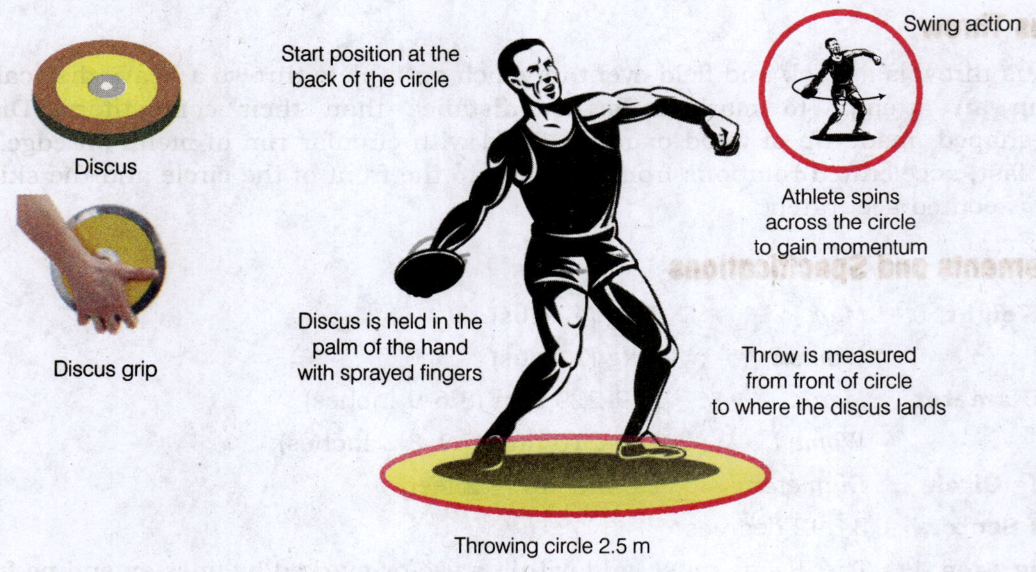

Discus Throw Technique

3. Javelin Throw

The javelin throw is a track and field event where the javelin, a spear about 2.5 m (8 ft 2 inch) in length, is thrown. It was introduced in 1908 Olympics for men and in 1932 for women.

Javelin is a smooth-surfaced, arrow-headed rod made up of steel or wood. Its fore part is very sharp and pointed, generally made up of metal. Its mid-part, also known as *grip,* is comparatively thick, having rope wrapped around it. Its third part or hind part is thin and conical in shape.

The current javelin throw specifications are as follows

S.No.	Javelin	For Men	For Women
1.	Weight of the javelin	800 gm	600 gm
2.	Length of runway	36 metres	
3.	Two parallel lines	4 metres apart	
4.	Length of the javelin	260 cm to 270 cm	220 cm to 230 cm
5.	Angle of sector	29°	

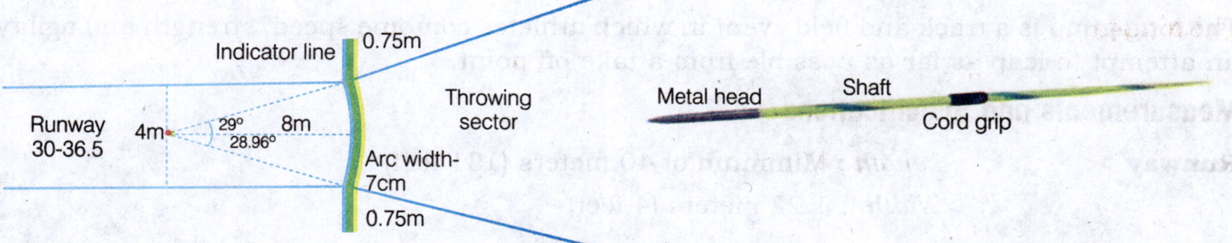

Runway for Javelin Throw and Javelin

Techniques

Grip

There are three types of grips, each depending on personal preference

1. *American Grip* Hold the javelin with the cord between the thumb and index finger.
2. *Finnish Grip* Extend the index finger under the shaft for control and grip the cord between the thumb and middle finger.
3. *V Grip* Grip the shaft between extended index and middle fingers.

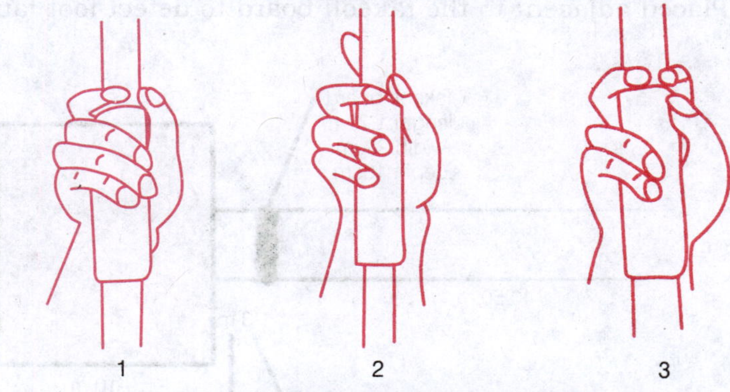

Javelin Throw Gripping Technique

Run-Up

- *Start* Hold the javelin high over your head, with your elbow level with your neckline and the javelin pointed slightly down.
- *Strides* Beginners take fewer than 10 strides; advanced throwers take 13 to 18 strides.

- *Positioning* Hips perpendicular to the target, planting foot pointed towards the target during the final strides.
- *Arm Position* Keep the throwing hand at shoulder height, arm straight, and pull the javelin back to throw.

Throw

- *Elbow Position* Keep your elbow high when coiling back to release.
- *Release Point* Ensure the point of release is in front of your planted foot.
- *Follow-Through* Complete the follow-through to maximise distance.

Jumping Events

Jumping is push oneself off a surface and into the air by using the muscles in one's legs and feet. There are four jumping events in field athletics : Long jump, triple jump, high jump and pole vault.

Long Jump or Broad Jump

The long jump is a track and field event in which athletes combine speed, strength and agility in an attempt to leap as far as possible from a take off point.

Measurements and Specifications

Runway	*Length* : Minimum of 40 meters (131 feet)
	Width : 1.22 meters (4 feet)
Takeoff Board	*Distance from Pit* : Generally, 1 meter (3.3 feet) from the sand pit.
	Width : 20 cm (7.87 inches)
	Length : 1.22 meters (4 feet)
	Material : Typically made of wood or synthetic material and painted white
Landing Pit	Width : Minimum of 2.75 meters (9 feet)
	Length : At least 9 meters (29.5 feet)
	Depth : The sand should be leveled and at least 30 cm (11.8 inches) deep
Plasticine Board	Placed adjacent to the takeoff board to detect foot faults.

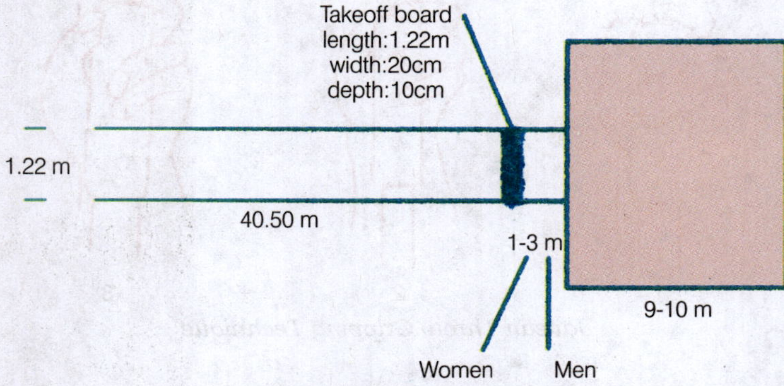

Long Jump Measurements

Techniques

Approach Run

Approach Run

- *Start* Begin with a controlled, consistent sprint from the start of the runway.
- *Acceleration* Gradually increase speed, maintaining balance and control.
- *Stride* Keep strides even and maintain an upright posture, focusing on speed and rhythm.

Takeoff

Takeoff

- *Last Two Strides* Shorten slightly to prepare for the jump, with the penultimate stride being longer and the final stride shorter.
- *Takeoff Foot* Plant firmly on the takeoff board, slightly ahead of the body's centre of gravity.
- *Body Position* Lean slightly backward, swing the opposite leg forward and upward to generate lift, and use arm drive for additional propulsion.

Flight

- *Hang Style* Extend your body, with arms and legs stretched outward. Tuck the legs under the body just before landing.
- *Hitch-Kick Style* Simulate a running motion in the air by cycling your legs, which helps maintain balance and control.
- *Sail Style* Extend both arms and legs forward, keeping your body in a pike position to maximise distance.

Landing

Landing

- *Legs Forward* Extend legs forward with feet aiming to touch the ground first.
- *Arms Backward* Swing arms backward to help lift the hips and extend the legs further.
- *Absorb Impact* Bend your knees and hips upon landing to absorb the shock and prevent falling backward.

Recovery

Recovery

- *Momentum* Use the forward momentum to push off from the landing position.
- *Balance* Maintain balance to avoid falling backward, ensuring the maximum distance is recorded.

Triple Jump

The triple jump, sometimes referred to as the hop, step and jump or the hop, skip and jump, is a track and field event similar to the long jump. As a group, the two events are referred to as the horizontal jumps.

Measurements and Specifications

Runway *Length* : Minimum of 40 meters (131 feet)
Width : 1.22 meters (4 feet)

Takeoff Board *Distance from Pit* : 9 meters (29.5 feet) to 13 meters (42.7 feet)
Width : 20 cm (7.87 inches).
Length : 1.22 meters (4 feet).
Material : Made of wood or synthetic material, painted white.

Landing Pit *Width* : Minimum of 2.75 meters (9 feet).
Length : 9 meters (29.5 feet)
Depth : The sand should be leveled and at least 30 cm (11.8 inches) deep.

Plasticine Board Placed adjacent to the takeoff board to detect foot faults.

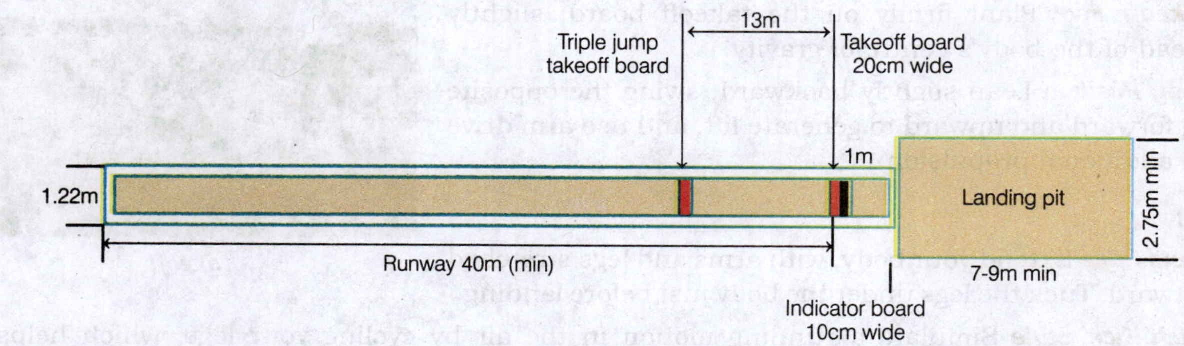

Triple Jump Measurements

Hop, Step and Jump

- *Hop* The first phase where the athlete takes off on one foot and lands on the same foot.
- *Step* The second phase where the athlete lands on the opposite foot.
- *Jump* The third phase where the athlete lands in the sand pit with both feet.

Techniques

- *Approach Run* Start with a controlled, accelerating run-up to build speed and momentum.
- *Hop Phase* Jump off one foot, drive the opposite knee forward, and land on the same foot.
- *Step Phase* Push off the takeoff foot, switch feet in the air, and land on the opposite foot.
- *Jump Phase* Use the momentum to drive into the final jump, extending both legs forward.
- *Landing* Land with both feet together in the sand pit, knees bent to absorb impact, and arms swinging forward for balance.

High Jump

The high jump is a track and field event where athletes aim to leap over a horizontal bar placed at measured heights without dislodging it. High jump was one of the nine original sports which featured at Athens 1896 – the first-ever Olympics of the modern era.

High Jump

Measurements and Specifications

Crossbar *Material* : Usually made of fiberglass or other flexible materials

Length : 4 meters (13 feet, 1.5 inches)

Diameter : Approximately 30 mm (1.2 inches)

Standards (Uprights) *Height*: Adjustable, typically up to 2.5 meters (8 feet, 2.5 inches) or higher

Distance Apart : 4 meters (13 feet, 1.5 inches), matching the length of the crossbar

Landing Area (Mat) *Length* : Minimum 5 meters (16 feet, 5 inches)

Width : Minimum 3 meters (9 feet, 10 inches)

Thickness : Minimum 0.5 meters (1 foot, 8 inches)

Runway *Length* : 15-25 meters (49-82 feet)

Width : Minimum 1.22 meters (4 feet)

Techniques

Approach

- *Run-Up* Athletes take a curved approach run towards the bar, usually from the left or right side, to generate speed and momentum. The curve helps in converting horizontal speed into vertical lift.

Takeoff

- *Jumping Leg* Plant the takeoff foot close to the bar and drive the opposite knee upward.
- *Arm Swing* Use the arms to generate additional lift.

Flight

- *Body Position* Arch the back to clear the bar with a technique called the Fosbury Flop, where the jumper goes over the bar head and shoulders first, with the back facing the bar.
- *Legs* Tuck the legs to avoid knocking the bar.

Landing

- *Mat* Land on a padded mat to cushion the fall.
- *Position* Typically, athletes land on their upper back and shoulders.

Famous Indian Athletes in Different Categories

Names	Categories
Hima Das	Sprinter
Dutee Chand	Sprinter
Muhammed Anas	Sprinter
Jinson Johnson	Middle Distance Runner
Bahadur Prasad	Middle Distance Runner
Sunita Rani	Long Distance Runner
Deep Chand	Long Distance Runner
Jyothi Yarraji	Hurdles
Joseph Abraham	Hurdles
Manjit Walia	Hurdles
Muhammad Ajmal Variyathodi	Relay racer

Subha Venkatesan	Relay racer
Kutty Saramma	Relay racer
Vikas Shive Gowda	Discus thrower
Seema Punia-Antil	Discus thrower
Kamalpreet Kaur	Discus thrower
Tajinderpal Singh Toor	Shot putter
Inderjeet Singh	Shot putter
Neeraj Chopra	Javelin thrower
Devarakeshavi Prakasha Manu	Javelin thrower
Murali Sreeshankar	Long jumper
Jeswin Aldrin	Long jumper
Reeth Abraham	Long jumper
Tejaswin Shankar	High jumper
Sahana Kumari	High jumper

Famous International Athletes and their Categories

Names	Categories	Countries
Christian Coleman	Sprinter	USA
Shelley-Ann Fraser-Pryce	Sprinter	Jamaica
Steve Mullings	Sprinter	Jamaica
Doug Lowe	Middle Distance Runner	England
Meseret Defar	Long Distance Runner	Ethiopia
David Oliver	Hurdles	USA
Liu Xiang	Hurdles	China
Dawn Harper	Hurdles	USA
Tianna Bartoletta	Relay racer	USA
Gabrielle Thomas	Relay racer	USA
Nesta Carter	Relay racer	Jamaica
Michael Frater	Relay racer	Jamaica
Mykolas ALEKNA	Discus thrower	Lithuanian
Piotr MALACHOWSKI	Discus thrower	Poland
Alex ROSE	Discus thrower	Samoa
Ryan Crouser	Shot putter	USA
Sarah Mitton	Shot putter	Canada
Lijiao Gong	Shot putter	China
Maddison-Lee Wesche	Shot putter	New Zealand
Jakub VADLEJCH	Javelin thrower	Czech Republican
Arshad Nadeem	Javelin thrower	Pakistan
Wayne PINNOCK	Long jumper	Jamaica
Mattia FURLANI	Long jumper	Italy
Jeremiah DAVIS	Long jumper	USA
Shelby MCEWEN	High jumper	USA
Hamish KERR	High jumper	New Zealand

Viva-Voce

Q.1 What does the word "Athletics" mean?

Ans. Athletics means contest or competition, derived from the Greek word "Athlos."

Q.2 Where and when was the first organized athletics competition held?

Ans. The first organized athletics competition was held in Olympia, Greece, in 776 BC.

Q.3 When were women first allowed to compete in Olympic track and field events?

Ans. Women first competed in Olympic track and field events in 1928 at the Amsterdam Olympics.

Q.4 Name the two main categories of athletics events.

Ans. Track events and field events.

Q.5 What is the minimum length of the runway used in long jump and triple jump?

Ans. The Minimum length of the runway used in long jump and triple jump is of 40 meters.

Q.6 Name the four main jumping events in athletics.

Ans. Long jump, triple jump, high jump, and pole vault.

Q.7 What is the purpose of the plasticine board in long jump and triple jump?

Ans. The purpose of the plasticine board in long jump and triple jump is to detect foot faults at the takeoff board.

Q.8 What is the angle of the throwing sector in shot put and discus throw?

Ans. The angle of the throwing sector in shot put and discus throw is 34.92 degrees.

Q.9 What is the standard width of each lane on an athletics track?

Ans. The standard width of each lane on an athletics tracks is 1.22 meters.

Q.10 Name the two primary combined events in athletics and state who participates in each.

Ans. Decathlon (men) and heptathlon (women).

Q.11 What is the difference between the running radius and the marking radius on a track?

Ans. The running radius is used for actual running distance calculation, while the marking radius is measured 30 cm inside the running radius for lane marking.

Q.12 What are the three main finishing techniques in sprint races?

Ans. The three main finishig techniques in sprint races are run through, drop finish, and shoulder shrug.

Q.13 What are the three phases of the triple jump?

Ans. The three phases of the triple jump are hop, step, and jump.

Q.14 What is the minimum depth of the landing pit in long jump?

Ans. The minimum depth of the landing pit in long jump is 30 cm.

Q.15 Name two types of grip used in javelin throw.

Ans. American grip and Finnish grip.

Q.16 What is the length of the men's javelin?

Ans. The length of the men's Javelin is 260–270 cm.

Q.17 Who is a famous Indian long jumper?

Ans. Murali Sreeshankar is a famous Indian long jumper.

Q.18 What is the main purpose of the stop board in shot put?

Ans. To prevent the athlete from stepping out of the front of the circle during the throw.

Q.19 List one famous international sprinter and their country.

Ans. Christian Coleman, USA.

Q.20 What is the function of the takeoff board in jumping events?

Ans. It marks the point from which athletes must jump, ensuring fair measurement of the jump.

Game 5

Basketball

History

The game of basketball was introduced by *Dr James Naismith* in USA during 1891. He was a Physical Education instructor at the International Young Men's Christian Association (YMCA), Training School in Springfield, Massachusetts, USA.

At the 1992 Barcelona Games, the overwhelming dominance of the American men's team nicknamed *The Dream Team* made NBA Basketball popular around the world.

Federation Internationale de Basketball (FIBA), also known as the International Basketball Federation, was founded in Geneva on 18th June, 1932.

In 1924, basketball was introduced as a demonstration sport in the Olympic Games held in Paris. In 1936, International Basketball Federation (FIBA) organised the first official match of the European Championship. Men's basketball was included for the first time in 1936 at Berlin Olympics and women's basketball was allowed only in 1976 Montreal Olympics.

This sport was introduced in Europe by Americans during the Second World War. The First National Basketball Game in India was held in 1934 in Delhi. Basketball Federation of India (BFI), which controls the game in India, was formed in 1950. It is affiliated to FIBA. Basketball has been part of the Asian Games since 1951.

Measurements and Specifications

(i) Dimensions of court = 28 m × 15 m (excluding 5 cm thickness of lines)

(ii) Radius of centre circle = 1.80 m

(iii) Height of lower edge of board = 2.90 m from floor

(iv) Dimensions of backboard = 1.8 m ×1.05 m (1.2 m inside the end line)

(v) Thickness of backboard = 3 cm

(vi) Height of basket from ground = 3.05 m

(vii) Diameter of basket ring = 45 cm

(viii) Length of net of basket = 60 cm

(ix) Circumference of ball = 75-78 cm

(x) Weight of ball = 600 gm to 650 gm

(xi) Number of players of a team = 5 + 7 (extra) = 12

(xii) Number of officials = 5 (1-Referee, 1-Umpire, 1-Scorer, 1-Timekeeper, 1-24 second operator)

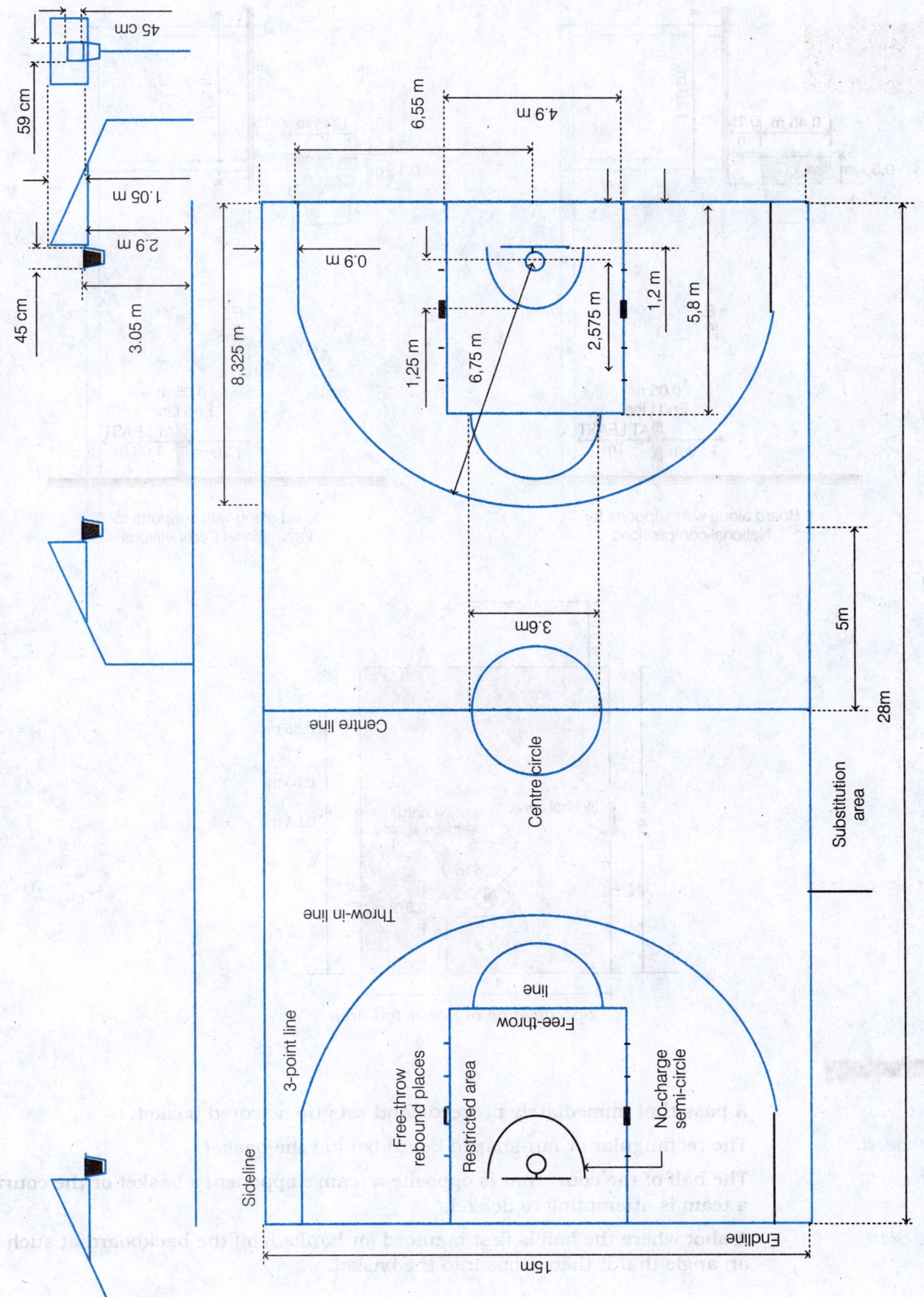

Layout of Basketball Court

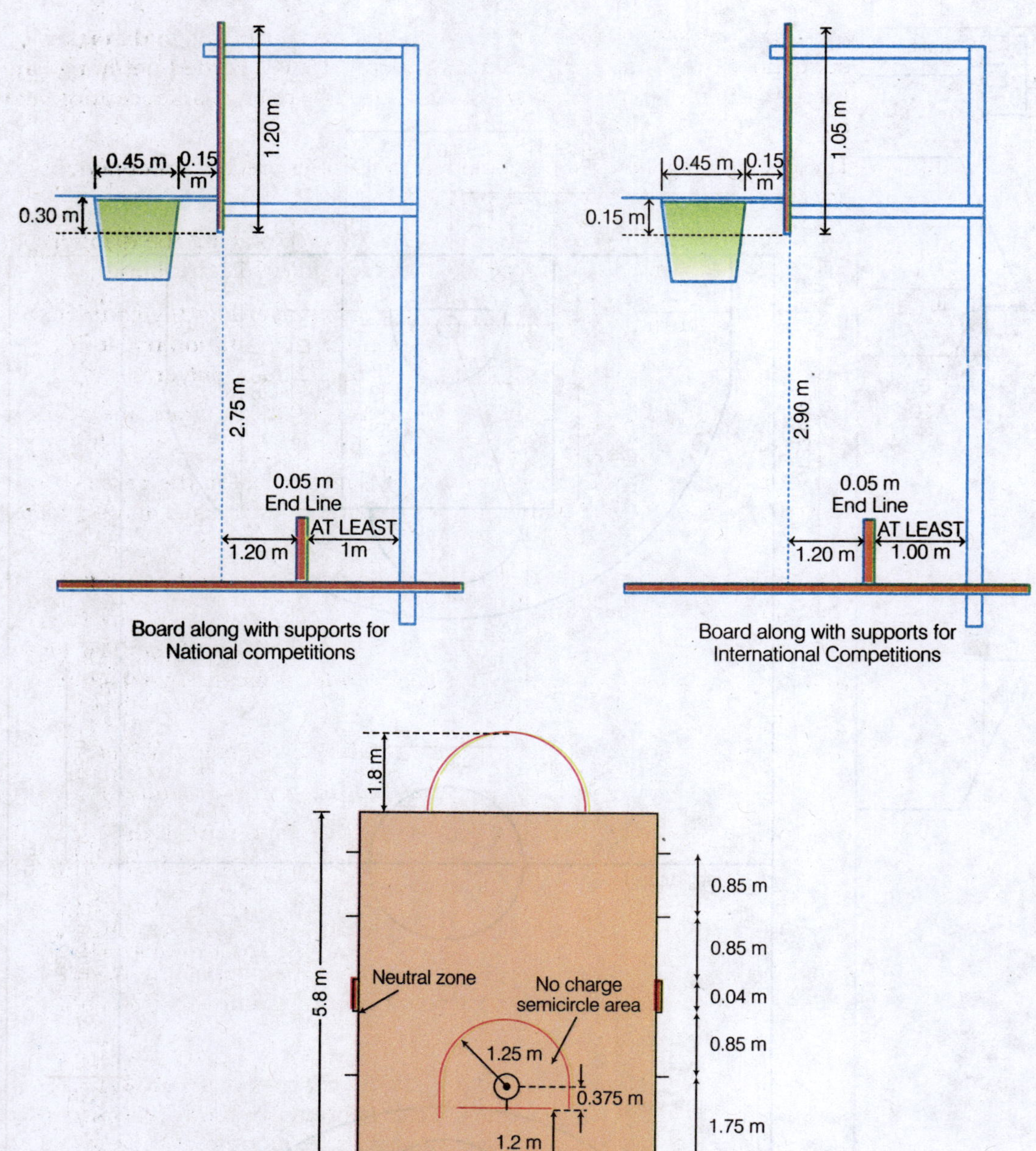

Specification of Restricted Area

Terminology

Assist	A pass that immediately proceeds and sets up a scored basket.
Backboard	The rectangular or fan-shaped board behind the basket.
Backcourt	The half of the court that is opposite a team's opponent's basket or the court a team is attempting to defend.
Bank Shot	A shot where the ball is first bounced (or banked) off the backboard at such an angle that it then drops into the basket.

Basket	Attached to the backboard, it consists of a metal rim 18″ in diameter suspended 10″ from the floor, from which a 15-18″ corded net hangs and through which points are scored. Also, used to refer to a successful field goal.
Blocking	The use of a defender's body position to illegally prevent an opponent's advance; the opposite of charging.
Carrying the Ball (also called palming)	A violation committed by a dribbler that involves placing the dribbling hand under the ball and shortly holding or carrying it while dribbling.
Charging	A personal foul committed when an offensive player illegally contacts a defensive player who has established position or is stationary. It is preventing defence from rear of player or backside of player.
Cut-in	It is the fast movement of a player towards the basket when one or more players of the opposite team are chasing after it.
Dead Ball	It occurs whenever the official blows the whistle to stop the game temporarily in case the ball lands out of bounds or in case of any violation, fouls etc.
Dodging	Pretending to move or throw the ball in one direction, but actually moving or throwing it in another direction.
Dribble	Process by which a player repeatedly bounces the ball off the floor so that it returns to his/her possession. It is the only legal means by which a player may move the ball across the court.
Foul	A violation resulting from illegal contact with an opposing player.
Free Throw	An unguarded shot taken from behind the free-throw line after a foul.
Front Court	This consists of the opponents' basket, the inbound part of the backboard, the sidelines and the inner edge of the centre line nearest to the opponents' basket.
Goal	A basket scored on a shot, except for a free throw, worth two or three points.
Jump Ball	A technique used to start or restart the game. Two opposing players jump for a ball that an official tosses above and between them.
Pass	An intentional throw to a teammate.
Personal Foul	Contact between players that may provide one team with an unfair advantage; players may not push, hold, trip, hack, elbow, restrain or charge into an opponent; these are also counted as team fouls.
Player-to-Player Defence (also called man-to-man defence)	A team defence in which each player is assigned to guard a particular opponent.
Possession	To be holding or in control of the ball.
Rebounding	When a player grabs a ball that is coming-off the rim or backboard after a failed shot attempt.
Shooting	An attempt to goal or basket scoring.
Shot Clock	A clock that limits the time allotted to a team with the ball and has to shoot it.
Substitute	A player who comes into the game to replace a player on the court.

Technical Foul A foul that does not involve contact with an opponent; or a contact foul committed by a player while the ball is dead.

Time-out When play is suspended by an official. Time-outs are 1 minute long. Each team may be granted 2 time-outs during the first half, 3 time-outs during the second half.

Violation An infringement of the rules that is not a foul. The penalty for a violation is the awarding of the ball to the opposing team.

Latest/General Rules

1. Basketball is played by 2 teams of 5 players each. There are extra 7 players in each team that may substitute the players if they need replacement.
2. The aim of each team is to score in the opponents' basket and to prevent the other team from scoring in their basket.
3. The game consists of 4 periods of 10 minutes each. First 2 periods are called first half and last 2 periods are called second half. In between I to II and III to IV periods there is an interval of 2 minutes and in between II and III periods, there is an interval of 5-10 minutes.
4. The game begins when the referee tosses the ball in the air and players jump to collect the ball.
5. A goal is made when a live ball enters the basket from above and remains within or passes through the basket.
6. A goal of 2 points is counted if the ball is thrown from a 2 points field goal area and 3 points if it is thrown from a 3 points field goal area. A goal of 1 point is counted if ball is thrown from free throw area.
7. After gaining possession of the ball, players must attempt a goal within 24 seconds.
8. The ball should not be held by a player for more than 5 seconds.
9. A player should not remain in opponents restricted area for more than 3 seconds.
10. The ball must be moved from rear (back) half of the court to the front within 8 seconds.
11. Personal fouls are counted if there is intentional or illegal contact with an opponent player. A player committing 5 personal fouls is not allowed to play any further.
12. In case of a tie, extra time of 5 minutes is given again and again to end the tie.

Fouls

It is the most common type of foul. It results from personal contact between two opposing players. A player is eliminated from the match if he consists personal fouls. Most personal fouls are called against a defensive player. A personal foul that is committed by a player of the team in possession of the ball is called an offensive foul. When neither team is in clear possession of the ball, a foul is called a loose-ball foul. Personal fouls includes charging, illegal blocking, guarding from behind, holding or pushing opponent, illegal screening, etc.

- **Technical Foul** When a coach or player performs misconduct or violent act deliberately consider as Technical Foul. In this foul, opponent gets two free throws alongwith throw in centre.
- **Intentional Foul** This foul is also known as Unsportsmanlike foul. This is a serious foul in which opponent gets two free throws along with side pass from centre line.
- **Multiple Foul** When two players are involved in the foul at almost the same time. Throw in taken from sideline is taken in alternate manner.
- **Team Fouls** These are the total fouls of the team. When team fouls exceed more than four fouls in each quarter then opponent team is awarded with two free throws on each foul.

Duties of Referee and Umpire

Referee

(i) He is responsible for fair play in the match.
(ii) He is the final authority on the rules and regulations from the start to the end of the match.
(iii) Referee performs toss before the start of the match.
(iv) He has the final say on every decision related of the match.

Umpire

(i) He assits the referee by enforcing rules during the match.
(ii) He signals fouls, violations or other rule breaches committed by players.

Duties of Scorer

(i) He takes notes of all the proceedings of the match in a chronological order, alongwith the points gained, time and substitutions made.
(ii) He makes a record of all the fouls made by each player of each team.
(iii) He records personal and technical fouls separately.
(iv) He maintains a score sheet with all the details of each player.

Duties of Timekeeper

(i) He notifies and assists the referee regarding the issues of the game.
(ii) He is responsible for notifying referee about the time at which each part of the match has to begin. This needs to be done atleast three minutes before the actual start of the game.
(iii) He shall start timeout watch for charged timeout.
(iv) The timekeeper also keeps record of the various times and situations when the match was paused and resumed.

Duties of 24 Second Operator

(i) His main duty is to check the 24 Second Rule.
(ii) He keeps a record of every time when possession of ball changes.

Fundamental Skills and Techniques

The brief description of some of the fundamental skills of basketball is given below

1. **Basic Stance**
   (i) *Defensive* There are two types of team defence: zone and man-to-man. In zone defence, each player is assigned a particular area of the court to defend, whereas in man-to-man defence, each player is assigned one of the opposing players.
   (ii) *Offensive* Attacking strategies may involve a number of passes and movement by all attacking players. The fast break is used to score quickly after the attacking team gets the possession of the ball.
2. **Jump Ball** To start the game, the ball is tossed and players jump for collecting the ball. They are not allowed to push or hit the opposing player.
3. **Passing** It is an act of throwing the ball to a teammate.
   (i) *Chest Pass* It is a direct pass to an own teammate at chest level. For performing a two handed chest pass perfectly, the player should hold the ball in front of the chest.
   (ii) *Bounce Pass* Player passes the ball to his teammates after beating defender with a bounce and it reaches the teammate at normal height.
   (iii) *One Hand Pass* After dodging an opponent, the player having the ball passes the ball to his own teammate. It can either be done by one hand or both hands.
   (iv) *Overhead Pass* The two-handed overhead pass is used for taller players. This pass keeps the ball away from defending players; that is why it is more safe.

(v) ***Baseball Pass*** This pass is given with one hand and is used for long passes.

(vi) ***Pivoting*** It is a restricted motion with the ball. A player rotates around while keeping one foot stationary.

4. **Dribbling** The ball is always controlled with fingers. The ball should not bounce higher than the waist; while dribbling, knees should be slightly bent.
   (i) ***High Dribble*** is an attacking dribble. Bounce is high at waist height to provide a fast running movement.
   (ii) ***Low Dribble*** is a defensive dribble. The ball is bounced at low height up to knee height and the player's body shields the opponent.
   (iii) ***Double Dribble*** Dribbling the ball with two hands at the same time is known as double dribble.
   (iv) ***Crossover Dribble*** It is a basketball movement in which the player possessing the ball rapidly switches the ball from one hand to the other, to make a change in direction.

Dribbling Technique

Popular Tournaments

International

- Olympic Games
- European Cup
- Africa Championship
- Euro-Basket
- Services Trophy
- Asia Cup
- FIBA World Championship
- American Cup
- FIBA Basketball World Cup

National

- Federation Cup Basketball Championship
- Don Bosco Invitational Tournament
- Bangalore Blues Challenge Cup
- Youth National Basketball Championship
- All India Ramu Memorial Trophy
- William Todd Memorial Trophy

Popular Basketball Awardees

Arjuna Award

- 1961 Sarbjit Singh
- 1968 Gurdial Singh
- 1970 Gulam Abbas Moontasir
- 1973 SK Kataria
- 1975 Hanuman Singh
- 1979-80 Om Prakash
- 1983 Radhey Shyam and Km Suman Sharma
- 2001 Parminder Singh
- 2017 Prashanti Singh
- 1967 Khushi Ram
- 1969 Hari Dutt
- 1971 Man Mohan Singh
- 1974 AK Punj
- 1977-78 T Vijayaraghavan
- 1982 Ajmer Singh
- 1999 Sajjan Singh Cheema
- 2014 Geetu Anna Jose
- 2019-20 Vishesh Bhriguvanshi

Popular International Players

USA Michael Jordan, Kareem Abdul-Jabbar, Magic Johnson and Ms. Sheryl Swoopes.

France Tony Parker

Viva-Voce

Q.1 Who invented basketball and when?

Ans. Dr. James Naismith invented basketball in 1891 at the YMCA Training School in Springfield, Massachusetts, USA.

Q.2 Why was basketball created?

Ans. Basketball was created as an indoor sport to keep students active during the winter months.

Q.3 Which event made basketball globally popular?

Ans. The 1992 Barcelona Olympics, especially the performance of the American men's team known as The Dream Team, made basketball globally popular.

Q.4 When was the International Basketball Federation (FIBA) founded and where?

Ans. FIBA was founded in 1932 in Geneva.

Q.5 When did men's basketball become an official Olympic event?

Ans. Men's basketball became an official Olympic event in 1936 (Berlin).

Q.6 When was women's basketball included in the Olympics?

Ans. Women's basketball was included in the Olympics starting from the 1976 Montreal Olympics.

Q.7 What are the standard court dimensions in basketball?

Ans. 28 meters in length and 15 meters in width (excluding the 5 cm line thickness).

Q.8 What is the height of the basket from the ground?

Ans. The height of the basket is 3.05 meters from the ground.

Q.9 How many players are on the court per team during a game?

Ans. 5 players are on the court per team.

Q.10 What is an assist in basketball?

Ans. An assist is a pass that directly leads to a basket.

Q.11 What is a free throw?

Ans. A free throw is an unopposed shot from the free-throw line awarded after a foul.

Q.12 What is the purpose of the shot clock?

Ans. The shot clock limits the time a team has to take a shot to 24 seconds after gaining possession.

Q.13 What happens if a player commits 5 personal fouls in a game?

Ans. The player is disqualified from the game.

Q.14 Name two types of defence in basketball.

Ans. Zone defence and man-to-man defence.

Q.15 Name one international and one national basketball tournament.

Ans. International FIBA Basketball World Cup and National Federation Cup Basketball Championship.

Game 6

Hockey

History

Hockey, i.e. field Hockey began a long time ago. The modern game as we know it today developed in England in the 19th century in public schools and in various clubs in London. Subsequently, the British army spread the popularity of Hockey all through the British Empire. 'English Hockey Association' was constituted in 1875.

The First International Competition in this sport was held in 1895. The First Club in India was formed in 1885 in Calcutta.

By 1908, the game was recognised for the Olympics. However, as Hockey was omitted from the 1924 Olympics in Paris, the International Hockey Federation (FIH) was formed in Paris in that year. From 1928 onwards, the Olympic Games have permanently included men's Hockey as a competitive sport and women's Hockey was introduced in 1980 Olympics.

Indian team dominated Olympic Games from 1928 to 1956 by winning Gold Medals in Hockey. They also won Gold Medals in 1964 and 1980. Hockey was introduced in Asian Games in 1958.

Measurements and Specifications

- Length of the field = 100 yards or 91.40 m
- Breadth of the field = 60 yards or 54.86 m
- Weight of the ball = 5½ to 5¾ ounces (156 g)
- Circumference of the ball = 22.4 cm to 23.5 cm or 8 inches to 9 inches
- Weight of stick (women) = 23 ounces (652 g)
- Weight of stick (men) = 28 ounces (793 g)
- Length of the goal post = 4 yards or 3.66 m
- Height of the goal post = 7 feet
- Height of the back board = 18 inches
- Depth of the back board = 4 feet
- Hockey should pass through = 2 inches (diameter of the ring)
- Distance of 'D' from back line = 16 yards
- Distance of penalty stroke = 7 yards
- Dotted shooting circle = 21 yards
- Game Duration = 60 minutes (four quarters of 15 minutes each)
- Break/Intervals = 2 min break after 1st and 3rd quarter and 15 min interval after the second quarter, which is halftime.
- No. of Player = 16 Players each team (10 players, 1 goalkeeper and 5 substitutes.)

Hockey Stick

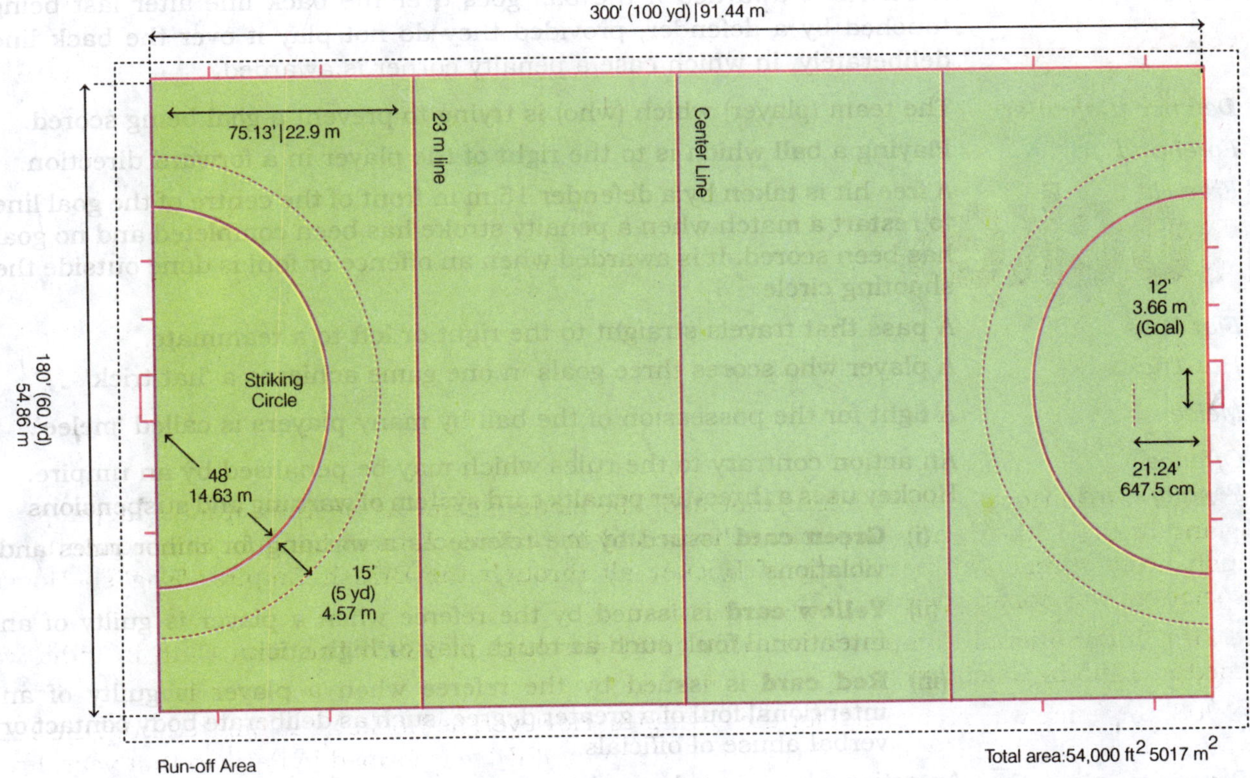

Hockey Ground

Terminology

16 yard hit A free hit for the defence that comes 16 yards from its goal after an opposing player hits the ball over the end line or commits a foul within the shooting circle.

Attack (Attacker) The team (player) which (who) is trying to score a goal.

Astroturf A synthetic material used for the field of play in place of grass.

Back Line The shorter (55 m) perimeter line.

Back Stick A foul called for hitting the ball with the rounded face of the Hockey stick.

Blind Pass Passing the ball without first looking to see if there is a teammate prepared to accept possession.

Bully A call used to start or restart play. The referee puts the ball between two opposing players. The players tap the flat sides of their sticks three times and then go for the ball.

Carried When ball touches the leg or feet of the player, it is said to have 'carried' away. It is also a violation.

Circle The area enclosed by including the two quarter circles and the lines joining them at each end of the field opposite the centre of the back line.

Center Line A line that divides the field in half. The field is 100 yards (91.4 m) long, so this is the 50 yard (45.7 m) line.

Center Pass A pass used to begin the game or the second half or to restart action following a goal.

Corner — A corner is awarded if the ball goes over the back line after last being touched by a defender, provided they do not play it over the back line deliberately, in which case a penalty corner is awarded.

Defence (Defender) — The team (player) which (who) is trying to prevent a goal being scored.

Forehand — Playing a ball which is to the right of the player in a forward direction.

Free Hit — A free hit is taken by a defender 15 m in front of the centre of the goal line to restart a match when a penalty stroke has been completed and no goal has been scored. It is awarded when an offence or foul is done outside the shooting circle.

Flat Pass — A pass that travels straight to the right or left to a teammate.

Hat Trick — A player who scores three goals in one game achieves a 'hat trick'.

Melee — A fight for the possession of the ball by many players is called 'melee'.

Offence — An action contrary to the rules which may be penalised by an umpire.

Penalty Card — Hockey uses a three-tier penalty card system of warning and suspensions

(i) **Green card** issued by the referee as a warning for minor rules and violations.

(ii) **Yellow card** is issued by the referee when a player is guilty of an intentional foul, such as rough play or high stick.

(iii) **Red card** is issued by the referee when a player is guilty of an intentional foul of a greater degree, such as deliberate body contact or verbal abuse of officials.

Pass — An action where one player gives possession of the ball to another. Common forms of passing include pushes, slaps, hits, aerials and deflections.

Penalty Corner/ Short Corner — The short or penalty corner is awarded

(i) for an offence by a defender in the circle which does not prevent the probable scoring of a goal.

(ii) for an intentional offence in the circle by a defender against an opponent who does not have possession of the ball or an opportunity to play the ball.

(iii) for an intentional offence by a defender outside the circle, but within the 23 meter area they are defending.

(iv) for intentionally playing the ball over the backline by a defender.

(v) when the ball becomes lodged in a player's clothing or equipment while they are defending inside the circle.

Penalty Shootout — It is a method used to decide which team progresses to the next stage of a tournament (or wins the tournament) after a tied game.

Penalty Spot — A spot marked seven yards from the goal. Penalty shots or strokes are taken from this position.

Penalty Stroke — A penalty stroke is awarded when a defender commits a foul in the circle (accidental or otherwise) that prevents a probable goal or commits a deliberate foul in the circle or if defenders repeatedly run from the back line too early at a penalty corner.

Side Line — The longer (91.40 m) perimeter line.

Slap — By slapping the ball, a player scores a goal. In this technique, the player holds his hand slightly apart on the stick and hits the ball with considerable force.

Shooting Circle An area in the shape of a capital 'D' and made up of two quarter-circles. It measures 16 yards out from each goal post and is joined by a short straight line. An attacking player must be within this area to score. It is also known as the 'D'.

Tackle An action to stop an opponent retaining possession of the ball.

Team A team consists of a maximum of 16 persons composed of a maximum of 11 players on the field and up to 5 substitutes. This may be amended by regulation to a maximum of 18 players.

Fouls for Penalty It is awarded only when a player or team has clearly been disadvantaged by opponent's offence. Intentional offence by defending player in circle which deprives attacker for the ball possession or unintentional foul during defense by defenders in circle or defenders intentionally plays the ball over back line. In these cases, penalty corner is given.

Sudden-Death After tie of score in extra time period of 10 min (in two halves) then sudden-death is followed. In this, five players of both teams take penalty strokes alternatively to break the tie. If tie still exists, then one to one sudden death is followed to break the tie to decide the winning team.

Latest/General Rules

1. Each team consist of 11 players, which includes one goalkeeper and 10 outfield players. Rolling substitution is implemented in Hockey which means that only number of players can be substituted at anytime except at the time of tie-breakers.
2. A hard ball is used in Hockey along with each player having a wooden stick. Only the flat side of the stick can be used. If ball touches any part of the player's body, it will be considered as carried. A face mask, helmet, padded gloves, chest pad and leg guards are all part of the attire for a goalkeeper. Some players wear eye and face masks also.
3. The game lasts for 60 minutes which is divided into 4 quarters of 15 minutes each (earlier it consisted of two 35 minutes halves with a 5 minutes rest in between). A 40 second timeout is given after penalty corner is awarded and after a goal is scored. There are 2 minutes break after the first and third quarters. The earlier 10 minutes half time break is now given between the second and third quarters.
4. A goal is scored when a player hits the ball in between the goal posts and over the line from within the 16-yards area. The ball must be struck with the player's stick and any use of the body will be an infringement.
5. Goals can be scored from penalty corners which are awarded when a foul is committed in the 16 yards area. From a penalty corner, the defending team all line up on their goal line. The attacking team must all be outside the 16 yards area when one player hits the ball to them from 10 yards either side of the goal line.
6. Goal keeper cannot be changed during the call of penalty corner or penalty stroke except when the goal keeper is injured.
7. No player will play the ball coming at a height of shoulder. Only a defender can stop such ball with stick.

Duties of Referee and Umpire The referee or umpire is responsible for ensuring fair play throughout the match. The act as the final authority on the rules and regulations from the start to the end of the match. Referee performs toss before the start of the match. He has the final say on every decision of the match.

Equipments of Referee and Umpire He has to carry all necessary equipment e.g. whistle, watch, green, yellow and red cards, etc.

Signals of Referee and Umpire The referee and umpire use various signals to communicate decisions during the match. Some important signals are given below.

Signals of Referee

Fundamental Skills and Techniques

Hockey is a game requiring high skills and needs highly skilled players. The major skill required is manoeuvring the ball. Another skill is to score a goal with speed and precision.

1. **Holding the Stick** A right-handed player must hold the stick firmly from the top edge of the grip with the left hand. The right hand is used to support the stick from the middle of the grip and is adjusted according to the requirements of the skill.
2. **Tackling** Here, the player tries to tackle the ball by putting the stick in the path of the ball coming from another player. He puts the stick close to the ground where the ball is moving. The stick works as a barrier for the ball.

   The different tackling skills in Hockey are

   (i) *Dribble* Dribbling is a technique used by a player when he moves the ball along the floor.

   (ii) *Push* Moving the ball along the ground using a pushing movement of the stick after the stick has been placed close to the ball.

   (iii) *Hit* This technique is used when a ball is hit with a considerable force but less than what constitutes an offence.

   (iv) *Flick* Pushing the ball so that it is raised off the ground. It is used for penalty strokes.

   (v) *Scoop* Raising the ball off the ground by placing the head of the stick under the ball and using a lifting movement.

(vi) *Dodge* It is a technique of dribble, in which the coming opponent is deceived in other direction by fake body movement. It prevents opponent from interfering or from possessing the ball.

(vii) *Corner Push* In this skill, player has to push the ball with power so that it should quickly reach a player of his own team.

Basic Grip *Tackling* *Dribble*

Hit *Flick* *Scoop*

Popular Tournaments

International Level Olympic Games (both Men and Women), World Cup (both Men and Women), Champions Trophy (both Men and Women), Sultan Azlan Shah Hockey Tournament (only Men), Hockey Asia Cup (only Men), Euro Hockey Nations Championship (both Men and Women), Commonwealth Games.

National Level MCC Murugappa Gold Cup Hockey Tournament, Indian Oil Surjit Hockey Tournament, Chhatrapati Shivaji Hockey Tournament, Agha Khan Hockey Tournament, Bombay Gold Cup Hockey Tournament, Jawaharlal Nehru Hockey Tournament, Lal Bahadur Shastri Hockey Tournament, KD Singh Babu Memorial Invitational Prize Hockey Tournament, Hero Hockey India League, Azlan Shah Cup Tournament.

Popular Hockey Awardees

Arjuna Award

- 2000 Raghbir Singh Bhola
- 2000 Jalaluddin Rizvi
- 2000 Balkrishan Singh
- 2001 Sita Gossain
- 2002 Mamta Kharb
- 2003 Devesh Chauhan
- 2004 Helen Mary
- 2005 Viren Rasquinha
- 2007 Prabhjot Singh
- 2009 Ignace Tirkey
- 2010 Sandeep Singh
- 2000 Tingongleima Chanu
- 2000 Baljit Singh Saini
- 2000 Madhu Yadav
- 2001 Dilip Tirkey
- 2002 Gagan Ajit Singh
- 2003 Suraj Lata Devi
- 2004 Deepak Thakur
- 2006 Jyoti Sunita Kullu
- 2009 Surinder Kaur
- 2010 Jasjeet Kaur Handa
- 2011 Rajpal Singh

- 2012 Sardar Singh
- 2015 P. R. Sreejesh
- 2016 Ritu Rani
- 2018 Savita Punia
- 2019 Chinglensana Kangujam
- 2020 Deepika Thakur
- 2021 Vandana Katariya
- 2021 Harmanpreet Singh
- 2021 Surender Kumar
- 2021 Birendra Lakra
- 2021 Nilakanta Sharma
- 2021 Vivek Sagar Prasad
- 2021 Mandeep Singh
- 2021 Lalit Kumar Upadhyay
- 2021 Simranjeet Singh
- 2023 Krishan Bahadur Pathak,
- 2024 Abhishek
- 2024 Jarmanpreet Singh
- 2024 Salima Tete
- 2013 Saba Anjum Karim
- 2016 V. R. Raghunath
- 2017 S. V. Sunil
- 2018 Manpreet Singh
- 2020 Akashdeep Singh
- 2021 Monika Malik
- 2021 Dilpreet Singh
- 2021 Rupinder Pal Singh
- 2021 Amit Rohidas
- 2021 Sumit Valmiki
- 2021 Hardik Singh
- 2021 Gurjant Singh
- 2021 Shamsher Singh
- 2021 Varun Kumar
- 2022 Deep Grace Ekka
- 2023 Shushila Chanu Pukhrambam
- 2024 Sukhjeet Singh
- 2024 Sanjay

Dronacharya Award

- 2000 Gurdial Singh Bhangu
- 2003 Rajinder Singh Sr.
- 2010 Ajay Kumar Bansal
- 2012 Harendra Singh
- 2017 P. A. Raphael
- 2019 Merzban Patel
- 2020 Jude Felix
- 2021 Pritam Rani Siwach
- 2002 Maharaj Krishan Kaushik
- 2009 Baldev Singh
- 2011 Rajinder Singh Jr.
- 2013 Narender Singh Saini
- 2018 Clarence Lobo
- 2020 Romesh Pathania
- 2021 Sarpal Singh
- 2023 Shri Shivendra Singh

Dhyan Chand Award (For Lifetime Contribution)

- 2002 Ashok Diwan
- 2003 Dharam Singh Mann
- 2005 Rajinder Singh
- 2007 Varinder Singh
- 2012 Gundeep Kumar
- 2014 Gurmail Singh
- 2016 Sylvanus Dung Dung
- 2018 Bharat Kumar Chetri
- 2020 Ajit Pal Singh
- 2022 Dharamvir Singh
- 2024 Harmanpreet Singh
- 2003 Charles Cornelius
- 2004 Hardayal Singh
- 2006 Nandy Singh
- 2008 Mukhbain Singh
- 2013 Syed Ali
- 2015 Romeo James
- 2017 Sumrai Tete
- 2019 Manuel Fredericks
- 2021 Davinder Singh Garcha
- 2023 Shri Vineet Kumar Sharma

Rajiv Gandhi Khel Ratna (formerly)/ Major Dhyan Chand Khel Ratna

- 1999–2000 Dhanraj Pillay
- 2017 Sardara Singh
- 2020 Rani Rampal
- 2021 P.R. Sreejesh, Manpreet Singh
- 2024 Harmanpreet Singh

Popular International Hockey Players

(i) **Men** Sohail Abbas (Pakistan), Ric Charlesworth (Australia), Hassan Sardar (Pakistan), Shahbaz Ahmed (Pakistan), Teun de Nooijer (the Netherlands/Holland), Ties Kruize (the Netherlands/Holland), Jamie Dwyer (Australia), Fergus Kavanagh (Australia).

(ii) **Women** Luciana Aymar (Argentina), Alyson Annan (Australia), Natascha Keller (Germany), Fanny Rinne (Germany), Alex Danson (United Kingdom), Delfina Merino (Argentina).

Popular Venues

Major Dhyan Chand National Stadium, New Delhi (India), Shivaji Hockey Stadium, New Delhi (India), Gachibowli Stadium, Hyderabad (India), KD Singh Babu Stadium, Lucknow (India), Surjit Hockey Stadium, Jalandhar (India), Riverbank Arena, London (England), State Netball and Hockey Centre, Melbourne (Australia), Estadio Mundialista de Hockey, Rosario (Argentina), North Harbour Hockey Stadium, Auckland (New Zealand), Warsteiner Hockey Park, Monchengladbach (Germany)

Viva-Voce

Q.1 Where did modern field hockey develop?

Ans. Modern field hockey developed in England.

Q.2 When was the English Hockey Association formed?

Ans. English Hockey Association formed in 1875.

Q.3 When was the first hockey club established in India?

Ans. In India, the first hockey club established in 1885.

Q.4 When did hockey first appear in the Olympics?

Ans. Field hockey first appear in the Olympics for men in 1908 at the London games.

Q.5 In which year was the International Hockey Federation (FIH) formed?

Ans. FIH formed in 1924.

Q.6 How long is a standard hockey field?

Ans. The length of a standard hockey field is 91.40 meters.

Q.7 What is the weight of a standard hockey ball?

Ans. The weight of a standard hockey ball is 156 grams.

Q.8 How many players are on the field from one team during a match?

Ans. In a hockey match there are 11 players on the field from men team.

Q.9 What is the total duration of a modern hockey match?

Ans. The total duration of a modern hockey match is 60 minutes.

Q.10 How many minutes is each quarter in hockey?

Ans. In most major field hockey competitions, including the Olympics, each quarter is 15 minutes long.

Q.11 **What is a 16-yard hit in hockey?**

Ans. A 16-yard hit is a free hit for the defending team.

Q.12 **What does a green card indicate in hockey?**

Ans. In hockey green card indicates warning.

Q.13 **What is the penalty stroke distance from the goal?**

Ans. The penalty stroke distance from the goal is 7 yards.

Q.14 **Name one international men's hockey tournament.**

Ans. World Cup.

Q.15 **Who was the first Indian woman to win the Khel Ratna in hockey?**

Ans. Rani Rampal is the first Indian woman who win the Khel Ratna award in hockey.

Game 7

Boxing

History

The first evidence of pugilism (boxing) was found in Egypt in around 3000 BC. Boxing as a sport was part of the ancient Olympics held in 688 BC. Boxing evolved from 16th-18th century prizefights, primarily in United Kingdom. Originally, only five weight classes were contested: Bantam, not exceeding 54 kilos; Feather, not exceeding 57 kilos; Light, not exceeding 63.5 kilos; Middle, not exceeding 73 kilos; and Heavy, any weight.

The first boxing competition at the Olympic Games of modern times was held in 1904 at St. Louis (USA). It included seven weight categories. Since its inclusion in the Olympics, boxing has been staged at each Olympics, except in 1912 in Stockholm, owing to Swedish law, which forbade the sport.

During the 1920 Summer Olympics in Antwerp, representatives from the national associations of England, France, Belgium, Brazil and the Netherlands met in a preliminary meeting for the foundation of an International Boxing Federation: The Fédération Internationale de Boxe Amateur (FIBA) and later renamed Association Internationale de Boxe Amateur (AIBA), is the global governing body for amateur boxing.

Indian Amateur Boxing Federation was founded on 25th February 1949, in Bombay (Mumbai). The first national championships were held at the Brabourne Stadium in Mumbai in March, 1950. Indian Boxing Federation was also known as Indian Amateur Boxing Federation (IABF) and was suspended by the International Amateur Boxing Association in 2014, following which BFI (The Boxing Federation of India) was recognised as the recognised body.

Measurements and Specifications

- Inside measurements of the ring = 12 feet square
- In International Championship, the size of the ring = 20 feet square
- Outside the rope platform = 18 inches
- Number of ropes in the boxing ring = 3 to 4
- Height of the platform from ground = 3 to 4 feet
- Colour of corner of rings = One red and another blue
- Headgear = Mandatory
- Cup Protector = Mandatory
- Gum-shield or Mouth-guard = Mandatory
- Officials = 1 Referee, 5 Judges, 1 Supervisor, 1 Ringside Doctor, 1 Chief Jury, 1 Time Keeper, 1 Bell Striker, 1 Technical Official, 1 Recorder.
- Bout Round = 3 for both (m/w)
- Duration of Round = 3 min each
- Break between Rounds = 1 minutes

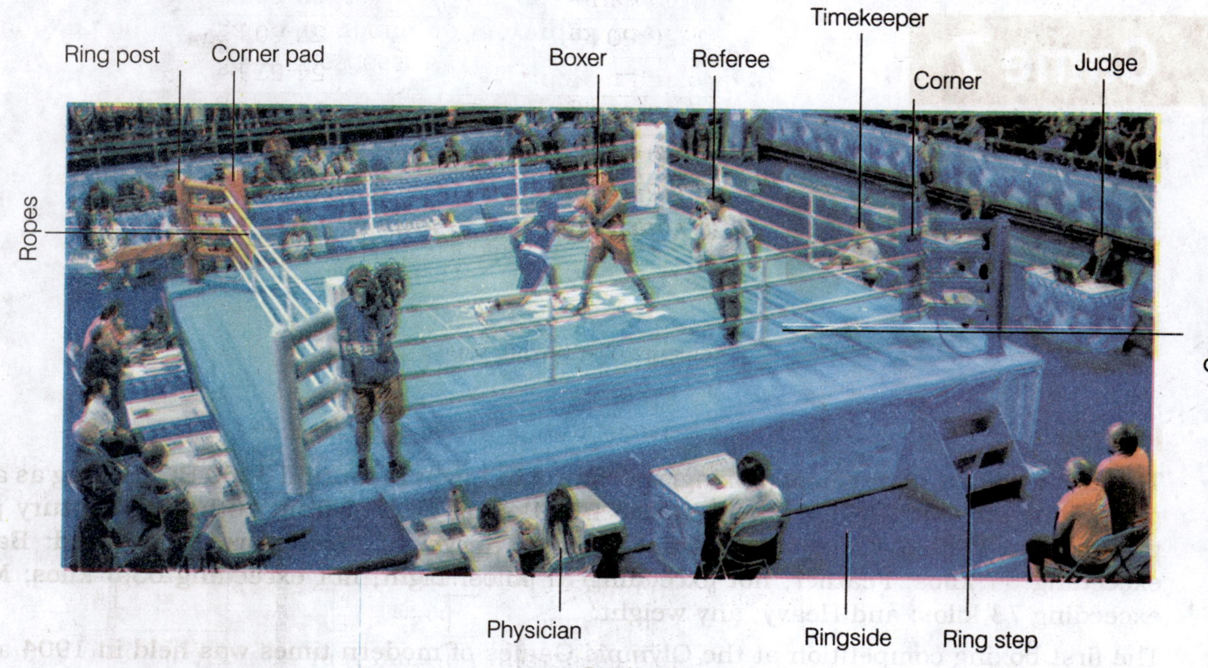

Boxing Ring

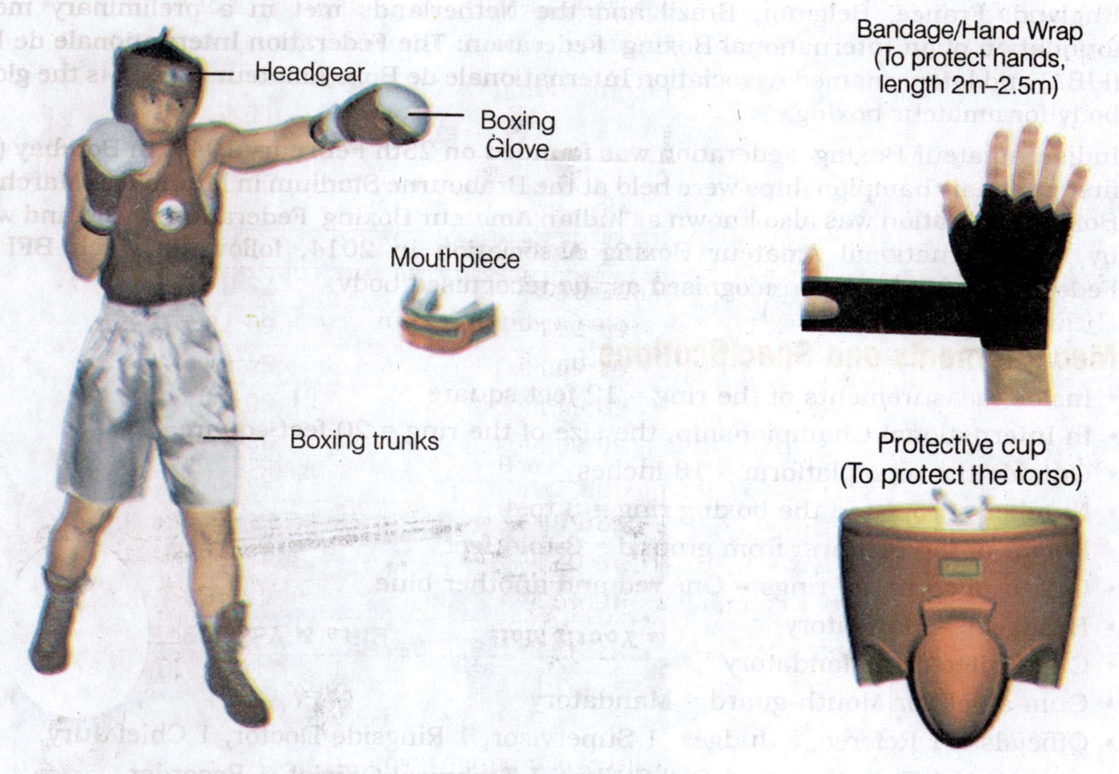

Boxing Equipments

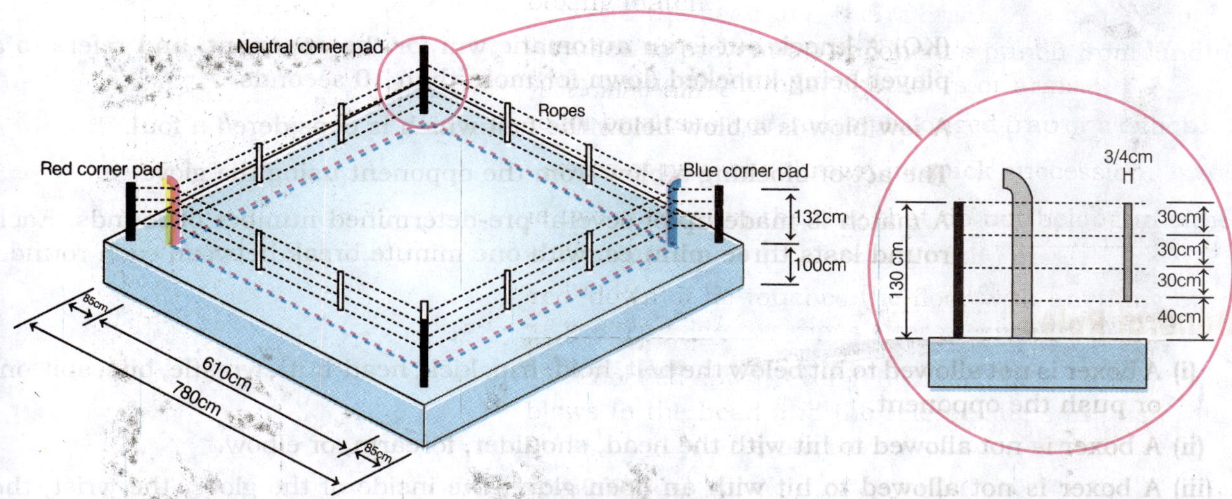

Measurements of a Boxing Ring

Weight Categories

Particulars	Elite & Youth Male	Elite & Youth Female
Light fly weight	46-49 kg	45-48 kg
Flyweight	49-52 kg	48-51 kg
Bantam weight	52-56 kg	51-54 kg
Feather weight	—	54-57 kg
Light weight	56-60 kg	57-60 kg
Light welter weight	60-64 kg	60-64 kg
Welter weight	64-69 kg	64-69 kg
Middle weight	69-75 kg	69-75 kg
Light heavy weight	75-81 kg	75-81 kg
Heavy weight	81-91 kg	81 kg
Super heavy weight	91+ kg	—

Terminology

Bout — A bout refers to a boxing match.

Blocking — A technique which is used to prevent an opponent's punch from landing on the head or torso by using the hands, shoulders or arms.

Break — A referee's command for boxers to free from a prolonged trap or a clinch.

Combination — A combination is a series of punches thrown in quick succession.

Corner — (Neutral) One of the two corners in the ring that do not belong to either fighter.

Down — A boxer is considered 'down' if he touches the floor with anything other than his feet or if he goes outside the ropes after receiving a punch.

Knock Down — A boxer is technically 'knocked down,' even if he hasn't fallen but he takes a serious blow or blows to the head and the referee steps in to stop the action.

Knock Out (KO) A knock out is an automatic win for the opponent, and refers to a player being knocked down for more than 10 seconds.

Low Blow A low blow is a blow below the belt which is considered a foul.

Parry The act of blocking a blow from the opponent using the glove.

Rounds A match is made up of several pre-determined number of rounds. Each round lasts three minutes, with one minute break between each round.

General Rules

(i) A boxer is not allowed to hit below the belt, hold, trip, kick, head-butt, wrestle, bite, spit-on, or push the opponent.

(ii) A boxer is not allowed to hit with the head, shoulder, forearm, or elbow.

(iii) A boxer is not allowed to hit with an open glove, the inside of the glove, the wrist, the backhand, or from the side of the hand.

(iv) A boxer is not allowed to hit opponent's back, or the back of his head or neck (rabbit punch), or on the kidneys (kidney punch).

(v) A boxer is not allowed to punch while holding on to the ropes to gain leverage.

(vi) A boxer is not allowed to hold the opponent and hit him at the same time, or duck so low that his head is below his opponent's belt line.

(vii) When the referee breaks the boxers from a clinch, then they are supposed to take a full step back, and they cannot immediately hit the opponent.

(viii) A Boxer is not allowed to spit out the mouthpiece.

(ix) If a boxer scores a knockdown on his opponent, then he is supposed to go to the farthest neutral corner while the referee makes the count.

(x) If a boxer 'floors' its opponent, then he cannot hit him when he is on the canvas.

(xi) A floored boxer has up to ten seconds to get back up on his feet before losing the bout by knockout.

(xii) A boxer who is hit with an accidental low blow has upto five minutes to recover. If he cannot continue after five minutes, then he is considered knocked out.

(xiii) If the foul results in an injury that causes the fight to end immediately, the boxer who committed the foul is disqualified.

(xiv) If the foul causes an injury but the bout continues, the referee orders the judges to deduct two points from the boxer who caused the injury.

Fundamental skills and Techniques

Stance and Footwork

- **Stance** The position a boxer adopts to balance, offense and defense. Common stances include orthodox (left foot forward) and southpaw (right foot forward).
- **Footwork** Moving efficiently to advance, retreat, or pivot, while maintaining balance and positioning.

Punching Techniques

- **Jab** A quick, straight punch with the lead hand, used for distance control and setting up other punches.
- **Cross** A powerful straight punch with the rear hand, often following a jab.

- **Hook** A punch delivered with a bent arm, targeting the side of the opponent's head or body.
- **Uppercut** A punch delivered from below, aimed at the opponent's chin or jaw.

Punching Techniques

Defence

- **Blocking** Using gloves and arms to absorb or deflect punches.
- **Parrying** Redirecting punches away from the body using quick hand movements.
- **Slipping** Moving the head and body to avoid punches by shifting the upper body.
- **Ducking** Bending the knees and lowering the body to avoid punches.

Defence Techniques

Popular Tournaments

International Boxing World Cup, World Series Boxing, Olympic Games, Youth Olympic Games, AIBA World Boxing Championships

National National Games, All India Boxing Tournament, Federation Cup Men and Women, Zonal Men and Women Competition

Popular Boxing Awardees

Arjuna Awardees

- 1961 L.Buddy D'Souza
- 1962 P.B. Mall
- 1966 Capt. Hawa Singh 1968 Dennis Swamy
- 1971 Capt. M. Venu
- 1972 Chandranarayanan
- 1973 Capt. Mehtab Singh
- 1978 B.S. Thapa
- 1979 C.C. Machaiah

- 1980 Bakshish Singh
- 1981 Issac Amaldas
- 1981 G. Manoharan
- 1982 Padmashri Kaur Singh
- 1983 Jas Lal Pradhan
- 1986 Jai Pal Singh
- 1987 S. Jayaram
- 1989 Gopal Dewang
- 1991 Dharmender Singh Yadav
- 1992 Rajender Prasad
- 1993 Manoj Pingale
- 1994 Mukund Killekar
- 1995 V. Devarajan
- 1996 Rajkumar Sangwan
- 1998 Dingko Singh
- 1999 Gurcharan Singh
- 1999 Jitender Kumar
- 2002 Md. Ali Qamar
- 2003 Mary Kom
- 2005 Akhil Kumar
- 2006 Vijender Singh
- 2008 Varghese Johnson
- 2009 L. Sarita Devi
- 2010 Dinesh Kumar
- 2011 M. Suranjoy Singh
- 2012 Vikas Krishan
- 2013 Kavita Chahal
- 2014 Manoj Kumar
- 2015 Mandeep Jangra
- 2016 Shiva Thapa
- 2017 Sub. L. Debendro Singh
- 2018 Subedar Satish Kumar
- 2019 Sonia Lather
- 2020 Lovlina Borgohain, Manish Kaushik
- 2021 Simranjit Kaur
- 2022 Amit Panghal, Nikhat Zareen
- 2023 Mohammad Hussamuddin
- 2024 Nitu Ghanghas, Saweety Boora

Rajiv Gandhi Khel Ratna Awardees

- 2009 Vijender Singh
- 2009 Mary Kom
- 2021 Lovlina Borgohain

Drunacharya Awardees

- 2014 Ganapathy Manoharan
- 2015 Swatantar Raj Singh
- 2017 Brij Bhushan Mohanty
- 2020 Shiv Singh
- 1985 Om Prakash Bhardwaj
- 1998 G. S. Sandhu
- 1999 Hawa Singh
- 2003 Anoop Kumar
- 2005 M. Venu
- 2006 Damodaran Chandralal
- 2007 Jagdish Singh
- 2009 Jaydev Bisht
- 2010 L Ibomcha Singh
- 2011 Inukurthi Venkateshwara Roy
- 2012 B. I. Fernandez
- 2013 Mahavir Singh
- 2016 Sagar Mal Dhayal
- 2018 Subedar Chenanda Achaiah Kuttappa
- 2021 Sandhya Gurung
- 2022 Mohammed Ali Qamar

Viva-Voce

Q.1 Where did boxing originate around 3000 BC?

Ans. Boxing originated in Egypt around 3000 BC.

Q.2 In which Olympic Games was modern boxing first featured?

Ans. Modern boxing first featured in 1904 in St. Louis Olympics (USA).

Q.3 What is the name of the international boxing body formed in 1920?

Ans. AIBA (now IBA)

Q.4 When was the Indian Amateur Boxing Federation (IABF) established?

Ans. The Indian Amateur Boxing Federation (IABF) was established in 1949.

Q.5 What is the standard size of a boxing ring used nationally?

Ans. The standard size of a boxing ring used nationally is 12 × 12 feet.

Q.6 How many judges are there in a boxing match?

Ans. There are 5 judges in a boxing match.

Q.7 How many rounds are there in a boxing bout?

Ans. A boxing bout typically has 3 rounds.

Q.8 What is the duration of each boxing round?

Ans. The duration of each boxing round is 3 minutes.

Q.9 What is the break time between boxing rounds?

Ans. The break time between boxing round is 1 minute.

Q.10 Name the stance used by right-handed boxers.

Ans. Orthodox.

Q.11 Which punch is a quick, straight punch with the lead hand?

Ans. Jab is a quick, straight punch thrown with the lead hand.

Q.12 Which punch moves upward toward the opponent's chin?

Ans. An uppercut is a punch that moves upward towards the opponent's chin.

Q.13 What is the technique of avoiding a punch by head movement?

Ans. Slip is the technique of avoiding a punch by moving the head.

Q.14 What is a punch below the belt called?

Ans. A punch below the belt is called a low blow.

Q.15 What happens when a boxer is down for more than 10 seconds?

Ans. When a boxer is down for more than 10 second it is a Knock Out (KO).

Q.16 Which punch is thrown in a circular motion?

Ans. A hook is a punch thrown in a circular motion.

Q.17 What is the act of using the glove to deflect a punch?

Ans. The act of using the glove to deflect a punch is called a parry.

Q.18 Name the boxing corner not assigned to any boxer.

Ans. The boxing corner not assigned to any boxer is the neutral corner.

Q.19 Which tournament is India's top national boxing event?

Ans. Federation Cup is India's top national boxing event.

Q.20 Who won the Khel Ratna in boxing in 2009?

Ans. In 2009, Vijender Singh won the khel Ratna award in boxing.

Game 8

Football

History

Football is also known as *soccer.* Football has a very old history, with different versions played in many ancient cultures. The Greeks played a game called 'Sphirer', where they tried to take the ball to the opponent's end. The Romans had 'Calcio', where they used their legs to move the ball. In China, people played 'Tsuchu', kicking a leather-filled ball. On 8th December, 1863, the official rules of soccer were established in Sheffield Football Club in England.

In 1904, the First International Match outside England was played in Paris between France and Belgium. This led to the founding of Federation Internationale de Football Association (FIFA), an international organisation that regulates the rules and regulation of football worldwide. FIFA fixed the First World Cup to be played in Uruguay in 1930, since then, the World Cup is played every 4 years.

In India, this game was introduced by the British. The First Indian Federation, the Indian Football Association was founded in 1893. Later, All India Football Federation was formed in 1937. At the London Olympics in 1948, bare-footed Indians took everyone by surprise and almost caused an upset when they narrowly lost to France by 1-2 in the second round match.

Measurements and Specifications

The original dimensions were specified in yards/feet/inch because these were formulated in England. Later on, these have been converted to the metric system.

(i) Ground dimension = 100-120 yards (91-110 m) × 50-100 yards (46-91 m).

(ii) Officials of match (international) = 1 Referee, 2 Linesmen or Assistant referee, 1 Commissioner, 1 Time- keeper.

(iii) Weight of the ball = 14 to 16 ounces (410-450 gm).

(iv) Circumference of the ball = 27 to 28 inch (68-70 cm).

(v) Number of players in a team = 11 on the field at any time + 7 substitutes.

(vi) Number of players that can be substituted in a match = 3.

(vii) Duration of match = 2 halves of 45 minutes (40 minutes for women) each with a half-time interval of not more than 15 minutes.

(viii) Extra time (in case of a tie at the end of time) = 2 halves of 15 minutes each.

(ix) Goalpost dimension = 8 yards (7.32 m) × 8 ft (2.44 m) with 5 inches thickness of post.

(x) Width of lines = 5 inch (12 cm).

(xi) Player's equipment (compulsory) = Studs (football shoes), shin guard, T-shirt with number.

(xii) Centre circle radius = 10 yards (9.15 m).

(xiii) Quarter circle radius = 1 yard (91 cm).

(xiv) Height of flags 5 ft = (1.2 m).

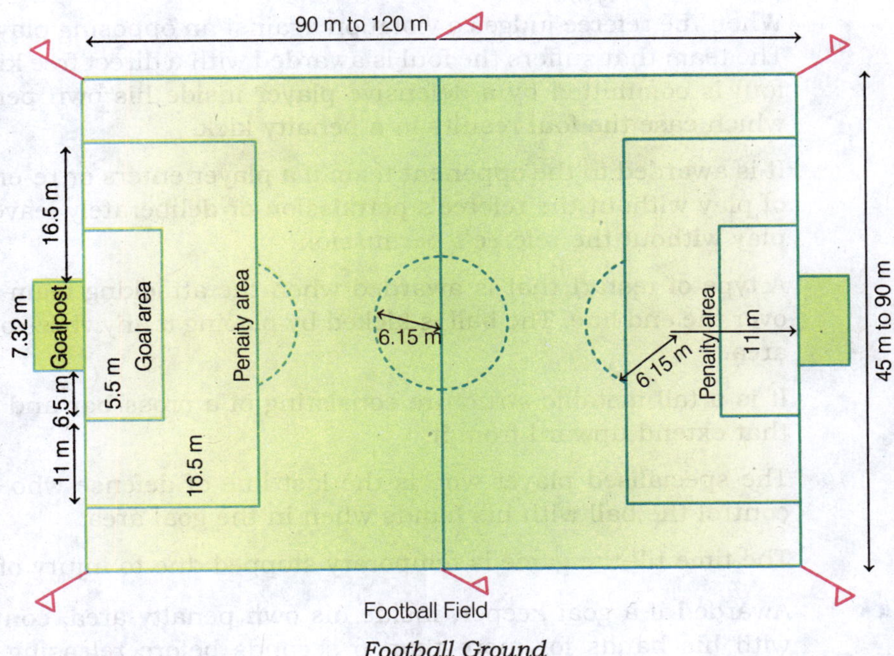

Football Ground

Terminology

Attacker Any player close to the opposing team's goal line is called an *attacker*, also called as *forward* or *striker*.

Advantage Rule The referee does not have to stop play every time, he detects a foul. If the offending team gains an advantage from the offence, he will certainly do so. But sometimes, a defender deliberately handles the ball to bring it under control but only succeeds in deflecting it to an opponent who is well placed for a shot at goal. To stop play at this moment would penalise the attacking team. In such a case, the referee would apply the advantage rule and allow play to go on.

Box The penalty area. Sometimes called the 18 yard box, to distinguish it from the goal area, which is the 6-yard box (16.5 m and 5.5 m).

Corner Kick A direct free kick that is awarded when the defending team puts the ball over the end line. A corner kick is taken by the offensive team from next to the corner flag.

Dead Ball When play is stopped and the ball is not moving, it is a dead ball. All free kicks, including penalty kicks, have to be taken from a dead ball.

Defender A player whose job is to stop the opposition attacking players from goal scoring.

Direct Free Kick Awarded against a player/team for kicking/attempting to kick an opponent, tripping or attempting to trip, jumping at, charging, striking or attempting to strike, pushing, tackling, holding or spitting at an opponent. It is also awarded if a player handles the ball deliberately (except goalkeeper in the goal area).

Drop Ball A method of restarting a game where the referee drops the ball between two players of opposing teams facing each other. The ball is dropped where it was last in play or at the nearest point outside the penalty area.

Foul	When the referee judges a violation against an opposing player it is a foul. The team that suffers the foul is awarded with a direct free kick unless the foul is committed by a defensive player inside his own penalty area, in which case the foul results in a penalty kick.
Free Kick	It is awarded to the opponent team if a player enters or re-enters the field of play without the referee's permission or deliberately leaves the field of play without the referee's permission.
Goal Kick	A type of restart that is awarded when the attacking team puts the ball over the end line. The ball is kicked by placing it anywhere on the penalty area.
Goalpost	It is a tall metallic structure consisting of a cross-bar and two uprights that extend upward from it.
Goal Keeper	The specialised player who is the last line of defense who is allowed to control the ball with his hands when in the goal area.
Injury Time	The time till the game is temporary stopped due to injury of a player.
Indirect Free Kick	Awarded if a goal keeper, inside his own penalty area, controls the ball with his hands for more than 6 seconds before releasing it. It is also awarded if a player commits any offence for which play is stopped or takes the ball again after releasing it himself to caution or send off a player.
Midfield	The line that divides the length of the field in half.
Offside	A violation that occurs when an offensive player crosses the goal line of opposing side before the ball reaches him/her. Players cannot be called offside if they are in their own half of the field. When a player is called offside, the opposing team is awarded an indirect free kick.
Obstruction	A foul in which a defensive player, instead of going after the ball, illegally uses his/her body to prevent an offensive player from playing it.
Penalty Kick	Awarded for any of the above fouls committed by a player inside his own penalty area, irrespective of the position of the ball, provided it is in play.
Red Card	A Red Card is a signal that the player has been banned from the rest of the match. A Red Card can be shown for a single serious offence, violent striking, attacking the opponent or as the result of being shown a second Yellow Card in the same game. Such a rejected player cannot be replaced by a substitute.
Sending Off	A rejection resulting from a player being shown a Red Card.
Throw-in	A way to restart play when the ball goes out over the side lines. The team that did not touch the ball last is allowed an overhead throw.
Yellow Card	A card the referee shows a player as a disciplinary action for violating a soccer rule. It is a warning issued by the referee. No elimination or rejection takes place in this case.

Latest/General Rules

1. The objective of soccer or football is to send the ball into the goal of opposing team, by kicking it with the feet or by any other part of their body.
2. A football match is played by two teams, with each allowed no more than 11 players on the field, one of whom is a goalkeeper. A match is played in 2 halves of 45 minutes (40 minutes for women) each.
3. The game begins with the toss of a coin and the winning captain decides which goal to defend or to take the first kick-off.
4. All players must use their feet, head or chest to play the ball. Only the goalkeepers are allowed to use their hands and only within their designated goal area.
5. A goal is scored when the whole of the ball passes over the goal line, between the goalposts and under the cross-bar, provided that no infringement of the laws of the game has been committed previously by the team scoring the goal. (see the given diagram)

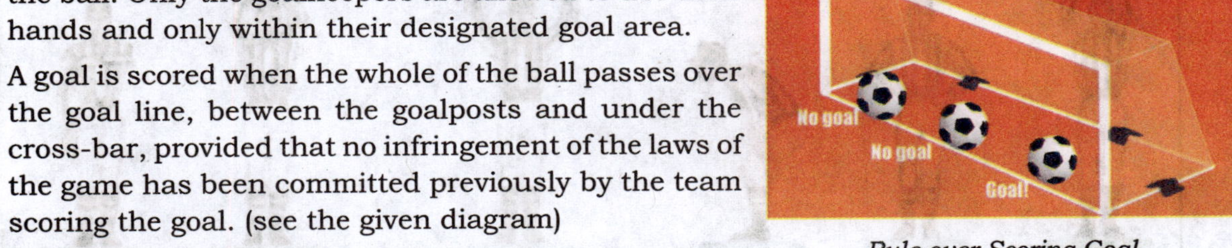

Rule over Scoring Goal

6. If the ball touches or crosses the side line, it is thrown back in the team that was not the last to touch the ball.
7. The game is controlled by a central referee and two linesmen. They award free kicks and penalties when rules are broken. For continual breaking of rules or for a bad foul, a player may be sent off from the field.
8. Substitutes (total 7 substitutes are there in each team, out of which 3 replacements are allowed during a match).
9. In a knockout tournament, if the score is tied after regulation time, the game goes into 30 minutes of extratime, divided into two 15-minute halves. The first team to score during this period wins. Previously, the golden goal rule applied, but now the silver goal rule is used.
10. If the score remainstied after extra time, a penalty shoot-out occurs. The referee selects the goal for the penalties, and a toss decides which team kicks first. Each team selects 5 players to take one penalty kick each, and the team with the most goals after 5 kicks wins.
11. The "sudden death" rule refers to a scenario where the first team to score a goal during extra time immediately wins the match. This rule was previously used in knockout tournaments but has been largely replaced by the "golden goal" or "silver goal" rules and now, for most competitions, the match proceeds with full extra time followed by a penalty shoot-out if necessary.

Duties of Match Referee

Referee is the person responsible for enforcing the **Laws of the Game** during the course of a match. He or she is the final decision-making authority on all facts connected with play, and is the only official on the pitch with the authority to start and stop play and impose disciplinary action against players during a match. He stops the game if player has been seriously injured and restarts the game after stoppage. He keeps the record of the game and act as timekeeper. At higher levels of play the referee may also be assisted by a **fourth official** who supervises the teams' technical areas and assists the referee with administrative tasks.

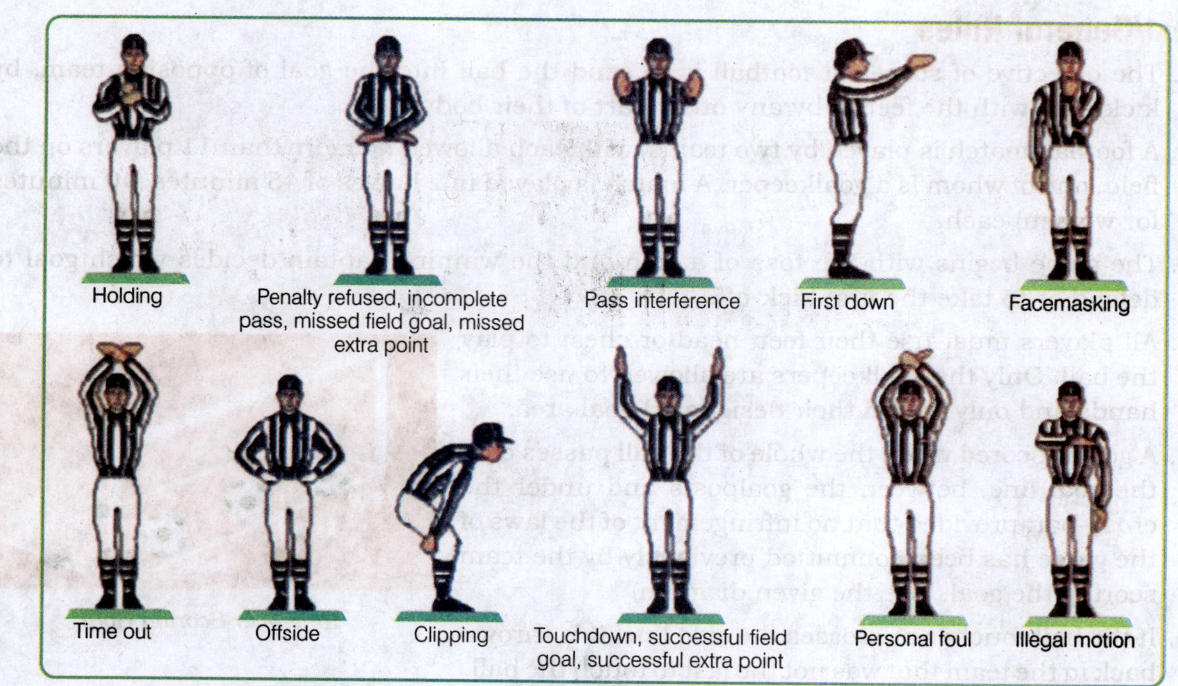

Referee Signals

Fundamental Skills and Techniques

These may be divided into the following major categories

1. *Dribbling* This is the ability to manoeuvre the ball with the feet to beat or dodge an opponent. *There are two techniques of dribbling*
   (i) Speed Dribbling (ii) Shielding Dribbling
2. *Receiving* Receiving refers to a player's first touch when he controls the ball using any part of the body except the hands and arms. When receiving a ball on the ground, the player should keep the eyes on the ball, choose which foot to receive the ball with.
3. *Passing* Passing the ball involves giving the ball to a teammate; so it is important that players know where their teammates are, so verbal communication is also required. Passing of ball is done while kicking it with a relaxed forward swing of the kicking leg.
4. *Kicking* This involves kicking the ball with the foot so that it lands in the area that the player wants. *There are two techniques of kicking*
   (i) Instep Kick (ii) Outstep Kick
5. *Shooting* Shooting uses the same technical elements as passing, the important difference being that the goal is to pass the ball beyond the goalkeeper. The ankle of the kicking foot is locked and the toe is pointed down if shooting with instep.The body weight is balanced on the kicking foot.
6. *Heading* Heading is the only way of contacting the ball when it is above the shoulders. Making contact with the ball with area between the eyebrows and hairline with mouth closed, eyes open and chin up. The neck should be kept stiff while heading to prevent the neck injury.
7. *Tackling* It involves tackling with the back foot and normally occurs in a 50-50 situation, when neither player has the ball. Key factors include a steady head, eyes on the ball, keeping a low centre of gravity, planting the support foot alongside the ball and contacting the ball with the inside of the foot.

8. *Tactics* Tactics involve the decisions the player must make about what to do with the ball, sometimes before receiving it. *These are basically of three types*

(i) Individual tactics (ii) Group tactics (iii) Team tactics

Dribbling

Kicking

Heading

Shooting

Popular Tournaments

International

- Olympic Games
- Merdeka Cup
- CONCAF Gold Cup
- UEFA European Championship
- FIFA World Cup
- African Cup
- Copa America
- AFC (Asian Football Confederation) Cup

National

- National Football League
- Santosh Trophy
- Durand Cup
- Subroto Cup
- Hero Federation Cup
- IFA Shield

Popular Football Awardees

Arjuna Award Winners

- 1961 PK Banerjee
- 1963 Chuni Goswami
- 1965 Arun Lal Ghosh
- 1967 Peter Thangaraj
- 1970 Syed Naeemuddin
- 1973 Magan Singh
- 1979-80 Prasun Banerjee
- 1981 Sudhir Karmakar
- 1989 S Bhattacharjee
- 1998 Baichung Bhutia
- 2010 Deepak Kumar Mondal
- 2011 Sunil Chhetri
- 2017 Oinam Bembem Devi
- 2020 Sandesh Jhingan
- 1962 Tulsi Balaram
- 1964 Jarnail Singh
- 1966 Yusuf Khan
- 1969 Inder Singh
- 1971 CP Singh
- 1978-79 Gurdev Singh Gill
- 1980-81 Mohammed Habib
- 1983 Shanti Mullick
- 1997 Brahmanand Sankhwalkar
- 2001 Bruno Coutinho
- 2003 IM Vijayan
- 2016 Subrata Pal
- 2019 Gurpreet Singh Sandhu

Dhyan Chand Award Winners

- 2017 Syed Shahid Hakim
- 2020 Sukhvinder Singh

Khel Ratna Award Winner

- 2021 Sunil Chhetri

Dronacharya Award Winner

- 1990 Syed Naeemuddin
- 2022 Bimal Prafulla Ghosh

Popular Venues

Wembley Football Stadium, London, England, The Allianz Arena, Munich, Germany, Old Trafford Football Stadium, Manchester, England, Camp Nou, Barcelona, Spain, Azteca, Mexico City, Mexico, Soccer City, Johannesburg, South Africa.

Viva-Voce

Q.1 When and where were the official football rules first framed?

Ans. The official football rules were first framed on 8th December 1863 in Sheffield, England.

Q.2 What are the ancient names for football-like games played by Greeks and Romans?

Ans. Greeks called it Sphirer, and Romans called it Calcio.

Q.3 In which year was FIFA established and where?

Ans. FIFA was established in 1904 in Paris.

Q.4 When and where was the first FIFA World Cup held?

Ans. The first FIFA World Cup was held in 1930 in Uruguay.

Q.5 When was the Indian Football Association (IFA) founded?

Ans. The Indian Football Association was founded in 1893.

Q.6 Who is the governing body for football in India today?

Ans. The All India Football Federation (AIFF) is the governing body for football in India, established in 1937.

Q.7 How many players are on the field per team in a football match?

Ans. There are 11 players on the field per team.

Q.8 What is the standard duration of a football match?

Ans. A standard football match consists of two halves of 45 minutes each.

Q.9 What is the maximum number of substitutions allowed in a match?

Ans. The maximum number of substitutions allowed is 3 (from a squad of 7 substitutes).

Q.10 What are the dimensions of a standard football field?

Ans. The standard football field is 91–110 meters in length and 46–91 meters in width.

Q.11 What are the dimensions of a football goalpost?

Ans. The goalpost is 7.32 meters in width and 2.44 meters in height.

Q.12 What is the circumference of a standard football?

Ans. The circumference of a standard football is 68–70 cm (27–28 inches).

Q.13 Who is the only player allowed to use hands within the penalty area?

Ans. The goalkeeper is the only player allowed to use hands within the penalty area.

Q.14 What is a corner kick and when is it awarded?

Ans. A corner kick is awarded when the ball crosses the goal line off a defender.

Q.15 What is the purpose of the advantage rule in football?

Ans. The advantage rule allows play to continue if stopping it would disadvantage the attacking team.

Q.16 What is the difference between a direct and an indirect free kick?

Ans. A direct free kick allows a direct shot at goal, while an indirect free kick requires another player to touch the ball before a goal can be scored.

Q.17 What is a red card in football?

Ans. A red card is shown to a player who is sent off the field for a serious foul or after receiving two yellow cards.

Q.18 Name one fundamental dribbling technique in football.

Ans. One fundamental dribbling technique is speed dribbling for quick movement.

Q.19 Name one popular international football tournament.

Ans. The FIFA World Cup is a popular international football tournament.

Q.20 Name one famous football stadium and its location.

Ans. Wembley Stadium is a famous football stadium located in London, England.

Game 9

Volleyball

History

The game of volleyball, originally called mintonette was invented in 1895 by William G Morgan of USA. He designed the game to be a combination of basketball, baseball, tennis and handball.

The first country outside the USA to adopt Volleyball was Canada in 1900. The United States Volleyball Association was formed in 1928. An International Federation, the Federation Internationale de Volleyball (FIVB) was founded in 1947 and the First World Championship was held in 1949 for men and in 1952 for women.

In 1964, a variation of this game, beach volleyball, was played for the first time. Volleyball was played for the first time in 1964 Olympics, held in Tokyo (Japan).

In 1951, the Volleyball Federation of India (VFI) was established and since then, the national team has participated in several International Championships like Asian Championship, Commonwealth Games, Asian Games, etc. In India, the first national championship was held at Chennai in 1952.

Measurements and Specifications

(i) Playing court = A rectangle measuring 18 m × 9 m

(ii) Free zone area = 3 m to 5 m on all sides of the playing court

(iii) Width of boundary lines = 5 cm

(iv) Officials of match (FIVB) = 2 referees, 1 scorer and 4 linemen

(v) Weight of the ball = 260 to 280 gm

(vi) Circumference of the ball = 65 to 67 cm

(vii) Dimensions of the net = 9.5 m × 1 m

(viii) Height of the net from ground = 2.43 m for men and 2.24 m for women

(ix) Number of players in each team = 6 (excluding extras)

(x) Number of substitutes in each team = 6

(xi) Number of Antennas = 2

(xii) Length of the Antenna = 1.80 m

(xiii) Thickness of Antenna = 10 mm

(xiv) Height of Antenna = 80 cm above net

(xv) Pole to pole distance = 10 m to 12 m

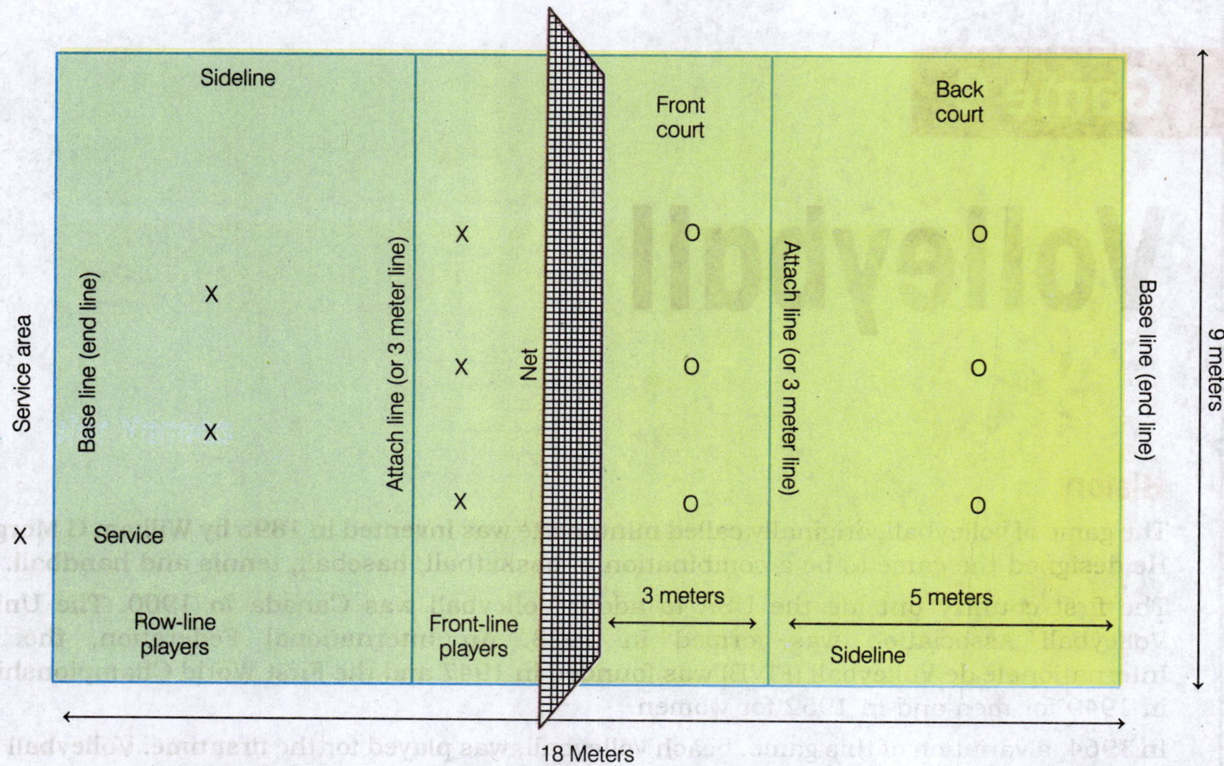

Volleyball Court Layout

Terminology

Ace	A serve that is not returned and results immediately in a point.
Antenna	The vertical rods (white and red) mounted near the edges of the net to indicate out-of-bounds along the sideline.
Approach	Fast stride towards the net by a spiker before he jumps in the air.
Assist	Passing the ball to a teammate who attacks the ball for a shot/smash.
Attack	The offensive action or attempt of hitting the ball.
Attack Error	An unsuccessful attack in which the ball lands out of bounds or the ball goes into the net. It directly results in a point for the opponent team.
Attacker	A player who attempts to hit a ball also called hitter or spiker.
Block	A defensive play by one or more players meant to deflect a spiked ball back to the hitter's court.
Boosting	Lifting the ball up for the smasher to smash. The player who does this, is called booster or setter.
Dig	Passing a spiked ball or passing an attacked ball close to the floor.
Dink	A legal soft push of the ball by the fingertips, around or over blockers.
Double Hit	Successive hits or contacts by the same player. (Illegal)
Expulsion	A player or coach is expelled and not allowed to play further, if he repeatedly performs misconduct. He is not even allowed to sit over team bench.

Hit	To jump and strike the ball with an overhand, forceful shot.
Jump Serve	A serve in which the server tosses the ball into the air, jumps-up and hits the ball in its downward motion.
Let Serve	A serve that contacts the net. If the ball dribbles over, it's playable just like any other ball.
Libero	A defensive player positioned at the rear half and is not limited by the regular rules of rotation.
Overhand Pass	A pass executed with both hands open, controlled by the fingers and thumbs, played just above the forehead.
Penetration	The act of reaching across the opponent area by crossing centre line by foot or hands over the net.
Rally	It is the continuous exchange of hits between the teams. Team winning the rally gets the service.
Red Card	A severe penalty in which an official displays a Red Card. The result of a Red Card may be a player is disqualified, the team loses the serve or the team loses a point. A Red Card may be given with or without a prior Yellow Card as a warning; it is up to the official's discretion.
Rotation	The clockwise movement of players around the court and through the serving position during the game.
Spike	Ball contacted with force by a player on the offensive team. The particular player is titled as spiker for the team.
Technical Time-out	A technical time-out of 60 seconds duration. It is taken when the leading team reaches the 8th and 16th points.
Underhand Serve	A serve in which the ball is given a slight underhand toss from about waist height and then struck with the opposite closed fist in an 'underhand pitching' motion.
Yellow Card	A warning from an official indicated by the display of a Yellow Card. Any player or coach who receives two Yellow Cards in a match is disqualified. A single Yellow Card does not result in loss of point or serve.

Latest/General Rules

1. Volleyball is a sport played by two teams on a playing court divided by a net. The object of the game is to send the ball over the net in order to ground it on the opponent's court and to prevent the same effort by the opponent.
2. Let service is allowed in volleyball.
3. Use of coloured ball is also permitted in competitions.
4. The ball is put in play with a service hit by the server over the net to the opponents. The rally continues until, the ball is grounded on either of the playing courts, goes 'out' or when a team fails to return it properly.
5. The team winning a rally, scores a point and the right to serve and its players rotate one position clockwise. Usually, 3 players are in the front row and 3 are in the back row. The front row is sectioned off by a line 10 ft from the net, called the *attack line* or the *10-foot line*.
6. During each possession of the ball, a team can only have three contacts with the ball known as a pass, a set and a hit, these are also called as *bump*, *set* and *spike*.

7. Positions are numbered from one to six, starting with the server in the back right corner and going in an anti-clockwise direction. After the server finishes, the other team gets the ball and when you get the ball back, everyone just shifts one spot to the right. Rotation, if not fully understood, can be a very confusing part of the game.
8. Teams score points whenever the other team cannot return the ball. Most matches are now played for winning three out of five games. The first four sets are of 25 points each and the fifth set is for 15 points.
9. A team can make a maximum of 6 substitutions per set. The ball can touch any part of the body and it must be hit (not held or thrown).
10. The player has 8 seconds to make service in a single attempt to get the ball over the net (it may touch net).

Duties of Referee He is the final authority on the rules and regulations from the start to the end of the match. Referee performs toss before the start of the match and he has the final say on every decision of the match.

Duties of Scorer He take notes of all the proceedings of the match in a chronological order, alongwith the points gained, time and substitutions made. He makes a record of all the fouls made by each player of each team and records personal and technical fouls separately. He maintains a score sheet with all the details of each player.

Duties of Linesmen There are 4 to 6 linesmen in a match. They basically are responsible for assisting the referee in case of infringement of boundary line rules. However, their assistance may be overruled by referee.

Fundamental Skills and Techniques

These may be divided into the following major categories

1. **Serving** Each point starts with a serve. The server steps behind the line at the back of the court, called *the end line* and has freedom to serve from wherever he pleases as long as the foot does not touch or cross the line. There are many techniques of serving. The underhand serving is done by beginners. Another technique is overhead serve where the ball is tossed in the air about 2 feet above the head. Topspin and jump serve are other overhead techniques.
2. **Hitting/Spike** Attacking the ball is all about timing and precision. The 'goal' of the third hit or 'spike', is to make the ball difficult for the opposing team to return. Players spiking should have excellent judgement to perceive the direction of the ball and balance the body to lift it while hitting the ball forcefully. The aim is to land the ball on the floor of the opponent's team.
3. **Blocking** This is a defensive technique where the players block the offensive shots and try it to shot them back to the opponent. The blocking can be done by one, two or three players according to the standard of match. For one man blocking, the player stands close to the net, face towards it. The player should try to interrupt the ball by taking a jump and raising his hands above the net.
4. **Lifts**

   (i) *Tip or Lift* It is a rally technique used during the match. The tip is a transitory move between reception and attack. It is made with an upward movement of the arms and legs. Contact with the ball is with the fingertips without touching palm. A player specialised in lifting is known as Booster or Setter.

(ii) *Bump or Underarm-Lift* Bump is a defensive skill keeping the ball from falling; receiving serve and offensive skill as it provides good chance to tip the ball for the spiker. Bump is the first contact of the ball (service reception). The bump provides the transition between defence and attack.

Tip or Lift

Bump or Underarm-Lift

(iii) *One Hand Lift* This is an advanced technique to lift the far away falling ball towards side. In this a player has less chance to move to the place where ball is falling towards side of players. Then, the extends one arm to lift the ball. Thus, ball can be raised up for further play.

(iv) *Dive Lift* In this, the players dive to lift the fast coming ball as there is less time to move forward or sideward. Thus, player dives for lifting the ball with underhand.

Popular Tournaments

International

- World Cup
- FIVB World Cup
- Italian Open
- Olympics
- Super Challenge Cup
- Canada Open
- New Zealand Open

National

- National Volleyball Championship (both Men and Women)
- Asian Volleyball Championship Cup for Men
- Shivani Gold Cup
- Federation Cup (India)
- All India Volleyball Tournament
- National Games

Popular Volleyball Awardees

Arjuna Award

- 1961 A Palanisamy
- 1962 Nripjit Singh Bedi
- 1972 Balwant Singh Sagwal ('Ballu')
- 1973 GM Reddy
- 1974 M. Shyam Sunder Rao
- 1975 R Singh, K.C. Elamma
- 1976 Jimmy George
- 1977 A Ramana Rao
- 1978 Kutty Krishnan
- 1979 SK Mishra
- 1982 GE Sridharan
- 1983 RK Purohit
- 1984 Saley Joseph
- 1986 Cyril C Valloor
- 1989 Abdul Bashith
- 1990 Dalel Singh
- 1991 K Uday Kumar
- 1999 Sukhpal Singh
- 2000 PV Ramana
- 2001 Amir Singh
- 2002 Ravi Kant Reddy
- 2010 KJ Kapil Dev
- 2011 Sanjay Kumar
- 2014 Tom Joseph
- 2015 Sanjay Kumar

Dhyan Chand Award

- 2003 Om Prakash
- 2015 TP Padmanabhan Nair

Dronacharya Award

- 1990 A Ramana Rao
- 1995 M Shyam Sunder Rao
- 2007 GE Sridharan

Popular Venues

- Polideportivo Gustavo Torito Rodriguez, Mendoza (Argentina)
- Gregory Gymnasium, Austin, Texas (USA)
- Indira Gandhi Indoor Stadium, New Delhi (India)
- YSR Indoor Stadium, Yanam, Puducherry (India)
- Jawaharlal Nehru Stadium, Chennai (India)
- Sree Kanteerava Indoor Stadium, Bengaluru (India)
- KVB Reddy Indoor Stadium, Hyderabad (India)

Viva-Voce

Q.1 Who invented volleyball and what was it originally called?

Ans. Volleyball was invented by William G. Morgan and it was originally called mintonette.

Q.2 When was volleyball invented?

Ans. Volleyball was invented in 1895 in Holyoke, Massachusetts, USA.

Q.3 What is the standard volleyball court size?

Ans. The standard volleyball court size is 18 meters × 9 meters.

Q.4 How many players are on a volleyball team during a match?

Ans. 6 players.

Q.5 What is the net height for men's volleyball?

Ans. The net height for men's volleyball is 2.43 meters.

Q.6 What is the net height for women's volleyball?

Ans. The net height for women's volleyball is 2.24 meters.

Q.7 How many contacts is a team allowed per possession?

Ans. A team is allowed a maximum of three contacts per possession to return the ball to opponent's side of the net.

Q.8 What is a spike in volleyball?

Ans. Spike is a powerful and overhand hit at the net.

Q.9 Who is the libero on a volleyball team?

Ans. The libero is a defensive spcialist who plays in the back row and cannot attack or serve.

Q.10 When did volleyball debut at the Olympics?

Ans. Volleyball debut at the Olympics in 1964 (Tokyo Olympics).

Q.11 What is an ace in volleyball?

Ans. A serve that lands in bounds and is not returned.

Q.12 What is blocking in volleyball?

Ans. Defensive move to stop a spike at the net.

Q.13 What is the maximum number of substitutions per set in volleyball?

Ans. Under FIVB (international) rules, a team is allowed a maximum of 6 substitutions per set.

Q.14 When was the Volleyball Federation of India formed?

Ans. Volleyball Federation of India formed in 1951.

Q.15 Name one international volleyball tournament.

Ans. FIVB World Cup.

Game 10

Badminton

History

Badminton is a popular game played by both men and women in singles and doubles. It was played in England's royal courts until 1873. The game grew in India, especially in Pune, where it was nick named 'Poona'. The rules of badminton were created in Pune in 1870. In March 1898, the first Open Tournament was held at Guildford, England. Denmark, USA and Canada became ardent followers of the game during the 1930s. In 1934, the International Badminton Federation (IBF) was formed.

The first major IBF Tournament was the **Thomas Cup** (World Men's Team Championship) held in 1948. Since then, the number of world events has increased with the addition of the Uber Cup (Women's team), World Championships (individual events), Sudirman Cup (Mixed team), World Junior Championships and the World Grand Pix Finals. Badminton was introduced in Commonwealth Games in 1966 and in Barcelona Olympics in 1992. The countries like China, Denmark, India, Indonesia, Japan, Korea, Malaysia and Russia have won medals in Badminton at Olympic Games since its introduction in 1992. Badminton Association of India (BAI) regulates the team selection, training and coaching to Indian players.

Badminton Court

65 mm
70 mm
25 mm

Shuttle

Measurements and Specifications

- Size of badminton court (Singles) = 13.4 m × 5.18 m (44 feet × 17 feet) including lines.
- Size of badminton court (Doubles) = 13.4 m × 6.10 m (44 feet × 20 feet) including lines.
- Height of poles = 1.55 m (5 feet 1 inch) over sideline for doubles.
- Height of net at centre = 1.52 m (5 feet).
- Weight of shuttlecock = 4.74 gm to 5.50 gm with 16 feathers.
- Width of lines = 4 cm as part of court.
- Number of points in game = 21 points game in best of three for all categories.
- Racket = 68 cm long and 23 cm wide head.

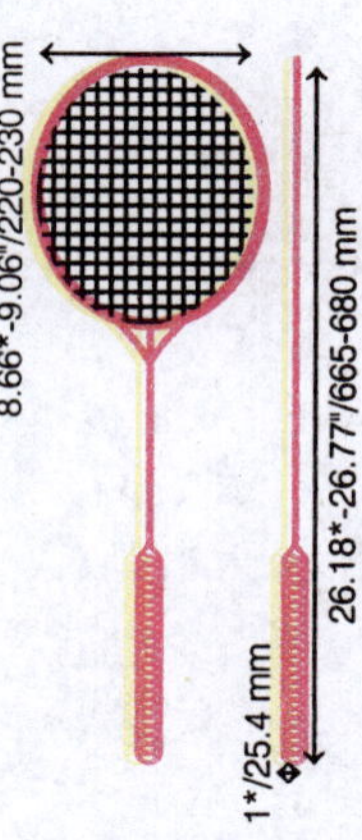

Racket

* **Officials = 1 Umpire, 1 Service Umpire, 4 to 8 Linesmen, 1 Match Referee**
* **Free space = 2 m on all sides of the court.**
* **Side galleries (each side) = 1 feet 6 inches.**
* Back gallery = 2 feet 6 inches.
* Number of max. sets = 3 sets.

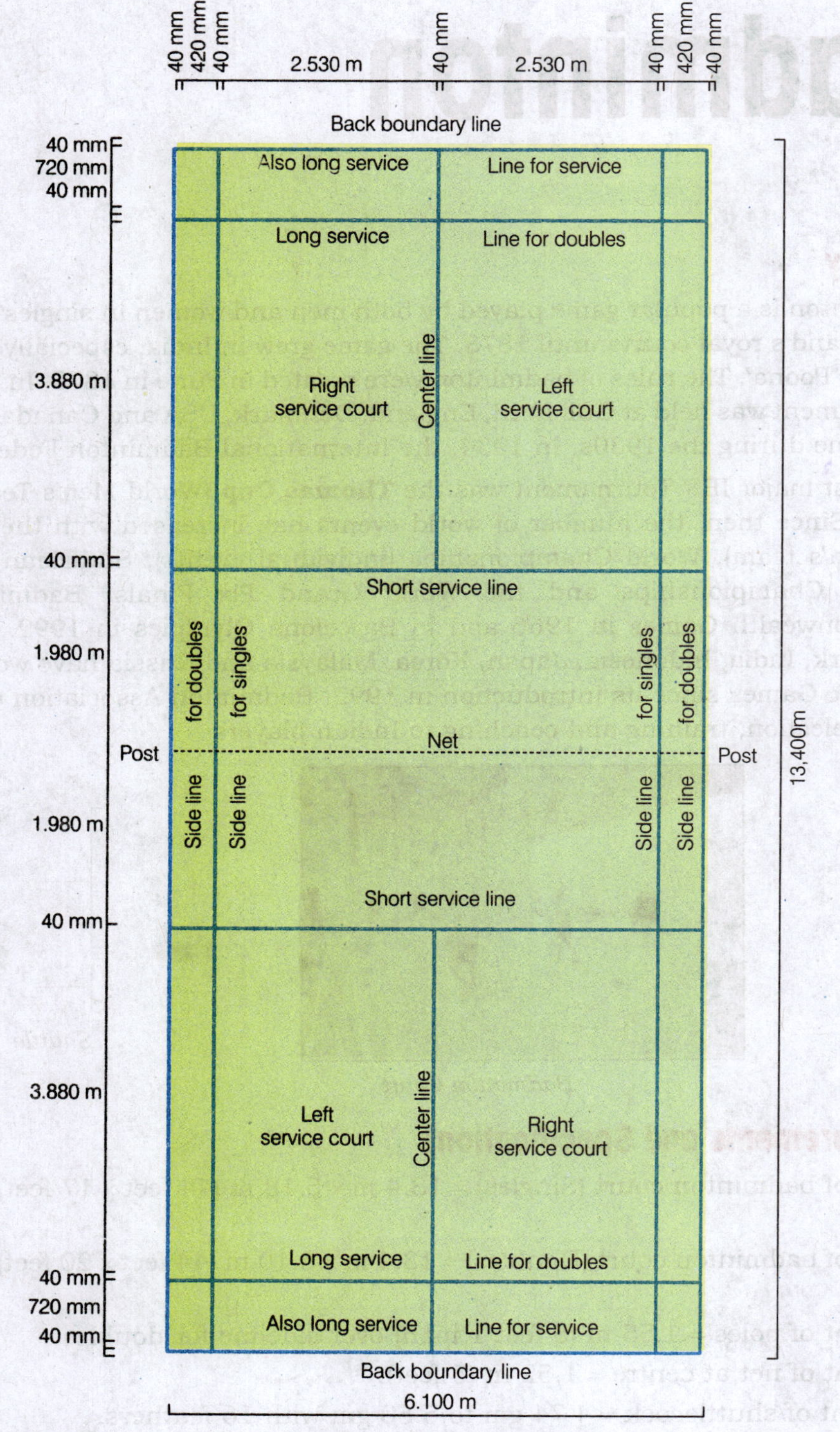

Layout of Badminton Court

Types of Badminton Tournaments

Traditionally, there are three types of competitive badminton games: singles, doubles and mixed doubles. Each event has a different pace, strategy and technique.

- **Singles** In a singles match, two players compete against each other. There are men's singles and women's singles contested at many badminton competitions. Singles matches can be a more strenuous workout, because the players must move to cover a larger area of the court than in doubles matches.
- **Doubles** In a doubles match, two pairs of players play against each other. At international badminton competitions, both men's and women's doubles are held. Playing in pairs requires teamwork, communication and focus.
- **Mixed doubles** In a mixed doubles match, one male and one female player team up to play an opposing team of the same composition.

Terminology

Ace	The shot which an opponent fails to return is called ace.
Attacking Clear	An offensive stroke hit deep into the opponent's court.
Back Hand	The stroke used to return balls hit to the left of a right-handed player or to the right of a left-handed player.
Base Line	The back boundary line at each end of the court, parallel to the net.
Bird	The term 'bird' is an informal term for the shuttlecock.
Centre Line	A line perpendicular to the net that separates the left and right service courts.
Court	It is the playing area enclosed between the back boundary lines and the side lines.
Doubles	A game where two players play against another team of two.
Doubles Side Line	The side boundary of a doubles court.
Drop Shot	A basic shot where a player strikes with a forehand, backhand or round the head action to direct it towards the top of net, so that after crossing the net, it falls in the opponent's court very close to the net.
Fault	A violation of the playing rule.
Inning	It is the time during which a player or pair holds service.
Let	The stopping of a play owing to any outside interference is called *let*. Lets may occur because of some unexpected disturbance such as a shuttlecock landing on court. It is called by the umpire or by a player to halt the game. The point is replayed in this case.
Love	The term is used to indicate zero score.
Love-All	It is the way of scoring in the beginning of game that means the score is nil at both sides.
Match Point	The point which, if won by the server makes him the winner of the match.
Net Strokes	These are the strokes which are executed to return a shuttle falling close to the net.
Racket	A bat with a round or oval frame strung with nylon, etc. used specially in tennis, badminton and squash.
Rally	The exchange of shots that decides each point.
Receiver	The player who receives the service.

Rotation	It is the system of play in doubles game in which the players keep on changing their positions during the play.
Server	The player who puts the shuttle into play by hitting it from the service area to start a rally.
Service Court	The area into which a service must be delivered.
Singles	A game where one person plays with another person.
Singles Side Line	The side boundary of a singles court.
Sling	An illegal stroke in which the shuttle is not hit, but caught and held on the racket before being released, also called a *carry* or *throw*.
Toss or Lob	It is a stroke that sends the shuttle high and deep towards the baseline of the opponent.
Wood Shot	A shot in which the shuttle hits the frame of the racket.

General Rules

There are some rules followed in playing badminton

(i) Before the beginning of the game, there will be a toss, where winner decides to choose an end of the court or to serve first. If winner of the toss chooses the court, the opponent will do first service.

(ii) Match is played on the basis of 'best of three' games.

(iii) Maximum 90 seconds break can be taken between games.

(iv) When the server serves, the shuttlecock must pass over the short service line on the opponent's court or it will count as a fault. At the start of the game, the server and receiver stand in diagonally opposite service courts. The server hits the shuttlecock so that it would land in the receiver's court. A badminton serve must be hit below waist height and with the racket shaft pointing downwards, the shuttlecock is not allowed to bounce and the players stand inside their service courts.

(v) In *singles*, the server stands in their right service court when their score is even, and in his/her left service court when the score is odd.

In *doubles*, if the serving side wins a game, the same player continues to serve, but he/she changes service courts so that he/she serves to a different opponent each time. If the opponents win the game and their new score is even, the player in the right service court serves, if odd, the player in the left service court serves.

(vi) Each game consists of 21 points. Of the best three games, the winner of the two games is declared victorious. In case of tie (deuce) at 20th point, whosoever scores two consecutive points first wins the game. If the score becomes 29 all, the player who scores 30th point will win the game. Continuous point scoring is followed according to new rules. In the beginning, the points are told as 'Love All'. Changes of sides are done after each game and also on the 11th point in the final game.

(vii) There are two ways to win a rally, either get the shuttlecock to hit the opponent's side court or force the opponent to commit a fault.

(viii) *A fault occurs in the following cases*

- A player serves 'out of turn'.
- Player serves from the wrong side of service court.
- Player tricking the serve, stands on wrong side of service court and receives the service.
- When the shuttlecock touches the court or does not go over the net.
- When the shuttlecock touches a player or his clothes or even the net.

Fundamental Skills

Following skills are very important for badminton

(i) *Service* In badminton, service is done from half side of the court to the diagonally opponent's court. It must be hit below the waist level so that it should reach the end of the opponent's court. There are many types of services like short service, long service, receiver in service, drive service, reverse hand service, flick service, etc.

(ii) *Strokes* There are mainly two types of strokes in badminton–forehand stroke and backhand stroke. Forehand stroke is played for returning a shuttle from the right side of the body of a player. Backhand stroke is applied to return a shuttle coming towards the left side of the body of a player.

(iii) *Drop Shot* It is a very gentle stroke in which a shuttle is struck with a forehand, backhand or round the head action to direct it towards the top of the net, so that it just crosses the net and lands near the net in opponent's court.

(iv) *Drive* It is a flat stroke in which the shuttle is sent over the net just clearing it and parallel to the floor and it should not be sent high towards the opponent.

(v) *Grip of the Racket* There are generally two types of grip, *viz.*, forehand grip and backhand grip. In forehand grip, the player holds the racket by the shaft in the left hand with the face of the racket perpendicular to the floor and shake hands with the grip. In backhand grip, the player turns the top edge of the racket frame slightly over to the right and puts the thumb along and parallel to the wide side of the handle.

(vi) *Clear or Toss* It is a high and deep shot sent to the back of the opponent's court.

(vii) *Smash* An offensive stroke which is powerfully hit in downward direction and gives no chance to the opponent to return it.

(viii) *Tap* It refers to a gentle, controlled shot, usually played at the net to quickly place the shuttlecock over the net, often used to finish a rally with precision.

(ix) *Flat Return* This offensive skill is mostly used in doubles game when the player returns the coming shuttle with force just at the height of net.

(x) *Footwork* The player must know the basics of movements on the court and practice them. The ready position in singles includes standing in the centre of the court and bending knees with relaxed body and waiting for the play. To move backward, the player must go fast, so that he gets behind the shuttle to hit it hard enough.

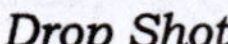
Drop Shot

Overhead Defence Technique

Short Serve

Smash

Popular Tournaments

Thomas Cup (World Team Men), Wills World Cup, European Cup, Olympic Challenge Cup (National Women), Naarang Cup (National Junior Team Men), China Cup, Asian Games, BWF World Championship.

Popular National Venues

Indira Gandhi Stadium (New Delhi), Hans Raj Stadium (Jalandhar), Sai Stadium Sports Complex (Chandigarh), Sports Centre (Lucknow), NIS Badminton Hall (Patiala, Gandhi Nagar, Bengaluru).

Popular Badminton Awardees

Arjuna Awardees

- 2005 Aparna Popat
- 2006 Chetan Anand, Rohit Bhakar (Disabled Category)
- 2007 Anup Sridhar
- 2008 Saina Nehwal, Parul D. Parmar
- 2011 Jwala Gutta
- 2012 Ashwini Ponnappa, P. Kashyap
- 2013 P.V. Sindhu
- 2014 V. Diju
- 2015 Srikanth Kidambi
- 2018 N. Sikki Reddy
- 2019 B. Sai Praneeth
- 2020 Satwiksairaj Rankireddy
- 2022 H.S. Prannoy, Lakshya Sen
- 2023 J.A. Jayarat Chagan

Padma Shree Awardees

- 1982 Prakash Padukone
- 1977 Meena Shah
- 2005 Pullela Gopichand
- 2006 Madhumita Singh Bisht
- 2010 Saina Nehwal
- 2012 Syed Mohammed Arif
- 2015 PV Sindhu
- 2022 Pramod Bhagat (Para-badminton)

Rajiv Gandhi (Major Dhyan Chand) Khel Ratan Awardees

- 2000-2001 Pullela Gopichand
- 2010 Saina Nehwal
- 2016 PV Sindhu

Dronacharya Awardees

- 2000 Syed Mohammed Arif
- 2009 Pullela Gopichand
- 2019 Vimal Kumar
- 2017 G.S.S.V. Prasad
- 2020 Gaurav Khanna (Para badminton)
- 2024 S. Muralidharan

Padma Bhushan Awardees

- 2014 Pullela Gopichand
- 2016 Saina Nehwal
- 2020 PV Sindhu

Viva-Voce

Q.1 Where did the modern game of Badminton originate?

Ans. England's royal courts

Q.2 What was badminton originally called in India?

Ans. Badminton was originally called Poona in India.

Q.3 In which year was the International Badminton Federation (IBF) formed?

Ans. The International Badminton Federation (IBF) formed in 1934.

Q.4 When did badminton become an Olympic sport?

Ans. Badminton officially become an Olympic sport in 1992 (Barcelona Olympics).

Q.5 What is the length and width of a singles badminton court?

Ans. The length and width of a single badminton court are respectively 13.4 m × 5.18 m.

Q.6 What is the standard height of the net at the centre of a badminton court?

Ans. The standard height of the net at the centre of a badminton court is 1.52 m.

Q.7 What is the maximum number of games in a badminton match?

Ans. Best of 3 games.

Q.8 How many feathers are used in a standard shuttlecock?

Ans. 16 feathers are used in a standard shuttlecock.

Q.9 What is the full length of a badminton racket?

Ans. The full length of a badminton racket is 68 cm.

Q.10 What is a powerful downward shot in badminton called?

Ans. A powerful downward shot in badminton is called Smash.

Q.11 What is the term for a score of zero in badminton?

Ans. The term for a score of zero in badminton is 'Love'.

Q.12 What is the stroke called that is played from the non-racket side?

Ans. The stroke that is played from the non-racket side is called backhand stroke.

Q.13 What type of serve travels flat and fast?

Ans. Drive serve is the type of serve that travels that and tast in badminton.

Q.14 What is the grip called where the thumb supports the flat side of the racket handle?

Ans. The grip where the thumb supports the flat side of the racked handle is called backhand grip.

Q.15 Which organization governs badminton in India?

Ans. Badminton Association of India (BAI).

Game 11

Swimming

History

Swimming emerged as a competitive recreational activity in England in 1830s. By 1837, the National Swimming society was holding regular competitions.
In other European countries also, swimming federations were established, e.g. in Germany in 1882, in France in 1890 and in Hungary in 1896. Swimming was included as a men's sport in 1896 Athens Olympics. It was included as women's sport in 1912 Summer Olympics, Stockholm, Sweden.

In 1908, the world swimming association, 'Federation Internationale de Natation Amateur (FINA) was established with 10 member nations.

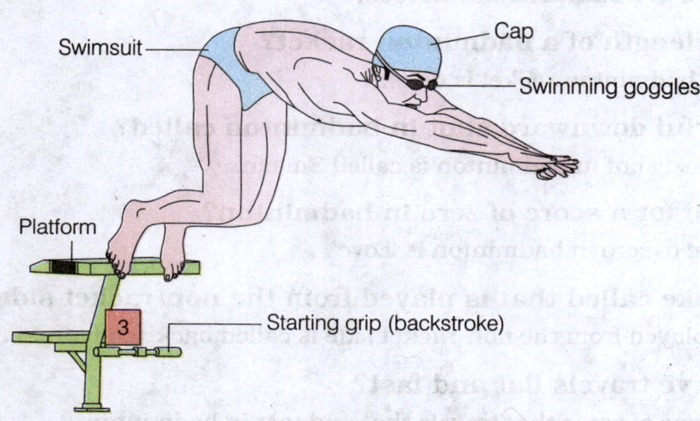

Swimming Equipments

Measurements and Specifications

- Length of the pool : 50 m
- Width of the pool : 25 m
- Depth of water : 1.8 m
- Number of lanes : 8; 10 at international events
- Width of lanes : 2.5 m
- Temperature of pool water : 24°C min
- Height of platform from water surface : 0.50-0.75 m
- Size of platform : 0.5 × 0.5 m
- Angle of platform : 10° max
- A standard swimming pool has 50 m length and 25 m breadth.

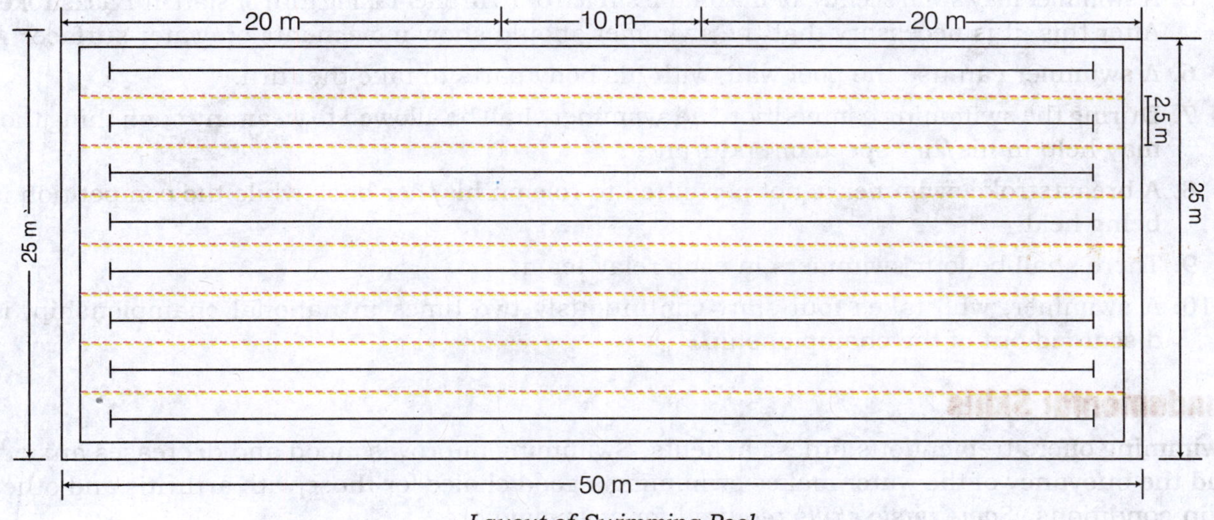

Layout of Swimming Pool

Terminology

Diving In competitive swimming, a good dive off the starting block is essential for winning races and improving the swimmer's time. It is jumping or falling into water from a platform or springboard. Diving evolved as a sport first in England, then in USA followed by Continental Europe. It is internationally recognised sport and a part of the Olympic games.

Front Crawl This is the fastest stroke and is used in freestyle races. In this stroke, legs and arms move alternately.

Gliding The swimmer is stretched with the arms to the front, the head between the arms and the feet to the back. This streamlined shape minimises resistance and allows the swimmer to glide.

Head-High Crawl This stroke is used by lifeguards to keep the victim in sight or those who simply want to see where they are going and breathe with ease. It is similar to front crawl, but with head above the water.

Individual Medley Individual medley consists of 4 equal portions with strokes used in this order–butterfly, backstroke, breaststroke and freestyle. When changing from one stroke to another, the swimmer has to follow the turn rules for the stroke just finished.

Lane Area in which each swimmer swims, which is separated by lane lines and floating markers. Lane markings are marked on the bottom of the pool.

Platform A diving platform or diving tower is a type of structure used for competitive diving. It consists of a vertical rigid tower with one or more horizontal platforms extending out over a deep pool of water.

Swim Wear According to the FINA rules of 2009, a swimmer must wear proper swim suit, swim cap, goggles for protection and maintain decency of the game.

General Rules

1. A swimmer who is the first to swim over the entire course is declared the winner of that event.
2. A swimmer is not allowed to change his lane during a swimming competition. If he is found doing so, he is disqualified.
3. Swimmers are not permitted to take any support from the bottom of the pool.
4. 4th lane is allotted to the top ranker swimmer.

5. A swimmer may swim silently for maximum stretch of 15 m after taking turn or start in 'Backstroke'. After this, it is necessary that the swimmer should show movements on water surface.
6. A swimmer can use the pool wall, with his body parts to take the turn.
7. During the swimming competition, no swimmer shall be allowed to wear any such thing that may help in his/her speed or endurance.
8. A breaststroke swimmer is not permitted to role on his/her back while the competition is being held.
9. There shall be four swimmers in each relay team.
10. A swimmer, who takes foul start continuously two times in national championship, is discarded out of the championship.

Fundamental Skills

Swimming offers tremendous fitness benefits. Swimming improves mood and decreases anxiety and the buoyancy of the water makes swimming a good choice for those with arthritis and other pain conditions. *Some basic skills required for swimming are*

1. **Strokes** Strokes are the arm movements used to pull the body through the water. The front crawl, sidestroke, breaststroke, backstroke and butterfly are the five most common swimming strokes. Each stroke uses different body positioning, breathing techniques and arm movements. Training with a qualified swimming coach is the best way to learn the various strokes. *The most common swimming strokes are*
   (a) **The Freestyle Stroke** Freestyle races are the most common of all swimming styles, with distances reaching 1500 m or 1650 yards. The stroke used almost universally in freestyle races is the front crack as this style is generally the fastest.
   (b) **The Breaststroke** Breaststroke is the most popular swim stroke of all. In breaststroke, both arms execute half-circular arm movement at the same time under water in front of the swimmer. The arm recovery also occurs under water. The legs simultaneously execute a whip kick. It is often the first swimming stroke taught to beginners. Infact, many casual swimmers can only swim this stroke.
   (c) **The Backstroke** As its name suggests, backstroke is swimming on the back. It uses alternating circular arm movements and an above water recovery. The legs execute a flutter kick similar to the one used in freestyle. Backstroke is faster than breaststroke, but slower than butterfly.
   (d) **Butterfly Stroke** The butterfly stroke stands out among the competitive strokes because of its unique and spectacular techniques. It uses a symmetrical arm stroke with an above water recovery. It also uses a wave-like body undulation and a dolphin kick. Butterfly is the second fastest swim stroke after freestyle. It has a reputation of being hard to learn and is quickly exhausting.
2. **Kicking** Kicking provides propulsion through the water. Once someone is comfortable with floating, kicking is the next logical step. Kicking is also used in treading water, which is the process of remaining in one place while keeping the swimmer's head above the water line.
3. **Diving** It is a sport where an athlete jumps or falls into water from a platform or springboard while performing acrobatic movements in the air. Here are different types of dives as follows
   - *Forward Dive* The diver faces forward and rotates forward.
   - *Backward Dive* The diver faces backward and rotates backward.
   - *Reverse Dive* The diver faces forward but rotates backward.
   - *Inward Dive* The diver faces backward but rotates forward.

• *Twisting Dive* Incorporates twists along with the somersaults.

Twisting Dive

Forward Dive

International Swimming Competitions

1. Olympics
2. World Championship
3. World Aquatics Championship (50 m pool)
4. European Aquatics Championships (50 m pool)
5. Open de Paris de Natation
6. United States Swimming National Championship
7. Commonwealth Games
8. Asian Games

Popular Venues

- Talkatora Stadium, New Delhi
- Kurukshetra University, Swimming Pool Kurukshetra
- Punjab University, Chandigarh
- HVPM Swimming Pool, Amaravati
- H.A.U Swimming Pool, Hissar
- Edmonton Swimming Pool, Edmonton, Canada
- War Heroes' Stadium, Ambala Cantt.
- Sports School, Rai, Haryana
- NIS, Patiala

Popular Swimming Awardees

Arjuna Awardees

- 1961 Bajrangi Prasad
- 1967 Rima Dutta
- 1967 Arun Shaw
- 1969 Baidya Nath
- 1971 Bhanwar Singh
- 1973 Dhanvir Khatu
- 1974 Avinash Sarang
- 1974 Manjari Bhargava
- 1975 Smita Divgikar
- 1975 M.S. Rana
- 1982 Persis Madan
- 1983 Anita Sood
- 1984 Khajan Singh
- 1985 Tara Nath Shenoy
- 1988 Wilson Cherian
- 1990 Bula Choudhary
- 1996 M.V. Kutraleeswaran
- 1998 Bhanu Sachdeva
- 1999 Nisha Millet
- 2001 Sebastian Xavier
- 2000 J. Abhijit
- 2005 Shikha Tandon
- 2010 Rehan Poncha
- 2011 Virdhawal Khade, Prasanta Karmakar
- 2012 Sandeep Sejwal
- 2015 Sharath Gayakwad
- 2020 Suyash Narayan Jadhav (Para Swimming)
- 2022 Swapnil Sanjay Patil (Para Swimming)
- 2024 Sajan Prakash

Dronacharya Awardees

- 2014 K. P. Thakkar
- 2015 Nihar Ameen
- 2020 Sachin Nag
- 2016 S. Pradeep Kumar
- 2021 Tapan Kumar Panigrahi (Life time)

Viva-Voce

Q.1 In which country did swimming emerge as a competitive sport in the 1830s?

Ans. Swimming emerged as a competitive sport in the 1830s in England.

Q.2 When was the National Swimming Society formed in England?

Ans. The National Swimming Society formed in England in 1837.

Q.3 In which year was swimming introduced in the first modern Olympic Games?

Ans. Swimming was introduced in the first modern Olympic games in 1896.

Q.4 When were women allowed to participate in Olympic swimming events?

Ans. Women were allowed to participate in Olympic Swimming event in 1912.

Q.5 What is the name of the international governing body for swimming formed in 1908?

Ans. FINA (Féderation Internationale de Natation Amateur)

Q.6 What are the standard dimensions of an Olympic-size swimming pool?

Ans. The standard dimensions of an Olympic-size Swimming pool is 50 m × 25 m.

Q.7 How many lanes are used in international swimming competitions?

Ans. 10 lanes are used in international swimming competition.

Q.8 What is the minimum water temperature required in swimming competitions?

Ans. The minimum temperature required in swimming competitions is 24°C.

Q.9 What is the size of a starting platform in swimming?

Ans. The size of a starting platform in swimming is 0.5 m × 0.5 m.

Q.10 What is the maximum allowed angle of a starting platform?

Ans. The maximum allowed angle of a starting platform is 10°.

Q.11 Name the fastest stroke in swimming.

Ans. Freestyle (Front Crawl)

Q.12 What is the second fastest but energy-intensive stroke in swimming?

Ans. The second fastest but energy-intensive stroke in swimming is butterfly.

Q.13 In which stroke do swimmers lie on their back with alternating arms?

Ans. Swimmers lie on their back with alternating arms in the backstroke.

Q.14 What is the name of the event that includes all four strokes in sequence?

Ans. The event that includes all four strokes in sequence is the individual medley.

Q.15 What is the rule for gliding distance after start/turn in backstroke?

Ans. The maximum allowed distance for gliding after a start/turn in back-stroke is maximum 15 meters.

Q.16 What is the penalty for changing lanes during a race?

Ans. The penalty for changing lanes during a race is disqualification.

Q.17 What is the name of the stroke with a circular arm motion and whip kick?

Ans. The swimming stroke that uses a circular arm motion combined with a whip kick is called the breaststroke.

Q.18 What kind of dive involves facing forward but rotating backward?

Ans. A reverse dive involves facing forward but rotating backward.

Q.19 Name two Indian swimmers who received the Arjuna Award.

Ans. Rehan Poncha and Sandeep Sejwal.

Q.20 Name any two popular swimming venues in India.

Ans. Talkatora Stadium (Delhi), NIS Patiala

Game 12

Kabaddi

History

The origin of Kabaddi has its roots in ancient India from the era of the Mahabharata. In Western India, Kabaddi is also known as Hutu Tu. Maharashtra was the pioneer state to bring the game to the national platform and give it further popularity.

Kabaddi is known as the 'Game of the masses', due to its popularity, simple and easy to comprehend rules, and public appeal. Standard rules and regulations were formulated in 1918 but were brought out in print in the year 1923. In the same year, an All India Tournament was organised at Baroda. Kabaddi received its first international exposure during the 1936 Berlin Olympics, demonstrated by Hanuman Vyayam Prasarak Mandal, Amaravati, Maharashtra. The Kabaddi Federation of India (KFI) also known as The All India Kabaddi Federation (AIKF) was formed in the year 1950.

Kabaddi is controlled by International Kabaddi Federation (IKF). The All India Kabaddi Federation (AIKF) was formed in the year 1950 to look after the promotion of the game and the Senior National Campionship started from the year 1952. Kabaddi was a demonstrative game in 1982, Asian Games held at New Delhi. Later, it was officially introduced in the Asian Games in 1990.

Measurements and Specifications

(i) Dimension of Playing Field = For Men, 13 m × 10 m, For Women, 12 m × 8 m
(ii) Width of Lobby = 1 m on sides
(iii) Duration of Game = 2 Halves of 20 min (5 min rest) Men, 2 Halves of 15 min (5 min rest) Women
(iv) Distance of Baulk Line = 3.75 m (men), 3 m (women) from Mid-line
(v) Number of Players = 12 (7 Playing, 5 Reserves)
(vi) Surface of Playing Field = Clay or Muddy/Synthetic
(vii) Officials = 1 Referee, 2 Umpires, 1 Scorer, 2 Linesmen (Assistant Scorers)
(viii) Width of marking lines and centre line = 5 cms
(ix) Block size = 1x 8 m (Men), 1x 6 m (Women and Juniors)

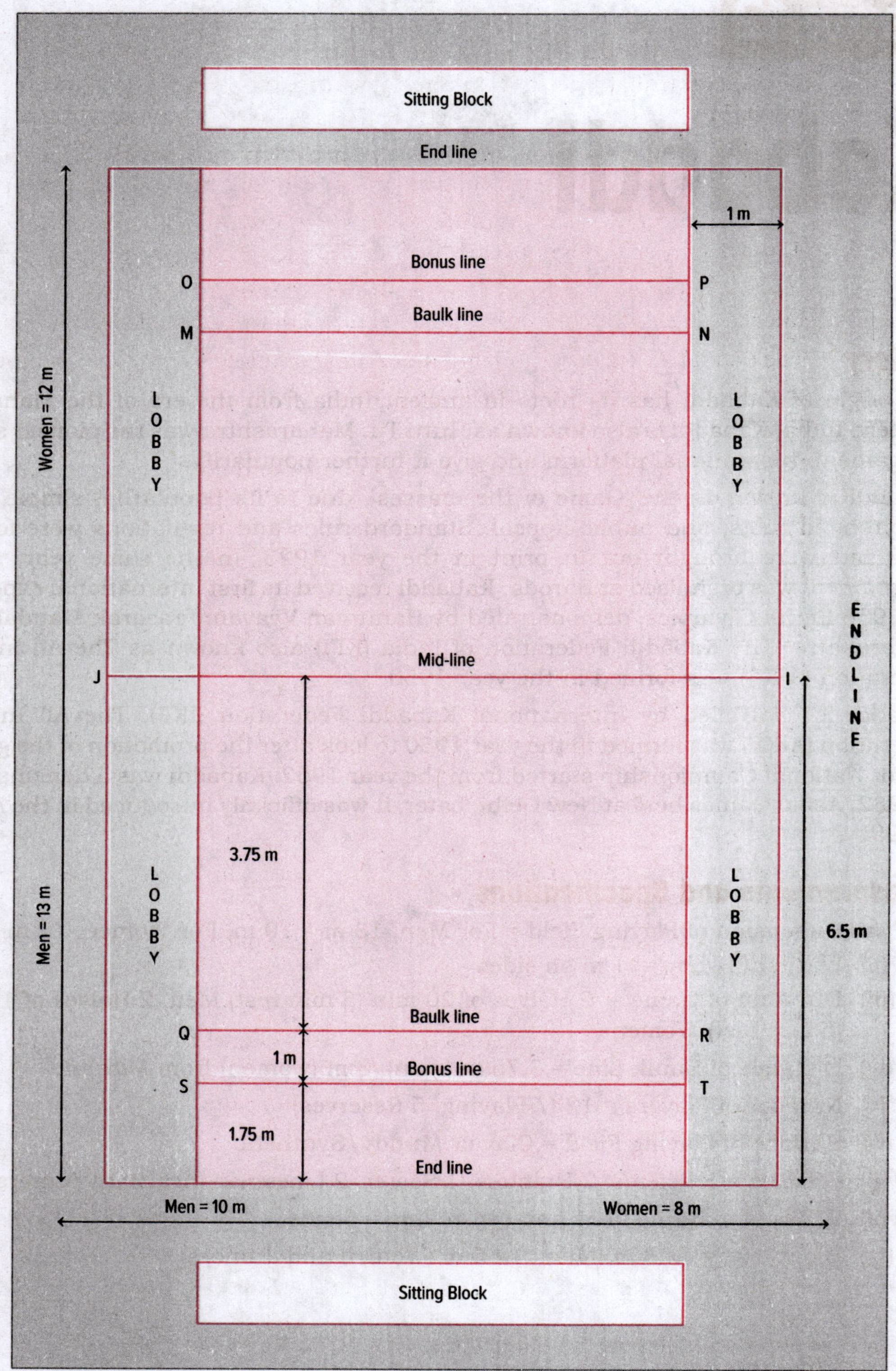

Kabaddi Court

Terminology

Anti-Raider Or Anti	Every player of the party in whose court the raid is being made shall be called an anti-raider or anti.
Baulk Line	The first parallel line from midline towards end line in each half is called as baulk line.
Bonus Line	The line parallel to baulk line towards end line in each half is known as bonus line. The distance between bonus line and baulk line will be 1 meter.
Chant	The continuous clear sounding recitation aloud of the approved word 'Kabaddi' in one single breath is called chant.
Broken Chant	When the continuous and clear repitition of the word 'Kabaddi' is broken by taking more than 1 breath in between repetitions, it is called broken chant.
Catch	The defensive player grabs the raider and completely over powers him, so that he cannot return safely to his own half.
Defender	Every player in whose half the raid is being made is called as defender.
Empty Raid	When the raider crosses the baulk line of the defending team at least once during the course of a raid and reaches his half with chant without scoring or losing a point is known as empty raid.
Entry	It means a raider's entry into the opponent team's court from right, left or centre depending on his decision to enter from any side.
Lobbies	The area on both the vertical sides of the playfield measuring one meter in width covering the entire length of the Field of Play (FOP) is known as the lobbies.
Raider	One who enters the court of the opponent with the chant is known as a raider. The raider must begin his chant before he touches the opponent's court.
Raid	When the raider enters the court of the opponent with cant, it is known as a raid.
Productive	A raid in which a point is scored by any team will be called as productive raid.
Sitting Block	Sitting blocks are placed outside the field of play where player who get out and extra players sit. There are two sitting blocks, one for each team.
Successful Raid	During the course of raid, if the raider crosses the baulk line of defending team at least once and returns back to his court without breaking its cant, it is known as successful raid.
Super Catch	If a raider is caught/self out/declared out, when 3 or fewer defenders are defending, then it is called as super catch.
Struggle	When a raider touches an anti or an anti touches a raider, the struggle begins.
TAG (Touch)	When the raider touches the defender or defenders by any part of his body or even the clothing, shoes or any other outfit, is called a touch (TAG).
To Put Out an Anti	If a raider touches an anti without the breach of the rules of play or if an anti touches any part of the body of the raider and then the raider touches his court with the chant, the anti is said to be put on.
To Reach Court Safely	If the raider after crossing the midline touches his court with any part of his body without breach of rules of play and with chant he is said to have reached his court safely.

Latest/General Rules

1. Each team consist of not more than 12 players with only 7 taking to the field at any one time.
2. The team that wins the toss will have the choice to elect either to raid or the side of the court.
3. To win a point when raiding, the raider must take a breath and run into the opposition's half and tag one or more members of the opposing team and then return to their own half of the pitch before inhaling again.
4. To prove that another breath hasn't been taken, the raider must continue to repeatedly chant the word 'Kabaddi'.
5. If a raider is coached, guided or in any way instructed by his team during the raid, then the Umpire or Referee may award one technical point to the opponent team.
6. During the timeout, the players on ground will not leave their halves of the play field, any violation will attract a technical point awarded to the opponent team.
7. If any player is suspended or disqualified from the match, no substitution is allowed for that particular player. The team will play with less number of players.
8. The player to be substituted should stand in the designated area with the permission of the assistant scorer in advance.
9. If a raider while crossing the bonus line is caught, then a point will be awarded to the defending team and no points will be given to raider's team.
10. In case of a tie, a fresh toss will be taken and the team that wins the toss will have the chance to raid, this is called Golden Raid.
11. Yellow Card is shown for temporary suspension of 2 minutes alongwith the gaining of one technical point by the opposite team.
12. Red Card is shown for suspension from the match. If the red card is shown second time in a tournament to the same player, then that player will be debarred from the tournament for rest of the matches.

Referee Signals

Fundamental Skills and Techniques

Two fundamental skills are involved in the game of kabaddi

1. **Offensive Skills** The offensive skills are used by the raider in order to touch the opponents and come back safely to their own half after the raid. These skills are side kick, toe touch, running hand touch, front kick, frog jump, dubki/mule-kick, etc.

2. **Defensive Skills** The defensive skills are performed to grab the raider. Some of the important defensive skills are thigh catch, knee catch, ankle catch, crocodile catch, wrist catch, washer man hold, chain formative, 3-2-2 formation, front back formation, waist hold, etc.

Popular Tournaments

International

- Kabaddi Asia
- Kabaddi Masters
- Kabaddi World Cup

National

- Pro Kabaddi League
- Federation Cup
- Departmental National Kabaddi Championship
- National Kabaddi Championships
- Beach National Kabaddi Championship

Popular Kabaddi Awardees

Arjuna Awardees

- **1973** Mr. Bholanath Guin
- **1972** Mr. Sahanand Mahadev Shetty
- **1980** Mr. Shantaram Jadhav
- **1978** Ms. Shakuntala Pandarinath Khatavkar
- **1983** Ms. Maya Kashinath
- **1981** Ms. Monika Nath
- **1990** Mr. Hardeep Singh
- **1986** Ms. Rama Sarkar
- **1994** Mr. Ashok Shinde
- **1994** Mr. S. Rajarathnam
- **1996** Mr. Shriram Bhavsar
- **1995** Mr. P. Ganeshan
- **1997** Mr. Randhir Singh
- **1996** Ms. Neeta Moreshwer Dadwe
- **1998** Mr. Bishwajit Palit
- **1998** Mr. Ashan Kumar
- **1999** Mr. Tirath Raj
- **1999** Mr. Balwinder Singh (Piddha)
- **2001** Mr. B.C. Ramesh
- **2000** Mr. C. Honnappa Gowda
- **2003** Mr. Sanjeev Kumar
- **2002** Mr. Ram Mehar Singh
- **2005** Mr. Ramesh Kumar
- **2004** Mr. Sunder Singh
- **2008** Mr. Pankaj Navnath Shirsat
- **2006** Mr. Navneet Gautam
- **2011** Mr. Rakesh Kumar
- **2010** Mr. Dinesh Kumar
- **2012** Mr. Anoop Kumar
- **2011** Ms. Tejeswini Bai V
- **2015** Mr. Manjeet Chhillar
- **2014** Ms. Mamtha Poojari
- **2015** Mr. Abhilasha Shashikant Mahatre
- **2018** G. Pranav Sai Reddy
- **2017** Mr. Jasvir Singh
- **2020** Deepak Niwas Hooda
- **2019** Ajay Thakur
- **2022** Sakshi Kumari
- **2021** Sandeep Narwal
- **2023** MS. Ritu Negi
- **2023** Shri Pawan Sehrawat

Dhyan Chand Awardees

- **2007** Shamsher Singh
- **2020** Manpreet Singh
- **2021** Vikas Kumar
- **2022** B.C. Suresh
- **2023** MS. Kavitha Selvaraj

Dronacharya Awardees

- **2002** E. Prasad Rao
- **2005** Balwan Singh
- **2012** Sunil Dabas
- **2017** Heera Nand Kataria
- **2019** Rambir Singh Khokhar
- **2020** Krishan Kumar Hooda
- **2021** Ashan Kumar
- **2023** Bhaskaran E.

Viva-Voce

Q.1 From which Indian epic is Kabaddi believed to have originated?

Ans. Kabaddi is believed to have originated from in Indian epic Mahabharata.

Q.2 What was Kabaddi traditionally known as in Western India?

Ans. In western India, Kabaddi was traditionally known as Hutu Tu.

Q.3 In which year were standard Kabaddi rules first framed?

Ans. The first standard Kabaddi rules were framed in 1918.

Q.4 Where was the first All India Kabaddi Tournament held?

Ans. The first All India Kabaddi Tournament was held in Baroda.

Q.5 In which Olympics was Kabaddi demonstrated internationally for the first time?

Ans. Kabaddi was demonstrated for the first time internationally at the 1936 Berlin Olympics.

Q.6 When was the All India Kabaddi Federation formed?

Ans. The All India Kabaddi federation was formed in 1950.

Q.7 Which year marked Kabaddi's inclusion as an official medal event in the Asian Games?

Ans. Kabaddi became an official medal event at the Asian Games in 1990.

Q.8 What are the field dimensions for a men's Kabaddi match?

Ans. The field dimensions for a men's kabaddi match are13 m × 10 m.

Q.9 How wide is the lobby area in Kabaddi?

Ans. The lobby area in kabaddi is 1 m on each side.

Q.10 How many players take the field from each team during a Kabaddi match?

Ans. 7 players from each team take the field during a kabaddi match.

Q.11 What is the total number of players in a Kabaddi team including reserves?

Ans. The total number of players in a kabaddi team including reserves is 12.

Q.12 What is the duration of a men's Kabaddi match (excluding rest)?

Ans. The duration of a men's kabaddi match is 40 minutes (2 halves of 20 minutes)

Q.13 Who is the player that enters the opponent's court chanting "Kabaddi"?

Ans. The player who enters the opponent's court is called a raider.

Q.14 What is called when a raider returns without scoring but crosses the baulk line?

Ans. When a raider returns with out scoring but crosses the boulk line is called empty raid.

Q.15 What is the term for a raid where a point is scored?

Ans. A raid where a point is scored is called a productive raid.

Q.16 Name any two defensive Kabaddi skills.

Ans. Thigh catch, Chain formation.

Q.17 What happens when a player steps outside the boundary line during play?

Ans. When a players steps outside the boundary line they are considered out.

Q.18 What colour card causes a 2-minute suspension and 1 technical point to opponent?

Ans. Yellow card causes a 2-minute suspension and 1 technical point.

Q.19 Name one international kabaddi tournament.

Ans. Kabaddi world cup

Q.20 Who received Arjuna Award in 1994 for kabaddi?

Ans. Mr. Ashok Shinde received Arjuna Award in 1994 for kabaddi.

Game 13

Kho-Kho

History

Kho-Kho is probably derived from the different strategies and tactics of the Kurukshetra War in Mahabharat, the Indian epic. The chariot fights during the war and the *zig zag* pathways followed by the retreating soldiers indicate the formation of chain play, a defence skill in this game. The word kho-kho is derived from Marathi language that means 'go and chase'.

Modern game of kho-kho was formed by 'Shree Hanuman Vyayam Pracharak Mandal', Baroda in 1929.

A committee was formed at the Poona Gymkhana in 1914 for framing the kho-kho rules and the first book describing these rules was published from the Baroda Gymkhana in 1924. Kho-Kho Federation of India (KKFI) was formed in 1958. Indian Kho-Kho Association was Constitution in the year 1960 and National Kho-Kho Championship for Men and Women was organised in the years 1960 and 1961, respectively. Initially, one player starts the game and 3 players are kept reserve. One team becomes the chasers while other the defenders or runners.

The Asian Kho-Kho Federation was established in the year 1987 and First Asian Championship was held in 1996.

The member countries were India, Bangladesh, Pakistan, Sri Lanka, Nepal and Maldives.

Measurements and Specifications

(i) Total area of field (including lobby) = 32 m × 19 m.

(ii) Dimension of playing field (including lobby) = 27 m × 16 m.

(iii) Lobby = 1.5 m on all sides to playing field.

(iv) Free zone area = 2.75 m × 16 m (beyond pole line) on both sides.

(v) Pole specification = Two poles of 1.20 m to 1.25 m high, 9 to 10 cm thick and 23.5 m away.

(vi) Sitting block area squares = 30 cm × 30 cm cutting of Cross lane and Centre lane.

(vii) Cross lane 35 cm × 16 m

(viii) Distance between cross lane = 2.50 m near pole and 2.30 m in others.

(ix) Match duration = Total 55 minutes, 2 innings, where each inning has 2 turns of 9 minutes duration with an interval of 5 minutes in each turn and 9 minutes interval in half time 9-5-9 interval 9 m 9-5-9.

(x) Officials = 1 referee, 2 umpires, 1 scorer and 1 timekeeper.

(xi) Number of players = 12 (9 playing + 3 substitutes).

(xii) Tie rule = Time noted and compared for 1 player in additional inning.

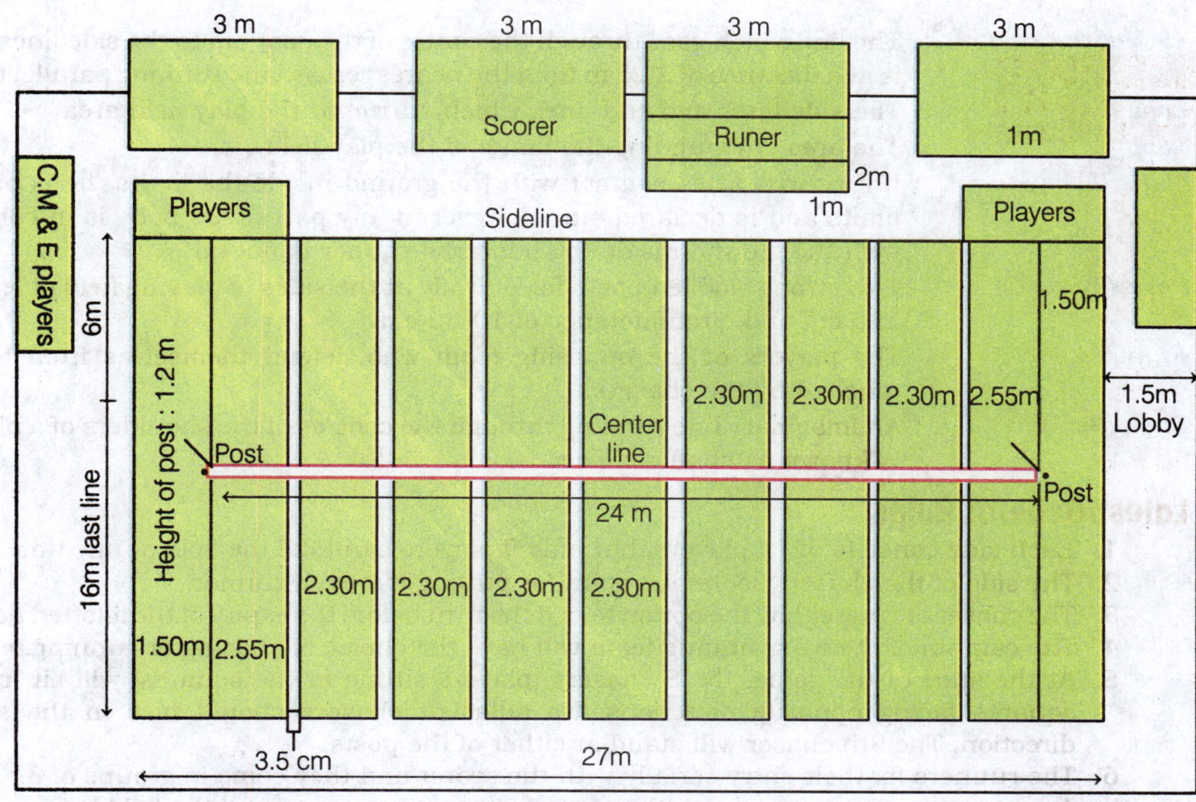

Kho-Kho Playing Field

Terminology

Active Chaser/ Attacker	An attacker is a player who pursues runners with a view to tag and touch them.
Centre Lane	Two parallel lines from one pole to other. It has its dimensions of 24 m by 30 cm. A chaser is not supposed to touch or cross the centre lane.
Chasers	Players of a team who sit in the squares to chase and touch the opponent with shoulder line parallel to the boundary line.
Contact In	If any part of a player's body, while going outside, touches the play field, he is declared contact in.
Contact Out	If while entering the play field, a player touches the ground outside the play area, he is declared contact out.
Cross Lanes	These are each of the lanes, 16 m × 30 cm, intersecting the central lane at right angles at regular intervals and themselves being divided into 2 halves. There are 8 cross lanes.
Defenders	The runners who actually come inside the limit, in a batch of three, are called defenders.
Entry	A runner is said to have entered the limits as soon as he loses the contact with the ground outside the limits with his feet and comes in contact with the ground inside the field with his feet.
Extra Period	Any period played after the end of a regular game in order to break a tie is called extra period.
Fake Kho	In such Kho, the chaser pretends to give Kho but actually he follows the runner.
Free Zone	Area by the side of the pole lines where runners and chasers can move in any direction.
Kho	The call 'Kho' is said to be given when an active chaser utters loudly and distinctly the word 'Kho', which means go or chase, simultaneously touching by hand a chaser from behind him. This is, therefore, a relay ensuring coverage of a certain minimum distance by an active chaser.

Line of the Post	The line which goes through the centre of the post, up to the side lines and is at a distance of 2.25 m from the nearest cross lane running parallel to it.
Limits	The side lines and end lines which surround the play field area.
Lobby	The area surrounding the limits of the play field.
Out of Limits	If a runner loses contact with the ground inside the limits, he is out of limits and is declared out. However, if any part of his body is in contact with the ground inside the limit, the runner is not out.
Posts/Poles	Two strong wooden posts fixed firmly at the sides of playing field of length 120 cm and circumference of 10-30 cm.
Runners	The players of the opposing team who defend themselves from being touched by the chasers.
Shoulder Line	An imaginary line running through the centres of the shoulders of a player is known as shoulder line.

Latest/General Rules

1. Each side consists of 12 players, but only 9 players can take the field at one time.
2. The side of the chasers score one point for putting out each runner.
3. The chaser or runner has the option to end the turn before the expiry of the allotted time.
4. The captain of the toss winning team will have the choice of chasing or running.
5. At the start of the game, the 8 chasers (players sitting in the squares) will sit in the squares facing opposite directions. No adjacent chasers should face in the same direction. The 9th chaser will stand at either of the posts.
6. The runners fix their entry serially with the scorer and they come in groups of 3.
7. As soon as a runner is put out, the next three runners must enter the field before a call 'Kho' is given.
8. A runner goes out/is put out by the following means:
   (i) If touched by a chaser.
   (ii) Crossing the boundary completely.
   (iii) Touching the seated chasers twice or after receiving a warning for a similar infringement.
9. Active chasers have to chase in one direction only, changing of the direction is not allowed.
10. Seated chasers become active only when they get a call for 'Kho'.
11. Changing the face of the square or leaving it without getting a 'Kho' from the chaser is considered a foul.
12. The game starts with one long and short blast of a whistle and ends with one long blast. Only one short blast signals the dismissal of a defender. A foul is indicated by continuous short blasts of the whistle. The penalty for a foul is to stop the chase and to take the direction indicated by the umpire. Various fouls are indicated by different signs.
13. In case of a tie, additional innings are held and the time taken to put out the first runner in a knock out contest is recorded.

Officials Duties

Duties of Referee/Umpire He is responsible for fair play in the match. He is the final authority on the rules and regulations from the start to the end of the match. Referee performs toss before the start of the match. He has the final say on every decision of the match.

Duties of Scorer He takes notes of all the proceedings of the match in a chronological order, alongwith the points gained, time and substitutions made. He makes a record of all the fouls made by each player of each team. He records personal and technical fouls separately. He maintains a score sheet with all the details of each player.

Duties of Timekeeper He notifies and assists the referee regarding the time issues of the game. He is responsible for notifying referee about the time at which each part of the match has to begin. This needs to be done atleast three minutes before the actual start of the game. He shall start timeout watch for charged timeout. The timekeeper also keeps record of the various times and situations when the match was paused and resumed.

Fundamental Skills and Techniques

- *Sitting Skills* *There are two methods and types of sitting in the square:*
  (i) Bunch or Bullet Method (ii) Parallel Thigh Method
- *Diving* It is gaining spontaneous speed and energy to touch an active runner by the chaser.
- *Tapping* This requires speed, balance, braking-power and perfect timing.
- *Single Chain* It is an important skill of defence.
- *Double Chain* It involves continuous running, but is a popular defence strategy.

Sitting

Dividing

Giving Kho

Tapping

Popular Tournaments

International Asian Kho-Kho Championship, South Asian Games

National National Kho-Kho Championship (both Men and Women), Federation Cup, All India Inter University Championship, Nehru Gold Cup, National Games, School Championship

Note Junior and sub-junior championships are not listed.

Popular Kho-Kho Awardees

Arjuna Award Winners

- 1970 Sudhir B Prabhakar
- 1971 Achala S Devre
- 1973 Bhavna H Parekh
- 1974 Nilima C Sarolkar
- 1975 Srirang J Inamdar, Usha V Nagarkar
- 1976 Shekhar R Dharwadkar
- 1981 Hemant M Takalkar
- 1983 Veena N Parab
- 1984 S Prakash
- 1985 Surekha B Kulkarni
- 1998 Shobha Narayan
- 2020 Kale Sarika Sudhakar
- 2023 MS. Nasreen

Dronacharya Award Winner for Coaches

- 2000 Phadke Gopal Purushottam

Viva-Voce

Q.1 From which Indian epic is the origin of Kho-Kho traced?
Ans. The origin of Kho-Kho is traced to the Mahabharata, where chariot movements resembled chain play.

Q.2 What is the meaning of the term 'Kho-Kho' and its language of origin?
Ans. 'Kho-Kho' means 'go and chase' and comes from the Marathi language.

Q.3 Who developed the modern version of Kho-Kho and in which year?
Ans. The Shree Hanuman Vyayam Pracharak Mandal, Baroda developed the modern version in 1929.

Q.4 When and by whom was the first Kho-Kho rule book published?
Ans. The first rule book was published in 1924 by the Baroda Gymkhana.

Q.5 In which year was the Kho-Kho Federation of India (KKFI) formed?
Ans. The Kho-Kho Federation of India was formed in 1958.

Q.6 When did the National Championships for men and women begin in Kho-Kho?
Ans. Men's started in 1960, and women's began in 1961.

Q.7 Name any three member countries of the Asian Kho-Kho Federation.
Ans. India, Bangladesh, and Sri Lanka are members of the Asian Kho-Kho Federation.

Q.8 What is the total field area including the lobby in Kho-Kho?
Ans. The total field area is 32 m × 19 m, including the lobby.

Q.9 How many players are there in a Kho-Kho team, and how many play at a time?
Ans. A Kho-Kho team has 12 players, with 9 playing at a time.

Q.10 What is the total match time and structure of Kho-Kho?
Ans. The match is 55 minutes long, with 2 innings having 2 turns of 9 minutes each.

Q.11 State any two conditions in which a runner is declared out.
Ans. A runner is out if touched by a chaser or completely crosses the boundary.

Q.12 What does the skill 'Giving Kho' involve?
Ans. It involves the active chaser tapping a seated chaser and saying "Kho" to pass the turn.

Q.13 Name the chasing technique where the chaser dives to touch the runner.
Ans. The technique is called Diving.

Q.14 What is the size of the sitting block area for chasers?
Ans. The sitting block area is 30 cm × 30 cm.

Q.15 What whistle signal indicates a runner's dismissal?
Ans. One short blast indicates a runner is out.

Q.16 How is a tie-breaker decided in knock-out rounds?
Ans. By recording the time taken to dismiss the first runner in an extra inning.

Q.17 What skill requires speed and perfect timing to touch a runner?
Ans. The skill is called Tapping.

Q.18 What is the distance between the two poles in a Kho-Kho field?
Ans. The distance between two poles is 23.5 meters.

Q.19 Name one international Kho-Kho tournament.
Ans. Asian Kho-Kho Championship.

Q.20 Who was the recipient of the Dronacharya Award in 2000 for Kho-Kho?
Ans. Phadke Gopal Purushottam received the award in 2000.

Game 14

Judo

History

'Judo' is a Japanese word which 'Ju' means gentle and 'do' means way, the word Judo means 'the gentle way'. Judo originated in Japan and its founder was *Jigoro Kano*. It originated as a derivative of the various martial arts developed and used by the Samurai and Feudal warrior class over hundreds of years in Japan. Although, many of the techniques of judo are derived from arts that were designed to hurt, maim or kill opponents in actual field, its objectives were mainly related to self-defence.

Students can practice Judo and apply the modified techniques safely and without hurting opponents. Judoka never resists his opponent rather turns his back on his attacker. Therefore, judo is a defensive art.

The regulatory body for Judo in India is the Judo Federation of India (JFI). It was formed in 1965. The JFI is affiliated with the International Judo Federation (IJF) and follows its guidelines and rules. The International Judo Federation (IJF) was founded earlier, in July 1951.

Judo Court

A well labelled diagram of judo court is given below

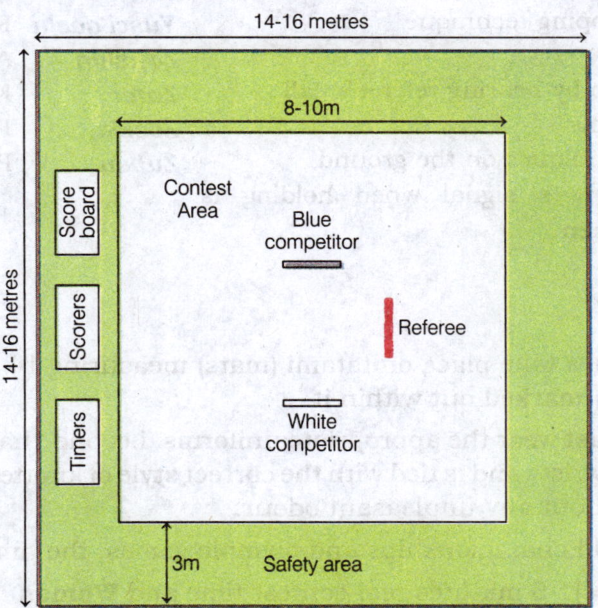

- Length of judo court (platform) = 14 - 16 m
- Width of judo court (platform) = 14 - 16 m
- No. of pieces of mat used to prepare the court = 50
- Size of each piece of mat = 3′ × 6′
- Area of danger zone = 8 × 8 m – 10 × 10 m

- Width of outer part of danger zone = 3 m
- No. of officials = 5 (1 Referee, 2 Judges, 1 Scorer, 1 Recorder)
- Shape of Arena = Square
- Distance between opponents standing point = 12 ft
- Bout Duration = 5 minutes for Men and 4 minutes for Women
- Penalty Points = minor (shido) or major (hansoku make)

Terminology

Ashi	Legs
Atemi	Striking
Budo	Martial arts
Dan	Black belt rank
Dojo	The hall where judo practice or competition takes place
Hajime	To start
Hiji	Elbow
Hidavi	Left
Hiki-wake	No decision
Hiza	Knee
Ippon	Winning 10 points
Jikan	Referee's call to stop clock
Kata	Forms
Koka	3 points
Kubi	Neck
Kumikata	Gripping technique
Koshi	Hip
Matte	Stop by hearing referee's call
Nage	Throw
Ne-waza	Techniques on the ground
Osakomi	Referee's signal when holding is broken
Randori	Free practice
Sansei	Judo teacher
Shiajo	Competition area
Shime waza	Choking technique
Shisei	Posture
Sona-mona	Referee's signal for remain as you are
Tatami	Mat for judo playing
Uchikomi	Repeated practice without completion
Ude	Arm
Waza	Technique
Waza-Ari	A controlled throw to the opponent which gives 7 points lead
Yame	Win
Yuko	5 points
Yusci-gachi	Restarting a passed game
Zanshin	Awareness
Zarei	Kneeling salutation
Zoseki	Father of Judo, Jigoro Kano
Zubon	Pants

General Rules

(i) Judo matches take place on tatami (mats) measuring 14 m × 14 m, with a combat area of 10 m × 10 m marked out within it.

(ii) Judokas must wear the appropriate uniforms, i.e. one that is no more than 5 cm above the ankles and wrists and is tied with the correct style of knotted belt. The Judogi must be clean, dry and without any unpleasant odour.

(iii) For the world championships and olympic games, the time duration of contest is

Men (seniors) : 5 minutes real contest time and **Women** : 4 minutes real contest time.

(iv) Any contestant is entitled to rest between contests for a period of 10 minutes.

(v) Bouts are won when one Judoka is awarded (ten points). If no (ten points) is awarded, the player with the highest score at the end of the bout is declared the winner.

(vi) Penalties are awarded for minor (Shido) or major (Hansoku make) infringements of the rules. Four Shidos result in the award of ippon to the opponent, as does one Hansoku make.

(vii) If players go outside the contest area and the referee says "sono-mona" (remain as you are), they are put back in their original positions. Restart is announced with "Yusci-guchi," and the time between these calls is not counted.

(viii) A successful throw or ground technique earns an ippon (10 points), ending the match. The referee indicates the winner by raising their hand.

(ix) The referee announces "waza-an" for a likely point. If the same player gets another waza-an, it becomes "usuza-ari awasete ippon" (10 points from two techniques), declaring that player the winner.

(x) If a holding technique (osakomi) is broken, the referee announces "osaekomi-loaketa" to indicate the end of the hold.

(xi) A judge can suggest changes to the referee's decision, but the referees final decision stands.

(xii) If a match ends in a draw and time expires, the referee says "sove made", meaning to stop the match.

(xiii) If a player refuses to compete, the opponent wins by default ('fusen-sho'). Persistent rule violations or forbidden actions after a warning result in "honsa-kumake" (disqualification). For injuries

- If caused by the opponent's errors, the injured player wins.
- If caused by the player's own mistakes, the opponent wins.

(xvi) The referee arranges and oversees the bout, and their decisions are final with no appeals.

Fundamental Skills and Techniques

(i) *Ready Position* The player tries to grab his opponent quickly and throws him off balance.

(ii) *Gripping* The player who successfully grabs his opponent (Kumi Kata) has the advantage.

(iii) *Positioning* The seized player tries to escape from his opponent, while his attacker prepares the next throw.

(iv) *Throwing* After throwing his opponent off the balance, the player destroys his power of self-defence.

(v) *Pinning* The attacker tries to increase the pressure on his opponent's body, especially on the shoulders.

(vi) *Choking* Using his hand and opponent's jacket, the attacker tries to cut off the breathing of the opponent by compressing his trachea.

(vii) *Arm Lock* The attacker holds his opponents arm and pulls it as straight as possible.

Popular Tournaments

- Olympic Games
- IJF World Judo Tour
- Pan American Judo Championships
- World Judo Championships
- European Judo Championships
- Asian Judo Championships

Popular Judo Awardees

Arjuna Awardees

- Cawas Billimoria (1993)
- Narender Singh (1998)
- Ms. Angom Anita Chanu (2004)
- Yashpal Solanki (2012)
- Kapil Parmar (Para Judo) (2024)
- Sandeep Byala (1992)
- Ms. Poonam Chopra (1996)
- Akram Shah (2003)
- Ms. Khumujam Tombi Devi (2007)
- Shushila Devi Likmabam (2022)

Dronacharya Awardees

- Shri Gurucharan Gogi (2014)
- Shri Jiwan Kumar Sharma (2018)

Viva-Voce

Q.1 What is the meaning of the word "Judo"?

Ans. The word "Judo" means "the gentle way".

Q.2 Who is the founder of Judo?

Ans. The founder of Judo is Jigoro Kano.

Q.3 What is a Judo practitioner called?

Ans. A Judo practitioner is called Judoka.

Q.4 In which year was the International Judo Federation (IJF) established?

Ans. IJF was established in 1951.

Q.5 When was the Judo Federation of India (JFI) founded?

Ans. JFI was founded in 1965.

Q.6 What is the total platform area of a Judo mat?

Ans. The total platform area of Judo mat is 14–16 m × 14–16 m

Q.7 What is the combat area size in Judo?

Ans. The combat area in Judo is 8–10 m × 8–10 m.

Q.8 What is the width of the danger zone?

Ans. The danger zone in Judo has a width of 3 meters.

Q.9 What is the shape of a Judo arena?

Ans. A Judo arena is square in shape.

Q.10 How many mat pieces are used in a Judo court?

Ans. 50 mat pieces are used in a Judo court.

Q.11 What is the duration of a senior men's Judo match?

Ans. A senior men's Judo match lasts for 5 minutes.

Q.12 What is the rest period between bouts?

Ans. The rest period between bouts is 10 minutes.

Q.13 How many referees are there in a Judo match?

Ans. There are 1 main referee in a Judo match.

Q.14 What score is awarded for a perfect throw (Ippon)?

Ans. 10 points are awarded for a perfect throw (Ippon).

Q.15 What does "Waza-ari" represent?

Ans. "Waza-ari" represents 7 points.

Q.16 Which penalty leads to immediate disqualification?

Ans. The penalty that leads to immediate disqualification is Hansoku-make.

Q.17 What is the term for minor penalty in Judo?

Ans. The term for a minor penalty in Judo is Shido.

Q.18 What is the command used by the referee to start the bout?

Ans. The referee's command to start the bout is Hajime.

Q.19 What does "Tatami" refer to?

Ans. "Tatami" refers to a Judo mat.

Q.20 What is the hall for Judo training called?

Ans. The hall for Judo training is called Dojo.

Q.21 What is "Randori"?

Ans. "Randori" refers to free practice in Judo.

Q.22 What is the Judo term for a choking technique?

Ans. The Judo term for a choking technique is Shime-waza.

Q.23 What are ground techniques called in Judo?

Ans. Ground techniques in Judo are called Ne-waza.

Q.24 What are throwing techniques in Judo called?

Ans. Throwing techniques in Judo is called Nage-waza.

Q.25 What does "Zubon" mean in Judo?

Ans. "Zuban" means pants in Judo Pants.

Q.26 Name any international level Judo tournament.

Ans. World Judo Championships.

Q.27 Who received the Arjuna Award in 2022 for Judo?

Ans. Shushila Devi Likmabam received the Arjuna Award in 2022 for Judo.

Q.28 Name the 1992 Arjuna Awardee in Judo.

Ans. Sandeep Byala

Q.29 Who received the Dronacharya Award in 2014 for Judo?

Ans. Gurucharan Gogi received the Dronacharya Award in 2014 for Judo.

Q.30 What is the referee's final call to end the match?

Ans. The referee's final call to end the match is Sore-made.

Game 15

Taekwondo

History

The earliest records of Taekwondo practice date back to about 50 BC. Taek Kyon (also called *Subak*) is considered the earliest known form of Taekwondo. Silla was a small kingdom of Korea which was always attacked by the Japanese pirates. During this time, a few selected Sillan warriors were given training in Taek Kyon by the early masters from Koguryo dynasty. The Taek kyon-trained warriors became known as the Hwarang.

The first taekwondo school started in Korea in 1945 in Yong Chun, Seoul.

Modern development of this game started in 1952 at a public function in Korea. There are eleven commandments in modern day Taekwondo. In 1961, the constitution of Korean Taekwondo Association (KTA) made Taekwondo popular all over the world. The World Championship of Taekwondo started in 1973.

In India, Taekwondo is regulated by Taekwondo Federation of India (TFI), found in 1979.

Taekwondo officially included in Olympic games in Sydney (2000).

Measurements and Specifications

Competion Area

- *Size* 12m x 12m with a 1m border.
- *Mat Thickness* 2-4 cm.
- *Zones* 8m x 8m active area

Timing

- *Rounds* Three rounds of 2 minutes each.
- *Sudden Death* Additional round if tied.

Uniform (Dobok)

- *Material* Cotton or cotton-polyester.
- *Jacket Length* To hips.
- *Sleeve Length* Covers wrists.
- *Pant Length* To ankles.
- *Belt* Wraps twice, hangs 20-30 cm on each side.

Protective Gear

- *Headgear* Full head coverage.
- *Chest Protector (Hogu)* Covers torso.
- *Arm and Shin Guards* Cover from wrist to elbow and knee to ankle.
- *Mouth Guard* Protects teeth.
- *Groin Protector* For males, covers groin.

Scoring System

- *Body Kick* 2 points.
- *Head Kick* 3 points.
- *Punch to Body* 1 point.
- *Spinning Kick to Body* 4 points.
- *Spinning Kick to Head* 5 points.

Ranking and Belts

- *Kup Ranks (Colour Belts)* 10th Kup (white) to 1st Kup (red with black stripe).
- *Dan Ranks (Black Belts)* 1st Dan to 9th Dan.

Terminology

Dobuk	Players' dress comprises of loose jacket and short pants comfortable for fight. Red belt and guards over dobuk are known as 'Chong'. Blue belt and guard over dobuk is known as *Hong*.
Diagi	Kicking to opponent which earns a point to player.
Joagi	Punching to opponent which earns a point to player.
Jumby	Ready position of players for fight at their positional marks over playing area.
Kaiso	Restart of fight after short break or interval.
Kalyeo	Means 'break'. The referee will call 'kalyeo' to keep an attacker from a downed opponent.
Keuman	Means 'stop'. The referee calls this to end each round.
Keysok	Means 'continue'. The referee calls 'keysok' when a downed contestant is ready to resume.
Shijak	Means 'start' or 'fight' indicated by the referee at the beginning of contest.

General Rules

1. Weighing-in of the contestants shall be done on the day of the competition, 1 hr prior to the beginning of the competition; weighing-in shall be done in the nude conditions only. Weighing-in for females shall be done by female officials only.
2. The player is awarded a point for the right punch or a valid kick on the torso of the opponent. Two points are awarded for a spining kick. The player is awarded four points for a legal turning kick on the head.
3. When a player scores four points in the negative, the referee can declare him as a looser depending on the penalties.
4. A player is declared as the winner of match, only if two or more than two corner referees give decision in favour of that player.

Procedure of the Contest

1. Contestants' names are announced three times, starting three minutes before the contest. Failure to appear within one minute of the scheduled start results in withdrawal.
2. Contestants must pass a physical and costume inspection, ensuring no harmful items or signs of aversion.
3. Contestants enter the competition area with one coach.
4. The contest starts with the re-referee's "shijak" (start) and ends with "keuman" (stop).

Fundamental Skills

For playing Taekwondo in fields, some skills are very important, which are as follows

1. Player must stand in ready position. He stands in slightly crouch position in the contest area and is ready for the fight. Very quickly the fighter changes his leg position and his hands are slightly flexed.
2. The player uses various **kick techniques**, like front kick, double front kick, round house kick, side kick, back kick and reverse round house kick.

3. The player uses different types of **punching techniques.** These include straight punch, side punch, hook punch, curve punch, etc.

Hook Punch

Side Punch

4. The player also uses various methods of **blocking** and **defensive techniques** for winning the game. These are face block, leg block, kick block, left block, right block, etc.

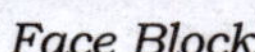
Face Block

Kick Block

Left Block

International Taekwondo Federation

International Taekwondo Federation (ITF) is an international Taekwondo organisation founded on 22nd March, 1966 by Choi Hong Hi in Seoul, South Korea. The ITF promotes and encourages the growth of the Korean martial art of Taekwondo.

Taekwondo Federation of India

The Taekwondo Academy of India (TAI) is assigned to look after the technical matter, such as promotion of Taekwondo philosophy, development of techniques, colour belt registration, black belt certificate from Korea, etc.

Other Taekwondo Associations

1. All European Taekwondo Federation
2. American Taekwondo Association
3. Belgian Taekwondo Association
4. Global Taekwondo Federation
5. United States Taekwondo Union
6. World Traditional Taekwondo Union
7. World Taekwondo Federation
8. World Taekwondo Alliance

Popular Taekwondo Players

1. Surender Bhandari (India)
2. Luo Wei (China)
3. Chen Zhong (China)
4. Chen Shih-Hsin (Chinese Taipei)
5. Dae Sang Moon (South Korea)
6. Jang Ji-Won (South Korea)
7. Steven Lopez (USA)
8. Hadi Saei (Iran)
9. Nakul Malhotra
10. Latika Bhandari
11. Rudali Barua
12. Maria Espinoza

Popular Tournaments

- Asian Games
- SAF Games
- National Games
- World Taekwondo Championship
- Olympic Games

Viva-Voce

Q.1 From which ancient martial art did Taekwondo originate?

Ans. Taekwondo originated from the ancient korean material art Taek Kyon (also known as Subak).

Q.2 Which warrior can practiced early forms of Taekwondo in Korea?

Ans. Hwarang warriors, an elite youth group in ancient korea practiced early forms of Taekwondo.

Q.3 In which year was the first Taekwondo school opened in Seoul?

Ans. The first Taekwondo school in Seoul was opened in 1945.

Q.4 When was the Korean Taekwondo Association (KTA) established?

Ans. The korean Taekwondo Association (KTA) established in 1961.

Q.5 Since which year has the Taekwondo Federation of India (TFI) governed the sport in India?

Ans. The Taekwondo Federation of India has governed the sports in India since 1979.

Q.6 In which Olympic Games did Taekwondo become an official sport?

Ans. Taekwondo became an official Olympic sport in 2000 Sydney Olympics.

Q.7 What is the total size of the Taekwondo competition area?

Ans. The total size of the Taekwondo competition area is 12 m × 12 m.

Q.8 What is the thickness of Taekwondo mats used in competition?

Ans. The thickness of Taekwondo mats used in competition is 2–4 cm.

Q.9 How many rounds are there in a standard Taekwondo match?

Ans. A standard Taekwondo match consists of 3 rounds.

Q.10 What is the duration of each round in Taekwondo?

Ans. The duration of each round in Taekwondo is 2 minutes.

Q.11 What is the name of the uniform worn by Taekwondo players?

Ans. The uniform worn by Taekwondo players is called a Dobok.

Q.12 What is the protective chest gear in Taekwondo called?

Ans. The protective chest gear in Taekwondo called a Hogu.

Q.13 How many points are awarded for a spinning kick to the head?

Ans. A spinning kick to the head is awarded 5 points.

Q.14 What is the range of Kup ranks in Taekwondo?

Ans. The range of kup ranks goes from 10th Kup (white) to 1st Kup (red with black stripe).

Q.15 What does the command "Shijak" signify in a Taekwondo match?

Ans. The command "Shijak" signifies the start of the match.

Q.16 What does the command "Keuman" mean in Taekwondo?

Ans. The command "Keuman" means to stop the match.

Q.17 What may happen if a player receives 4 penalty points?

Ans. If a player receives 4 panalty points it may lead to disqualification.

Q.18 What is the basic stance of a Taekwondo fighter like?

Ans. The basic stance of a Taekwondo fighter involves a slight crouch, quick leg change, hands flexed.

Q.19 Name two renowned Indian Taekwondo players.

Ans. Surender Bhandari and Rudali Barua.

Q.20 Name one major international Taekwondo tournament.

Ans. World Taekwondo Championship.

Game 1

Boccia

History

Boccia traces its roots to ancient Greece and Egypt, where it was originally played using large stones. It is one of the oldest known games in human history. Initially developed for individuals with Cerebral Palsy, the game has now evolved to include players with various disabilities, gaining popularity in more than 50 countries.

Modern Development and Recognition

Boccia was introduced in the Paralympic Games in 1984 and has since then become one of the fastest-growing disability games. It is governed by the Boccia International Sports Federation (BISFed). At the recreational level, it welcomes participants with physical, sensory, and learning disabilities, promoting inclusivity and participation worldwide.

Measurements and Specifications of Boccia

- Boccia is mainly played indoors on smooth and flat surfaces.
- Court size: 12.5 m (length) × 6 m (width).
- Court is divided into 6 throwing boxes, each 2.5 m × 1 m.
- A V-shaped line (25 cm) is drawn at the front of each throwing box.

- A centre line divides the court into two halves.
- A target box (1 m × 1 m) is placed at the far end.
- The Jack Line, 1.5 m from the back, marks the minimum throw distance for the jack ball.
- Court boundaries are defined by sidelines along the length.

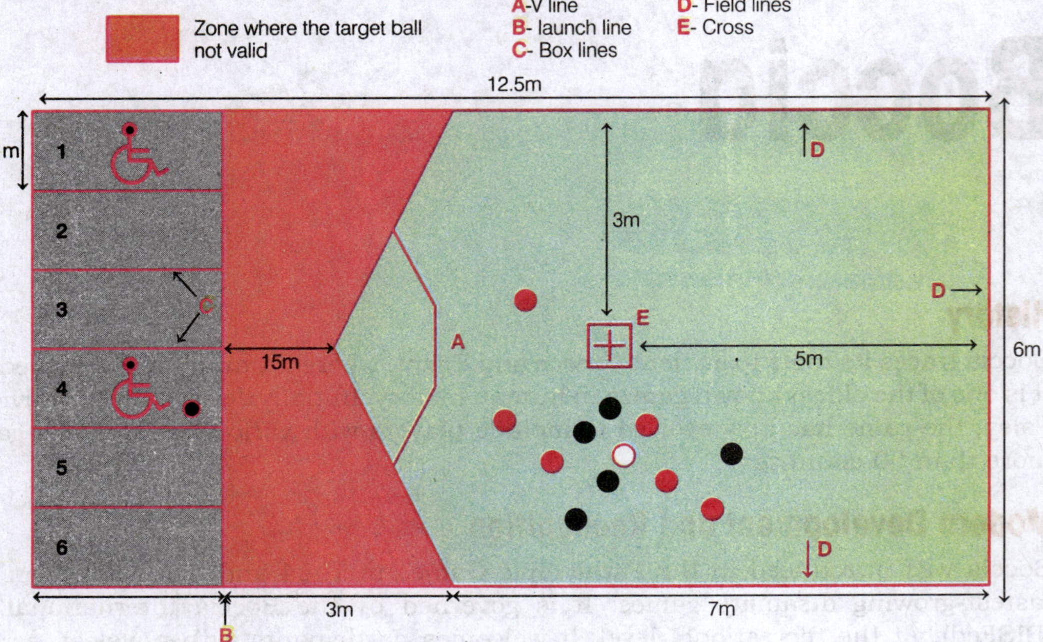

Balls and Equipment

- Each ball weighs 275–290 grams with a 270 mm circumference.
- Balls are made of leather or synthetic material for grip.
- Each team has 6 red or 6 blue balls, plus 1 white jack ball (same size and weight).
- Other equipment includes measuring devices used to determine the closest ball to the jack.

Assistive Devices

- Players with physical impairments may use ramps, head pointers, or other customized assistive devices.
- Devices must comply with BISFed regulations.

Key Terminology in Boccia

Jack	It is the white ball which is considered as a target ball in which players aim to get their balls closest to it.
Ball	Each team uses six coloured balls (red or blue).
Throw	Act of delivering a ball towards the jack.
Assistive Device	Tools like ramps or head pointers used by players to throw the balls.
Scoring	Determining the points based on proximity of balls to the jack. Only one team or player scores per end.
End	A segment of game where players or team throwes all their balls. The number of ends in a match can vary.
Classification	The system used to categories players based on their physical abilities to ensure fair competitions (BC1 – BC4)
Valid Line	Line 1.5 m from the back; jack must cross it to be valid.

Throwing Box	The marked area on the court from where players throw their balls.
Centre Line	It is the line in the middle of court and it divides the court into two equal halves.

Basic Rules of Boccia

- **Objective** Place your coloured balls (red or blue) closer to the white jack than your opponent.
- **Scoring** The side with the closest ball to the jack scores 1 point for each ball closer than the opponent's nearest ball

Game Partials

- Each game consists of several partials (rounds). The number of partials depends on competition format :
- Individual and Pairs : 4 rounds (partials)
- Team Competitions : 6 partials.
- Total score decides the winner. Tie-breakers are played if needed.

Competition Formats

- Individual: (one on one) – Each player uses 6 balls.
- Pairs: (two on two) – Each player uses 3 balls.
- Teams: (three on three) – Team consist of BC1 and BC2 player and each player uses 2 balls.

Starting the Game

- Coin toss decides colour and court side.
- Red team starts the game of ball by throwing the jack followed by their first ball.

Gameplay Flow

- After first throw, opponent throws ball.
- The team farther from the jack keeps playing until all their balls are thrown.
- Then, the other team throws their remaining balls.

End of Partial

- A partial ends after all 12 balls are thrown. The team with ball closest to the jack determines the scoring side.

Winning

- The side with the highest total score after all partials is declared the winner.
- In case of ties, additional tie-breakers are played.

Key Skill and Techniques

Skill/Technique	Description
Accuracy	Precisely placing the ball close to the jack.
Strategy	Planned throws to either score or block the opponent.
Ball Control	Managing force and direction for precise placement.
Chipping	Using a ball to move opponents' balls or reposition your own.

Blocking	Placing balls strategically to obstruct opponent's balls.
Trajectory Management	Controlling ball's path using different angles and forces.
Assistive Devices	Skillfully using ramps, head pointers, or other aids for throwing.
Timing	Knowing when to play defensively or offensively.
Endurance & Focus	Maintaining concentration and energy throughout the match.
Adaptability	Adjusting strategies as per match situation and opponents.

Viva-Voce

Q.1 Where did Boccia originate?

Ans Boccia originated in Ancient Greace Egypt.

Q.2 In which year was Boccia first included in the Paralympic Games?

Ans In 1984, Boccia was first included in the paralympic game.

Q.3 Which body governs international Boccia competitions?

Ans Boccia International Sports Federation (BISFed) governs international Boccia competition.

Q.4 What are the standard dimensions of a Boccia court?

Ans The standared dimensions of a Boccia court are 12.5 m long × 6 m wide.

Q.5 How many throwing boxes does a Boccia court have and what is their size?

Ans There are six throwing boxes in Boccia court and size of each box is 2.5 m × 1 m.

Q.6 What is the purpose of the Jack Line on the Boccia court?

Ans Jack line marks 1.5 m from the back as the minimum valid distance for the jack.

Q.7 What is the weight and circumference specification of a Boccia ball?

Ans The weight of Boccia ball is 270–290 gm and its circumference is 270 mm.

Q.8 How many balls does each team use in a standard Boccia match?

Ans Six coloured balls (red or blue) plus one white jack.

Q.9 Name two assistive devices permitted in Boccia.

Ans Ramps and head pointers are two assistive devies permintted in Boccia.

Q.10 What does the term "end" refer to in Boccia?

Ans The term end refer to a round in which each player or team throws all their balls.

Q.11 What classification categories are used to ensure fair play?

Ans BC1, BC2, BC3, and BC4 are the categories used to ensure fair play.

Q.12 How are points scored in Boccia?

Ans One point for each ball closer to the jack than the opponent's nearest ball.

Q.13 How many partials (rounds) are played in an individual Boccia match?

Ans Four partials are played in an individual Boccia match.

Q.14 What is the first action after the coin toss decides red and blue teams?

Ans The red team throws the jack, then its first ball.

Q.15 Name two key skills required in Boccia.

Ans Accuracy and strategy are the two key skills required in Boccia.

Game 2

Sitting Volleyball

History

Sitting Volleyball was born in Germany where a seated game called Sitzball was already popular but lacked the energy and excitement of traditional sports. In 1956, the Dutch Sports Committee decided to combine the structure of Sitzball with the dynamic elements of volleyball, creating a new and more engaging sport–sitting volleyball. The game features six players per side, a smaller court and a lowered net, making it not only more fast-paced and exciting but also more inclusive and accessible to athletes with physical disabilities.

Adaptation for Disabled Athletes

William G. Morgan adapted the game for athletes with disabilities, designing a simplified version and a classification system based on the degree of physical impairment. The sport was first included as a demonstration event at the 1976 Paralympic Games in Toronto and became an official medal event in the 1980 Arnhem Paralympics, promoting inclusive competition.

Terminology

Term	Definition
Ace	A serve that lands in the opponent's court without being touched.
Attack	An attempt by a player to win a point by hitting the ball over the net.
Attack Line	A line three metres from the net, limiting back-row player attacks.
Back-row Player	Any of the three players positioned at the back of the court.
Block	Attempt to stop a spike by jumping at the net with arms raised.
Centre Line	It is an imaginary line under the net dividing the court into two halves.
Chuck	It is a slang for pushing or throwing the ball instead of hitting it.

Court	The official playing area for the match.
Crossing Space	The area above the net between the antennae through which the ball must pass.
Dig	A defensive move using both arms to bounce a hard-hit ball upward.
End Line	The back boundary line of the court.
Facial	Slang for a spike that hits an opponent in the face.
Fault	Any foul or error resulting in the loss of the rally.
Front-row Player	One of three players positioned closest to the net.
Front Zone	Area between the net and the attack line.
Heater	Slang for a hard-hit or spiked ball.
Setter	Player who specializes in setting the ball for teammates to attack.
Sideline	The side boundary lines of the court.

Playing Court (Measurements and Specifications)

The court is 10 meters long and 6 meters wide. It is surrounded by a free zone that must be at least 3 meters wide on all sides, and the playing area must have a minimum height clearance of 7 meters.

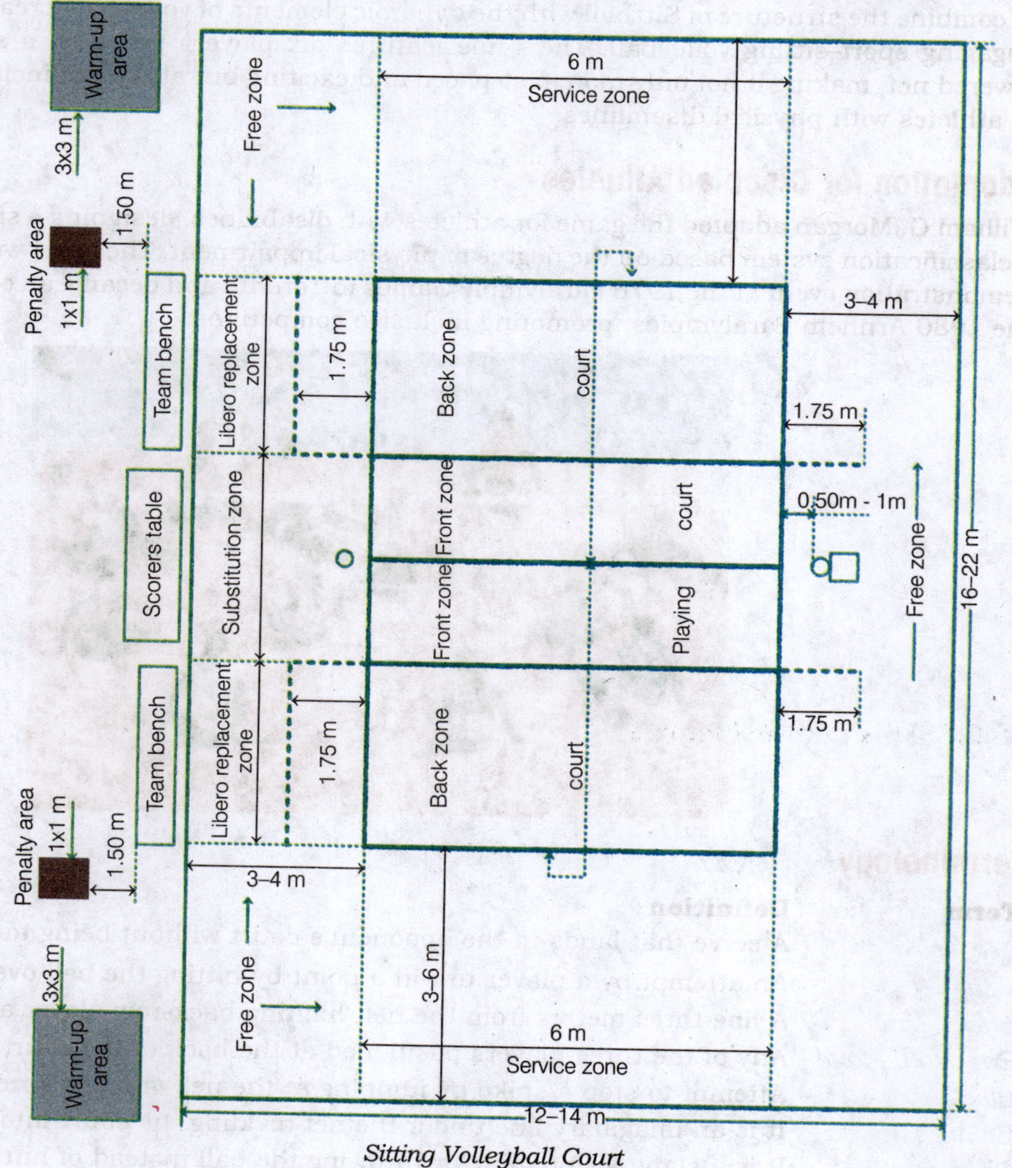

Sitting Volleyball Court

Team Composition

Each team has 6 players on the court, including a libero (a defensive specialist). A team can have up to 14 players in total, including substitutes.

Structural Elements of Sitting Volleyball

Element.	Description
Scoring System	Sitting Volleyball matches are played in a best-of-five sets format. A team wins a set by scoring 25 points (15 points in the deciding fifth set), but to secure victory the team must always maintain at least a two-point lead if the score reaches 24–24.
Antennae	The antennae are flexible rods attached to the net that mark the legal crossing boundary for the ball. They are made of fiberglass, measure 1.60 meters in length, and have a diameter of 10 millimeters.
Side Bands	Side bands are white vertical strips placed on each side of the net to define the crossing space for the ball. Each band is 5 centimeters wide and 0.80 meters long, making it easier for referees and players to judge whether the ball has passed legally.
Posts	The posts are used to hold and support the net in place. They are positioned 0.5 to 1 meter outside the sidelines and can be adjusted to a height of up to 1.25 meters, ensuring proper tension and stability of the net during the match.
Ball Specifications	The official Sitting Volleyball ball is round and made of flexible leather. It weighs between 260 and 280 grams, and its circumference ranges from 65 to 67 centimeters, providing a balance between control and speed for players.

General Rules of Sitting Volleyball

Rule	Explanation
Contact Rule	At least one buttock must stay in contact with the floor during play
Blocking the Serve	Allowed in sitting volleyball
Set Format	Best of 5 sets; first to 25 points (win by 2 points)
Touches per Side	Maximum 3 touches before sending the ball over the net
Front Row Attack Rule	Pelvis must touch the floor while attacking from the front zone
Libero	Defensive specialist preventing the ball from touching the court
Player Rotation	Rotates clockwise; positions 1 to 6, starting with the server at back right
Attack Hit Rule	Player cannot lift bottom off the court during attack
Body Contact Rule	Must keep upper body in contact with court (except in free zone defense)
Referee Signal Lifting	Hand and forearm raised parallel to floor

Fundamental Skills and Techniques

Skill	Description
Serving	Starts each point; techniques include underhand, overhead, topspin, and jump serves.
Passing	First touch to control the ball and direct it to the setter using forearms or fingers.
Setting	Second touch using finger pads in diamond shape to set the ball for attack.
Hitting/ Spiking	Third touch aimed at scoring; requires timing and body balance Blocking.
Blocking	It is a defensive skill to stop spikes using one, two, or three players by raising hands over the net.

Viva-Voce

Q.1 What is the origin of Sitting Volleyball?
Ans Sitting Volleyball originated in Germany as a mix of Sitzball and volleyball.

Q.2 Who adapted Sitting Volleyball for disabled athletes?
Ans William G. Morgan adapted it for athletes with disabilities.

Q.3 In which Paralympic Games was Sitting Volleyball first demonstrated?
Ans Sitting Volleyball was first demonstrated at the 1976 Toronto Paralympic Games.

Q.4 When did Sitting Volleyball become an official medal sport?
Ans Sitting Volleyball became an official medal event in the 1980 Arnhem Paralympics.

Q.5 How many players are on each Sitting Volleyball team on court?
Ans Each team or Sitting Volleyball has 6 players on the court.

Q.6 What is the size of a Sitting Volleyball court?
Ans The size of Sitting Volleyball court is 10 meters by 6 meters.

Q.7 What is the main condition for player contact with the ground during play?
Ans At least one buttock must remain in contact with the floor.

Q.8 What is the role of the Libero in Sitting Volleyball?
Ans The Libero is a defensive specialist preventing the ball from touching the court.

Q.9 What is the maximum number of touches allowed before the ball crosses the net?
Ans Before the ball crosses the net team is allowed a maximum of 3 touches.

Q.10 What is meant by a "Fault" in Sitting Volleyball?
Ans A fault in Sitting Volleyball is any foul or error resulting in the loss of a rally.

Q.11 What does the referee's lifting signal indicate?
Ans It indicates that a player has lifted off the court illegally during play.

Q.12 What is the required winning margin in a set?
Ans The required winning margin in a set is that a team must win by at least 2 points.

Q.13 What does the skill of "Setting" involve?
Ans Setting involves using finger pads to launch the ball for a teammate's attack.

Q.14 What is an "Ace" in Sitting Volleyball terminology?
Ans An Ace is a serve that lands in the opponent's court untouched.

Q.15 What is the purpose of the Antennae on the net?
Ans The antennae mark the legal crossing space above the net for the ball.

Wheelchair Basketball

History

Wheelchair basketball originated after World War II, in 1946, as a rehabilitation activity for injured soldiers in the United States. It was introduced to help wounded soldiers recover both physically and emotionally. The sport quickly gained popularity and spread internationally and becoming a structured competitive game for people with physical disabilities.

Wheelchair Basketball in the Olympics (Paralympics)

Wheelchair basketball is not a part of the Olympic Games but it is a major event in the Paralympic Games. It was first introduced at the 1960 Rome Paralympics for men and later included for women in 1968. Today, it is one of the most watched and competitive sports in the Paralympics, with teams from all over the world competing at elite levels.

Court and Basket Specifications

Specification	Measurement
Court Dimensions	28×15 meters
Height of Lower Edge of Board	2.90 meters from floor
Basket Height	10 feet / 3.05 meters
Diameter of basket Ring	45 cm
Length of Net	60 cm
Radius of Centre Circle	1.80 metres

Court Structure and Markings

Team Bench Area Designated zone near the sideline for substitutes and coaches.

Team Bench Seating area provided for team members who are not currently playing.

Scorer's Table Positioned centrally courtside, used for timekeeping and score keeping.

Sideline The boundary line running the length of the court.

Centre Circle Radius Used for jump balls and starting play, typically 1.80 meters in radius.

Court Dimensions Standard 28m (length) ~ 15m (width).

Spacing Standards 2 meters clearance behind baselines and line width of 5 centimeters defining all court margins.

Ball Specifications

Specification	Measurement
Weight of Ball	600 to 650 grams
Circumference of Ball	75 to 78 cm

Players, Timing and Officials

Specification	Details
Players on Court (per team)	5
Total Team Size	12 (5 on court + 7 substitutes)
Playing Time	4 quarters of 10 minutes
Number of Officials	5 (Referee, Umpire, Scorer, Timekeeper, 24-second operator)

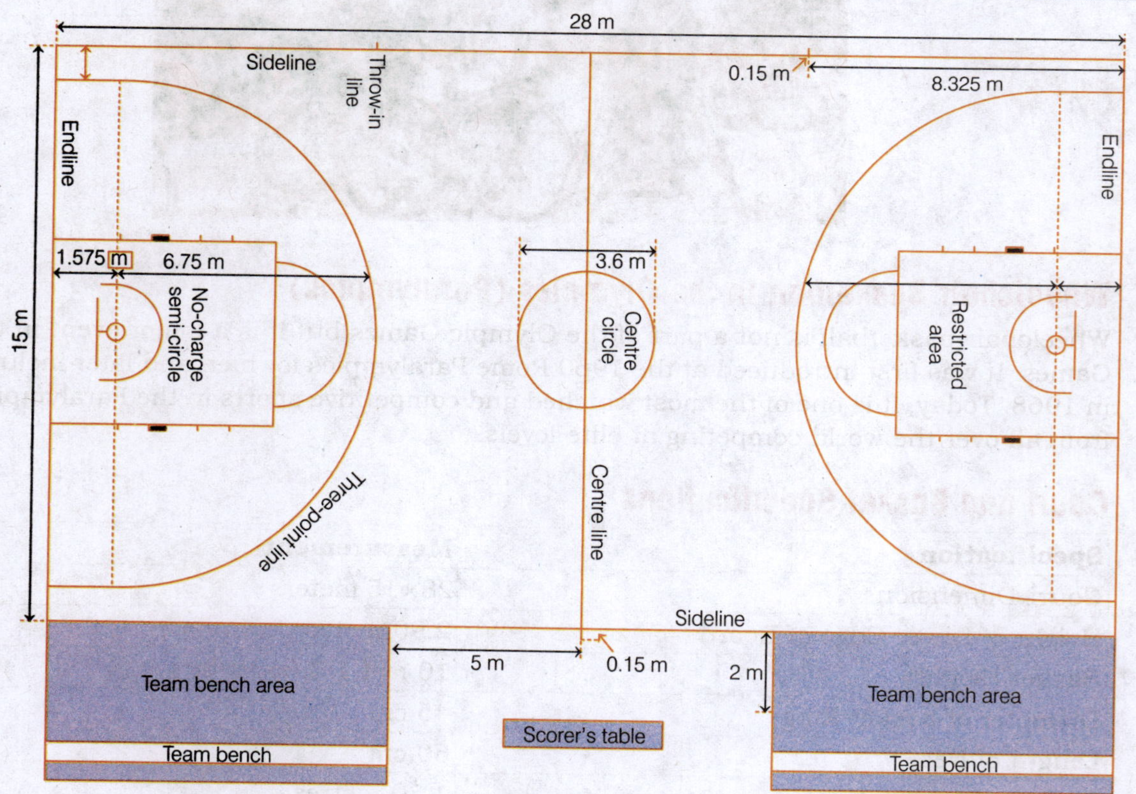

Wheelchair Basketball Playing Court

Terminologies Used in Wheelchair Basketball

Term	Meaning
Backdoor	Offensive move away from overplaying defender towards the basket.
Backpick	Pick on a transitioning defender to gain numerical advantage.
Banana Cut	Using in a curved path when moving into picking position.
Crossing	Moving side-to-side to create space during transitions.
Hand Position	Thumb pads on tires, making a D-shape motion like train wheels.
Help Position	Defensive position in the middle of the free throw lane.
Hi-Lo / Lo-Hi Pick	Vertical pick (parallel to sideline).
Integrated	Disabled and non-disabled players participating together.
Lifting	Illegally raising buttocks off the seat during play.
Travelling	More than two pushes without dribbling; turning allowed after two pushes.
Triple Switch	Defensive move to maintain low post and point position.
Turning	Types : 90° (corner), 180° (reverse), 360° (full circle), 45° (half - corner)
Volume of Movement	Range where an athlete can catch, pass, and shoot effectively.
Yo-Yo	Tandem defensive movement to block offensive post advantage.

Basic Game Rules

Rule	Description
Start of Play	Game begins with a jump ball (toss-up), players cannot push or hit opponents during the jump ball.
Dribbling / Traveling	Must pass or bounce after every two touches on the wheelchair to avoid travel.
Double Dribble	It is a violation in wheelchair basketball; players are allowed to stop, place the ball on their lap and then begin dribbling again stopping.
Player Classification	Players are rated from 1.0 to 4.5 based on their functional ability to ensure fair team composition.
Shot Clock	A team has have 24 seconds to attempt a shot after gaining possession of the ball.
Foul limit	5 fouls per player; the player must be replaced after reaching the limit.
Travel Violation	Occurs if a player pushes more than twice without dribbling.
Personal Foul	Illegal personal contact with an opponent.
3-Second Rule	Offensive players cannot stay in the free-throw lane for more than 3 consecutive seconds.

Equipment Related Rules

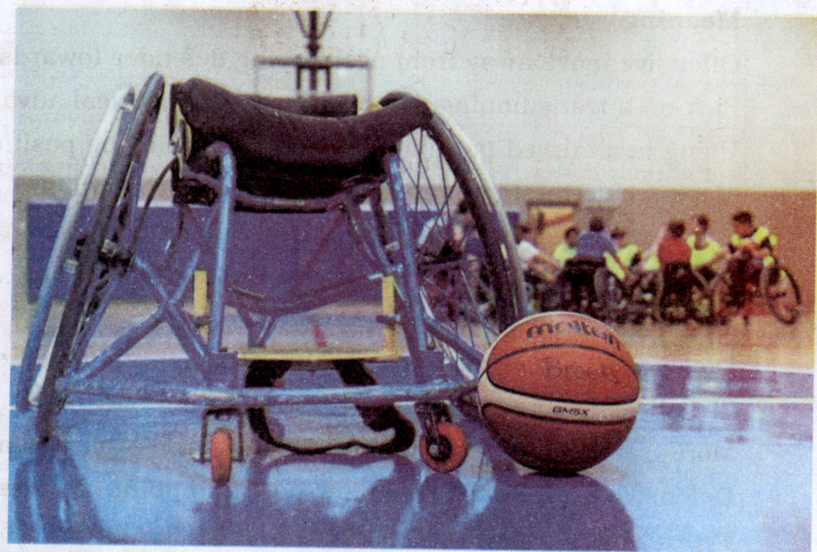

- Wheelchairs must have 3 to 4 wheels, with the rear 2 being large.
- Rear tyre diameter must not exceed 66 cm and must include hand support.
- Maximum seat height (accent): 63 cm (≈ 24.8 inches) from the floor.
- Cushion height limit is 10 cm (5 cm for players rated 3.0 or higher).
- Prohibited features: Brakes, gears, steering devices, mechanised/ motorised wheelchairs, flashing lights.
- Pivoting is allowed and, it occurs in place without directional movement.
- A protective horizontal bar must be 11 cm above the floor at its most forward point.
- The bar can be straight, angled or curved, but angles formed by joints should not be more than 20 degrees.
- In 3-wheelchairs, the front small wheel must be centrally located within the front bar.
- An optional second castor can be added to the front wheel.
- Each wheel must have one hand rim for propulsion.

Time-Related Rules

- Offensive lane time limit is of maximum 3 seconds and player is allowed to stay in the lane while in possession only.
- If a player is attempting to exit, the count is paused.
- If a player remains in the restricted area for more than 3 seconds and then calls for the ball, it is a violation.
- If another player shoots, the trapped player can still rebound legally.

Viva-Voce

Q.1 When and where did wheelchair basketball originate?

Ans Wheelchair basketball originated in 1946 in the United States as rehabilitation for injured soldiers.

Q.2 Is wheelchair basketball a part of the Olympics?

Ans No, it is not a part of the Olympics however, it is a part of the Paralympic Games.

Q.3 In which year was wheelchair basketball introduced in the Paralympics for men?

Ans In 1960 at the Rome Paralympics wheelchair basketball was introduced.

Q.4 What are the dimensions of a standard wheelchair basketball court?

Ans The dimensions of standard wheelchair basketball court are 28 meters × 15 meters.

Q.5 What is the height of the basket in wheelchair basketball?

Ans The height of basket in wheelchair basketball is 10 feet or 3.05 meters from the floor.

Q.6 How many players are allowed on the court from one team during play?

Ans 5 players are allowed on the court from each team during play.

Q.7 What is the weight and circumference range of the basketball used?

Ans The weight of basketball is 600 to 650 grams and its circumference range is 75 to 78 cm.

Q.8 Name the five officials involved in a wheelchair basketball game.

Ans The five officials involved in a wheel chair basketball game are Referee, Umpire, Scorer, Timekeeper, 24-second operator.

Q.9 What is the purpose of the player classification system in wheelchair basketball?

Ans The purpose of the player classification system is to ensure fair competition by rating players from 1.0 to 4.5 points based on motor impairment.

Q.10 What is a Backdoor move in wheelchair basketball?

Ans Backdoor move in wheelchair basketball is an offensive move where a player cuts behind an overplaying defender towards the basket.

Q.11 What is considered a travel violation in wheelchair basketball?

Ans Travel violation is considered when a player pushes their wheelchair more than twice without dribbling the ball.

Q.12 Is double dribble a violation in wheelchair basketball?

Ans No, it is allowed to dribble again after picking up the ball.

Q.13 What is the role of the protective horizontal bar on the wheelchair?

Ans The bar must be 11 cm from the floor and ensures safety during contact.

Q.14 Define the 3-second rule in wheelchair basketball.

Ans 3 second rule is a rule in which offensive players cannot remain in the free-throw lane for more than 3 seconds while in possession of the ball.

Q.15 What is the standard playing time in wheelchair basketball?

Ans The standard playing time in wheelchair basketball is 4 quarters of 10 minutes each.

Game 4

Unified Badminton

History

Unified Sports are an integral part of Special Olympics Unified Champion Schools, which was founded in 2008 and funded by the US Department of Education. The Special Olympics Movement was founded in the USA in 1968 by Late Eunice Kennedy Shriver, sister of President John F. Kennedy. She believed that the Olympic ideals of sports could give confidence and new hope to people with intellectual (learning) disabilities as well as to those who cared for them. In 1989, Unified Sports were adopted by Special Olympics International.

Since 1995, badminton has been a part of the Special Olympics World Games. In badminton, reaction time, muscle strength and endurance are the most important factors. The goal is to hit the shuttlecock over the net in such a way that the opponed cannot return it.

Special Olympics Badminton includes the following events

- Singles
- Target Serve
- Unified Sports Doubles
- Unified Sports Mixed Doubles
- Doubles
- Mixed Doubles
- Individual Skills Competition

Special Olympics also has meaningful competitions for athletes with lower abilities levels. These competitions include events such as Return Volley and Return Serve.

Unified Badminton

Court Measurements and Equipment

- The badminton court is rectangular, measuring 13.40 × 6.10 metres (and 5.18 metres wide for singles) with 4 cm wide white or yellow boundary lines.
- For international competitions, the ceiling height must be at least 12 metres.
- A minimum clearance of 2 metres should be maintained around the court.
- The posts are 1.55 metre high from the court surface and are placed on the doubles sidelines.
- The net is dark in colour and measures 1.524 meters in height at the centre.
- The net depth is 76 cm and its width is at least 6.10 metres.
- The shuttle cock consists of 16 feathers and weighs between 4.74 and 5.50 grams.
- The racket must not exceed a total length of 680 mm and a total width of 230 mm.

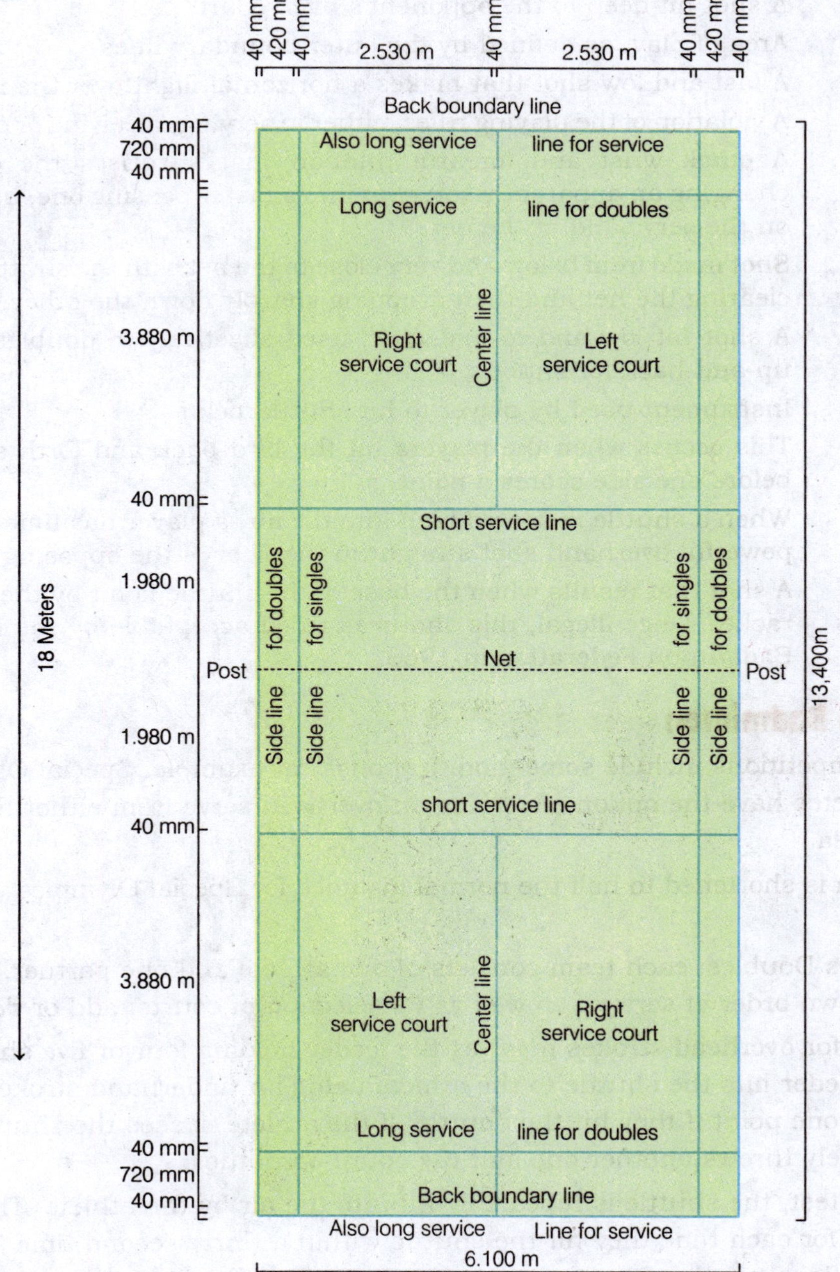

Badminton Court

Terminology

Alley	Side-extension of the court by 1½ feet on both sides that is used for doubles play.
Back Alley	Area between the back boundary line and the long service line for doubles.
Baseline	Back boundary line at each end of the court that runs parallel to the net.
Bird or Birdie	Another name for the shuttlecock.
Carry	An illegal tactic, also called a sling or throw, in which the shuttle is caught and held on the racket and then slung during the execution of a stroke.
Center Line	Line perpendicular to the net that separates the left and right service courts.
Clear	A shot hit deep to the opponent's back court.
Court	Area of play, as defined by the outer boundary lines.
Drive	A fast and low shot that makes a horizontal flight over the net.
Fault	A violation of the playing rules, either in serving, receiving or during play.
Flick	A quick wrist and forearm rotation that surprises the opponent by changing an apparently soft shot into a faster passing one, used primarily on the serve and at the net.
Hairpin Net Shot	Shot made from below and very close to the net with the shuttle rising, just clearing the net and then dropping sharply down the other side.
Halfcourt Shot	A shot hit low and to midcourt, used effectively in doubles against the up-and-back formation.
Racket	Instrument used by player to hit shuttlecock.
Rally	This occurs when the players hit the bird back and forth several times before one side scores a point.
Smash	When a shuttle is floated high into the air, a player has time to unleash a powerful overhand shot straight to the floor of the opposing court
Wood Shot	A shot that results when the base of the shuttle is hit by the frame of the racket. Once illegal, this shot was ruled acceptable by the International Badminton Federation in 1963.

Rules of Unified Badminton

- The rules of competitions include some modifications. For example, Special Olympics wheelchair athletes have the option of serving an overhead serve from either the left or right serving area.
- The serving area is shortened to half the normal distance for Special Olympics wheelchair athletes.
- In Unified Sports Doubles, each team consists of one athlete and one partner. Each team determines its own order of service, as well as its selection of courts, add or deuce.
- Racket Feeding for overhead strokes involves the feeder holding four or five shuttles at one time. The feeder hits the shuttle to the athlete using an underhand stroke. The athlete receives one point if they hit the shuttle. If the athlete misses the shuttle, the feeder immediately throws another one and the count continues.
- In the 'Ups' Contest, the shuttle is repeatedly hit into the air by the athlete. The athlete receives a point for each time they hit the shuttle within a thirty-second time frame. If the shuttle hits the floor, another shuttle is given and the count continues.

- The forehand stroke requires a Special Olympics athlete to stand two feet from the net with the feeder, who is positioned on the opposite side of the net. The feeder uses an underhand serve to hit a shuttle to the forehand side of the athlete. The athlete has five tries to hit the shuttle and receives one point for each successful forehand stroke.
- Where Return Volleys are concerned, athletes are also given ten tries to return the shuttle. A feeder, from the opponent's mid-court, hits the shuttle into the athlete's court.
- The athlete then attempts to send the shuttle back into their opponent's single court. Athletes are awarded one point for every successful hit into their opponent's single court.
- During the Return Serve, athletes are given ten attempts to return a served shuttle. A feeder, from the athlete's opponent's service area, serves a shuttle into the athlete's court, five serves from each side of the court. The athlete attempts to return the serve. Athletes are awarded one point for each successfully returned serve.
- The final score is determined by adding all of the scores together for each of the six individual skills competitions.

Equipments Required

Racket

The racket shall be a frame not exceeding 680 mm in overall length and 230 mm in overall width. The handle is the part of the racket intended to be gripped by a player. The stringed area is the part of the racket with which it is intended that a player hits the shuttle. The stringed area shall be flat and consists of a pattern of crossed strings either alternately interlaced or bonded where they cross. It shall not exceed 280 mm in overall length and 220 mm in overall width. The width of the extended stringed area should not exceed 35 mm. The overall length of the stringed area should not exceed 330 mm. The head bounds the stringed area.

- The shaft connects the handle to the head.
- The throat (if present) connects the shaft to the head.

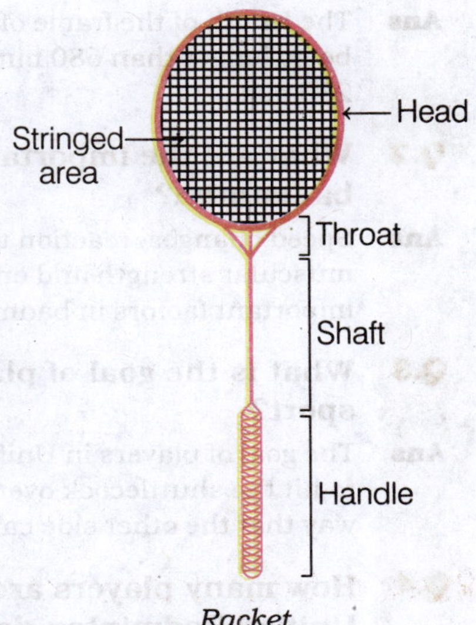

Racket

Shuttle

The shuttle shall be made of natural and/or synthetic materials. Regardless of the material, the flight characteristics generally shall be similar to those of a natural feathered shuttlecock which features with a cork base covered by a thin layer of leather.

Feathered Shuttle

The shuttle shall have 16 feathers fixed in the base. The feathers shall have a uniform length between 62 mm to 70 mm when measured from the tip to the top of the base. The tips of the feathers shall lie on a circle with a diameter from 58 mm to 68 mm. The feathers shall be fastened firmly with thread or other suitable material. The base shall be 25 mm to 28 mm in diameter and rounded on the bottom. The shuttle shall weight from 4.74 to 5.50 grams.

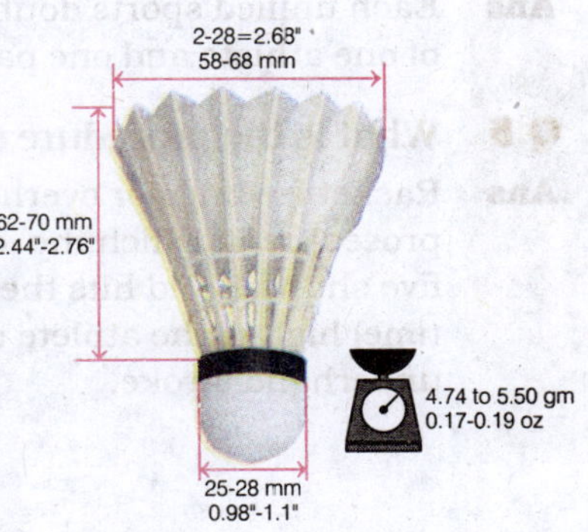

Shuttlecock Weight and Dimensions

Non-Feathered Shuttle

The skirt, or simulation of feathers is made of synthetic materials, instead of natural feathers. Measurements and weight shall be same as feathered shuttle. However, because of the difference in the specific gravity and other properties of synthetic materials in comparison with feathers, a variation of upto 10 per cent shall be acceptable.

Non-Feathered Shuttle

Viva-Voce

Q.1 What is the length and width of a racket?

Ans The length of the frame of a racket should be no longer than 680 mm or wider than 230 mm.

Q.2 What are the important factors in badminton?

Ans Speed changes, reaction time demands, muscular strength and endurance are the important factors in badminton.

Q.3 What is the goal of players in this sport?

Ans The goal of players in Unified Badminton is to hit the shuttlecock over the net in such a way that the other side cannot hit it back.

Q.4 How many players are there in a Unified Badminton double team?

Ans Each unified sports double team consists of one athlete and one partner.

Q.5 What is the procedure of racket feeding?

Ans Racket feeding (for overhead strokes) is a procedure in which the feeder (coach) holds five shuttles and hits the shuttle (one at a time) high to the athlete using an underhand stroke.

Q.6 How is final score determined?

Ans Final score is determined by adding all the scores together for each of the six individual skills competition.

Q.7 What is flick?

Ans Flick is a quick wrist and forearm rotation that surprises an opponent by changing an apparently soft shot into a faster passing one, used primarily on the serve and at the net.

Q.8 In which year did wood shot become acceptable?

Ans Wood shot was ruled acceptable by the International Badminton Federation in 1963.

Q.9 What values does Unified Badminton promote?

Ans Unified Badminton promotes equality, inclusion and sportsmanship in a competitive setting.

Q.10 What promotes Unified Badminton?

Ans Unified Badminton is promoted by special Olympics as part of their Unified sports program.

Game 5

Unified Basketball

History

The Special Olympic Movement was founded in the USA in 1968 by Late Eunice Kennedy Shriver. She strongly believed that the ideals of the Olympics could inspire people with intellectual (learning) disabilities by building their confidence and offering them new hope. To test this belief, she organized a summer day camp to help such individuals discover their abilities in sports.

Entry into Olympics

This initiative led to the organisation of the first Special Olympics Summer Games in Chicago. Nearly 1,000 athletes from the United States and Canada participated in events such as track and field, swimming and floor hockey. This landmark event laid the foundation for the global Special Olympics movement that continues to empower individuals with intellectual disabilities through sports.

Measurement and Specification of Basketball Court

Specification	Details
Court Dimensions	28m × 15m
Boundary Line Width	5 cm
Backboard Thickness	3 cm

Official Events (Individual & Unified)

Event Type	Details
Full Court Competition	5-on-5
Half Court Competition	3-on-3
Unified Full Court Competition	5-on-5 (3 athletes + 2 partners)
Individual & Unified Skills	Dribbling, passing and shooting

Full Court Competition (5-on-5)

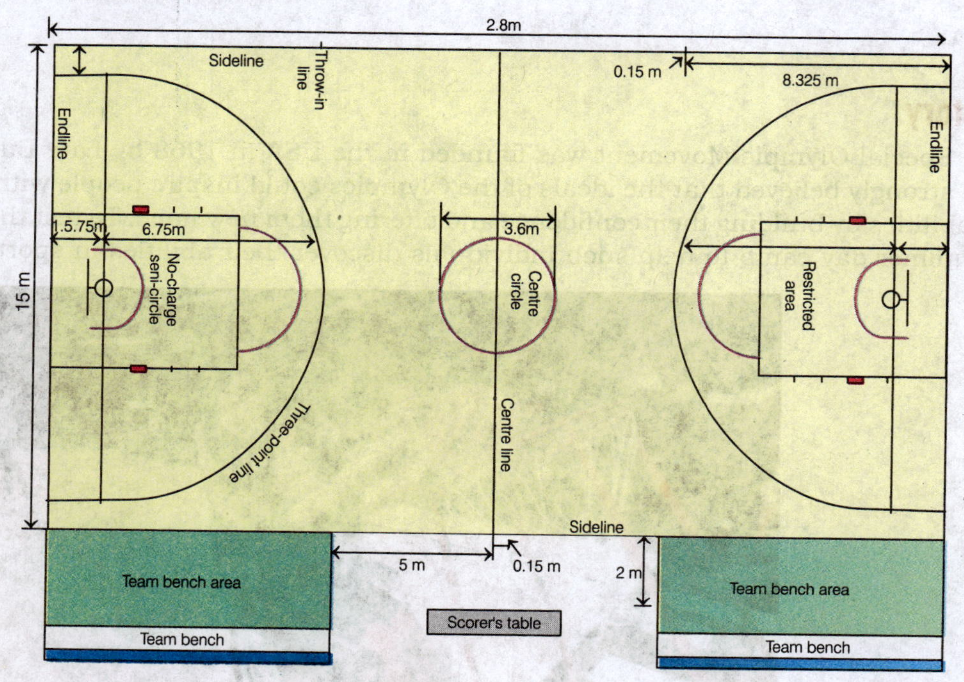

Specification	Details
On-Court Players	5 (3 athletes + 2 partners)
Total Team Size	Max 10, Min 9 (5 athletes + 4 partners)
Game Duration	Two halves of 20 minutes each

Half Court Competition (3-on-3)

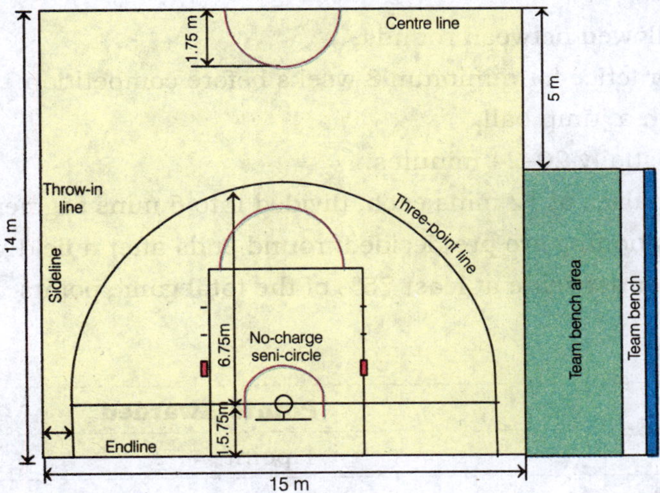

Specification	Details
On-Court Players	3 (2 athletes + 1 partner)
Total Team Size	5 players (3 athletes + 2 partners)
Game Duration	20 minutes or until a team scores 20 points

Unified Basketball Court Dimensions

- Full Court (5-on-5): 28 m × 15 m
- Half Court (3-on-3): 15 m × 14 m
- Includes: Centre Line, End Line, Throw-in Line, No-charge Semi-circle
- Team Bench Area: Located along the sideline for substitutes and coaches

Key Terminologies Related to Unified Basketball

Term	Meaning
Bounce Pass	A pass that hits the floor before reaching the teammate
Coach	Prepares strategy and guides the team
Dead Ball	The ball becomes inactive during fouls or when it goes out of bounds
Double Dribble	Dribbling with both hands or restarting dribble after stopping
Field Goal	A basket scored during play (2 or 3 points)
Perimeter Players	Players positioned outside the key area
Post Players	Players near the basket, often facing away from it
Rebound	Gaining possession after a missed shot
Time Outs	Two 60-second and one 30-second timeout per team; additional for injury as needed

General Rules

1. Each team can have a maximum of 22 members, including athletes, partners, and coaches.

2. On the court, there are always 3 students athletes and 2 student partners playing at all times.
3. Substitutions allowed between rounds.
4. Teams should practice for minimum 8 weeks before competition.
5. Game starts with a jump ball.
6. Match length: Usually 20–24 minutes.
   For 24 mins: 2 halves of 12 mins each, divided into 6 mins segments.
7. Passing and positioning are pre-decided; round ends after a field goal attempt.
8. Unified athletes must score at least 75% of the total game points.

Scoring Pattern

Action	Points Awarded
Correct Pass /Catch	1 point
Successful Field Goal	2 points

Shooting/Spot Shot (Individual Event)

1. This is an individual basketball skill-based event.
2. Each player attempts a total of 12 field goals.
3. Shooting Positions:
   - There are 6 marked spots (1 to 6) on both sides of the free-throw lane.
   - Each spot is 1.5 meters apart.

Shooting Sequence

1. The player takes 2 shots from each spot.
2. The shooting order is:
   - First from spots 2, 4 and 6
   - Then from spots 1, 3 and 5.

Viva-Voce

Q.1 Who founded the Special Olympic Movement and in which year?

Ans The Special Olympic Movement was founded by Eunice Kennedy Shriver in 1968.

Q.2 What was the aim of the first Special Olympics summer camp?

Ans The aim of the first Special Olympics summer camp use to help individuals with intellectual disabilities discover their abilities in sports.

Q.3 Where were the first Special Olympics Summer Games held?

Ans The first Special Olympics Summer Games were held in Soldier Field, Chicago, USA.

Q.4 How many athletes participated in the first Special Olympics Summer Games?

Ans Nearly 1,000 athletes from the USA and Canada participated in first Special Olympics Summer Games.

Q.5 What are the official dimensions of a Unified Basketball court?

Ans The official dimensions of a unified Basketball court are 28 meters × 15 meters.

Q.6 What is the thickness of the basketball backboard in Unified Basketball?

Ans The thickness of the basketball backboard in Unified Basketball is 3 cm.

Q.7 Name the two types of official Unified Basketball competitions.

Ans The two types of official Unified basketball competitions are Full Court Competition (5-on-5) and Half-Court Competition (3-on-3).

Q.8 How many players play on-court during a Full Court Unified Basketball game?

Ans During a Full-Court Unified Basketball game, 5 players (3 athletes + 2 partners) play on court.

Q.9 What is the total duration of a Full Court Unified Basketball match?

Ans Total duration of Full-Court Unified Basketball match is two halves of 20 minutes each.

Q.10 What is the total team size in a Half-Court Unified Basketball game?

Ans The total team size in a Half Court Unified Basketball is 5 players (3 athletes + 2 partners).

Q.11 What is the scoring pattern in Unified Basketball?

Ans The scoring pattern in Unified Basketball is 1 point for each correct pass or catch, and 2 points for each successful field goal.

Q.12 What is the minimum percentage of points that must be scored by Unified athletes in a game?

Ans At least 75% of the total points must be scored by unified athletes in a game.

Q.13 What are the dimensions of the Unified Basketball Half Court?

Ans The dimensions of Unified Basketball court are15 meters × 14 meters.

Q.14 How many total shots does a player attempt in the Spot Shot event?

Ans A player attempts total 12 shots (2 from each of 6 spots) in the spot shot.

Q.15 What is the shooting order in the Spot Shot individual event?

Ans The shooting order in the Spot Shot individual event is first from spots 2, 4, 6; then from spots 1, 3, 5.

Game 6

Unified Football

History

Unified Football is a version of soccer where players with and without intellectual disabilities play together on the same team and compet against other teams with similar compositions. It promotes inclusion, equality, and teamwork. This format is a part of Special Olympics Kansas, which follows National Federation of High School (NFHS) soccer rules. However, if NFHS rules conflict with unified play modifications, the Special Olympics Unified rules take precedence.

Game Format

- Team Composition: 5-a-side outdoor soccer (5 players per team).
- Teams include a mix of athletes (with intellectual disabilities) and partners (without disabilities) playing together.

Field and Equipment Specifications

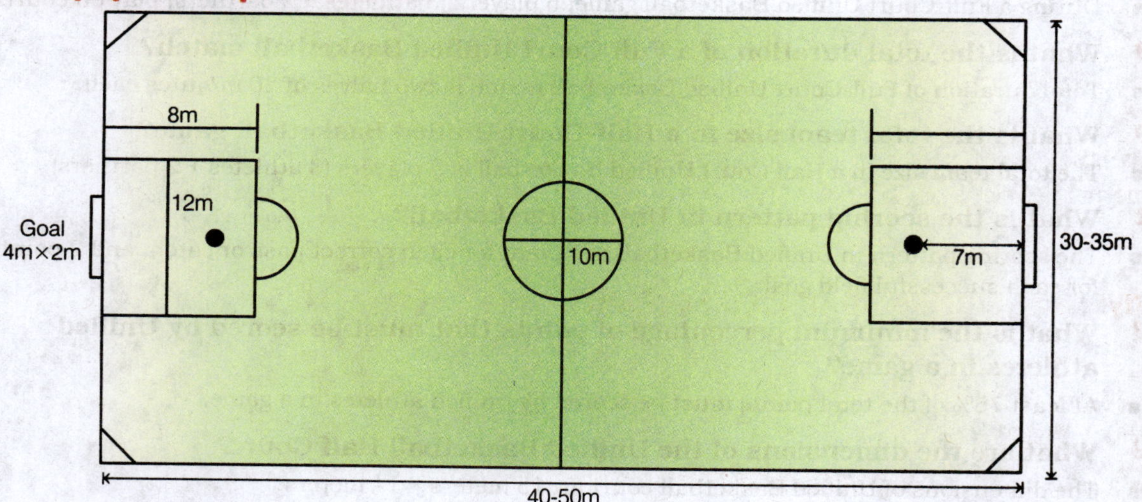

Field Measurement of the Court

Component	Specification
Field Shape	Rectangular
Maximum Field Size	50 meters × 35 meters
Minimum Field Size	40 meters × 30 meters (recommended for lower ability teams)
Goal Size	Between 4 meters × 2 meters and 3 meters × 2 meters
Goal/ Penalty Area	8 meters × 12 meters
Penalty Mark	7 meters from goal line (or 6 meters for smaller goals)
Recommended Surface	Grass
Ball Size	Circumference: 68–70 cm (27–28 inches)

Provisions of Unified Football

Heading	Description
Players and Substitutions	Each Unified Football team consists of 5 players, including 1 goalkeeper, and a minimum of 3 players are required to start or continue a match. Permissible team compositions must maintain a balance between athletes (with intellectual disabilities) and partners (without disabilities), such as 3 athletes + 2 partners, 2 athletes + 2 partners, or 2 athletes + 1 partner.
Special Provisions	At Level 3, a non-playing partner may assist a specific athlete on the field while wearing a distinct pinny, but cannot participate in active play. Players using wheelchairs or adaptive equipment may only participate in Level 3. Unified partners are also permitted to play as goalkeepers and may score goals.
Substitution Rules	Substitutions are unlimited and can be made when the ball is out of play, after a goal is scored, during time-outs, or between periods. Players may only enter the field after receiving the referee's signal, and the roster must always maintain the correct ratio of athletes and partners.
Player's Equipment in Unified Football	All players must wear proper uniforms that are distinguishable from opponents and referees, with numbered shirts for identification. Metal studs are prohibited, shin guards are compulsory, and players may not wear hats or jewellery during matches.
Duration of the Game	A standard game consists of two halves of 15 minutes each, separated by a 5-minute halftime interval. In extreme heat conditions, referees may allow a 3-minute water break midway through each half.
Overtime (only in tournaments)	If a tournament match ends in a tie, it proceeds to a 5-minute sudden-victory overtime period. If the game is still tied after this period, a penalty shootout is conducted to decide the winner.

Player's Equipment in Unified Football

- All players must wear team uniforms that are distinguishable from opponents and referees.
- Shirts must have numbered.
- Shin guards are mandatory.
- Metal studs are not allowed.
- Hats or jewellery are not permitted.

Rules of Play in Unified Football

Rule	Description
Kickoff	The kickoff starts each half and restarts play after a goal. The ball may be kicked in any direction from the centre spot, and a goal may be scored directly.
Ball In and Out of Play	The ball is out of play only when it completely crosses the sideline or end line. A sideline crossing gives a throw-in, while an end line crossing results in a goal clearance if last touched by attackers or a corner kick if last touched by defenders.

Scoring Method	A goal is awarded when the entire ball crosses the goal line between the posts and under the crossbar, with no rule violations by the scoring team.
Fouls and Misconduct	Tripping, pushing, charging, or handball are fouls. In Level 2, every handball is a re-do, while in Level 3, only advantageous handballs are repeated. Most fouls result in a direct free kick.
Free Kick	Free kicks are direct or indirect. Direct free kicks allow a goal to be scored directly, while indirect free kicks require the ball to touch another player. If within 5 meters of the goal line, the ball is moved back, and fouls in the penalty area restart with a goal clearance.
Throw-In	A throw-in is awarded when the ball crosses the sideline. It must be taken from the crossing point with both feet on the ground, the player stationary, and the ball thrown with both hands from behind and over the head.
Corner Kick	A corner kick is awarded when the defending team sends the ball over its own goal line, and it is taken from the nearest corner arc.

Viva-Voce

Q.1 What is Unified Football?

Ans Unified Football is a version of soccer where players with and without intellectual disabilities play together.

Q.2 Which organisation's rules does Unified Football follow primarily?

Ans Unified Football primarily follows the National Federation of High School (NFHS) rules, with special Olympics Unified modifications applied.

Q.3 How many players are there in each team in Unified Football?

Ans There are 5 players including 1 goalkeeper in each Unified Football team.

Q.4 What is the recommended field size for lower ability teams?

Ans The recommeded field size is 40 meters × 30 meters for lower ability teams.

Q.5 What is the size of the ball used in Unified Football?

Ans The size of ball is 68–70 cm (27–28 inches).

Q.6 What is the penalty mark distance from the goal line?

Ans 7 meters (or 6 meters for smaller goals).

Q.7 What are the permissible team compositions?

Ans Permissible team compositions are : 3 athletes + 2 partners, 2 athletes + 2 partners, or 2 athletes + 1 partner.

Q.8 What happens if the athlete-partner ratio is not maintained?

Ans If the athlete-partner ratio is not maintained the team may forfeit or the opposing team is awarded a penalty kick.

Q.9 Who may assist on the field in Level 3 and how?

Ans A non-playing partner wearing a pinny may assist on field in lavel 3 but not participate in active play.

Q.10 Can Unified partners play as goalkeepers and score?

Ans Yes, Unified partners play as goalkeeper and score.

Q.11 When can substitutions be made?

Ans Substitutions can be made when the ball is out of play, after a goal, during time-outs, or between periods.

Q.12 Name two player equipment rules.

Ans Players must wear numbered shirts and mandatory shin guards.

Q.13 What is the total duration of a Unified Football match?

Ans Total duration of Unified Football match is 2 halves of 15 minutes each with a 5-minute halftime.

Q.14 When is a corner kick awarded?

Ans A corner kick awarded when the defending team sends the ball over its own goal line. It is taken from the nearest corner arc.

Q.15 What is the condition for a goal to be awarded?

Ans The entire ball must cross the goal line between the posts and under the crossbar.

Game 7

Blind Cricket

History

Blind cricket was invented in Melbourne, Australia in 1922 by two blind factory workers who used a tin can filled with rocks as a ball. The game quickly gained popularity, leading to the establishment of the Victorian Blind Cricket Association in the same year. By 1928, the first dedicated sports ground and clubhouse for blind cricket was constructed at Kooyong, Melbourne. Thus, marking a major milestone in making the sport accessible for the visually impaired.

World Blind Cricket Council (WBCC)

The World Blind Cricket Council (WBCC) was founded in September 1996 during an international cricket meeting in New Delhi, India. The council was established with the aim of promoting and governing blind cricket globally. George Abraham from India was the founding Chairman of the WBCC. Under his leadership, the first Blind Cricket World Cup was organized in November 1998 in New Delhi, featuring participation from seven countries.

International Achievements and Championships

The first international Test match for blind cricket was played in 2000, where Pakistan defeated South Africa by 94 runs. Earlier, South Africa won the inaugural Blind Cricket World Cup (BCWC) in 1998, overcoming Pakistan in the final. Pakistan then went on to win the 2002 and 2006 BCWCs, defeating South Africa and India respectively. In 2014, India emerged victorious, defeating Pakistan in the final and securing India's first BCWC title.

Team Composition in Blind Cricket

Each team has 11 players, including:

- 4 totally blind (B1)
- 3 partially blind (B2)
- Up to 4 partially sighted (B3)

Rules of Blind Cricket

- Verbal signals are widely used both umpires and players.
- Bowlers must shout "Play!" while releasing the ball.
- Blind batsmen (B1) cannot be stumped and must be given LBW twice to be out.
- Blind fielders (B1) can take catches on one bounce.
- Bowling must be underarm, which means the arm has to be below the shoulder.
- The ball must pitch at least twice and not roll before reaching the batsman.

Runners

- B1 players must have a runner.
- B2 players may choose to have a runner.
- A batsman who has chosen a runner cannot serve as a runner for another batsman.
- A 'one-bounce' catch by a B1 fielder results in the batsman being declared out.

Sight Classification of Players

Classification	Vision Description	On Field Identification
B1	No light perception or inability to recognize a hand's shape at any distance or direction	White wristband (right wrist) or one white stripe
B2	Can recognize hand shape up to 2/60 visual acuity or visual field < 5° in better eye after correction	Red wristband or two white stripes
B3	Visual acuity from above 2/60 up to 6/60 or visual field < 20° in better eye after correction	Blue wristband or three white stripes

Equipment Used in Blind Cricket

Equipment	Specifications
Ball	Larger than standard cricket ball, filled with ball bearings to create sound for direction awareness
Stumps	Made of wood or plastic; fluorescent orange or yellow; no bails used
Bat	Standard cricket bat as per usual specifications
Pitch	22 yards long, surface made of turf or synthetic grass
Boundary	Ranges between 45 to 55 yards

Blind Cricket World Cup – Winners List

Year	Format	Host City / Country	Winner	Final Match Highlight
1998	40 over	New Delhi, India	South Africa	1st World Cup, called 'Kanishka World Cup'
2002	40 over	Chennai, India	Pakistan	Defeated South Africa
2006	40 over	Islamabad, Pakistan	Pakistan	Defeated India under Aga Shaukat Ali's captaincy
2014	40 over	Cape Town, South Africa	India	Defeated Pakistan on 7th December
2018	40 over	Sharjah, UAE	India	Defeated Pakistan on 20th January
2012	T-20	Bengaluru, India	India	Defeated Pakistan by 29 runs
2017	T-20	Bengaluru, India	India	India defeated Pakistan on 12th February
2022	T-20	Bengaluru, India	India	India defeated Bangladesh on 17th December
2024	T-20	Multan, Pakistan	Pakistan	Pakistan defeated Bangladesh on 3 December

Viva-Voce

Q.1 Where and when was blind cricket invented?

Ans The blind cricket was invented in 1922 in Melbourne, Australia.

Q.2 Who founded the World Blind Cricket Council (WBCC) and in which year?

Ans The world blind cricket council was founded by George Abraham in 1996.

Q.3 Which team won the first Blind Cricket World Cup and in which year?

Ans South Africa won the first Blind Cricket World Cup in 1998.

Q.4 How many players are there in a blind cricket team and what is the required classification ratio?

Ans Each blind cricket team has 11 players and the required classification ratio is : Minimum 4 (B1), 3 (B2), Maximum 4 (B3).

Q.5 What are the special features of the ball used in blind cricket?

Ans The ball used in blind cricket is larger than a standard cricket ball and is filled with ball bearings to produce sound.

Q.6 What special rule applies to B1 batsmen regarding LBW and stumping?

Ans B1 batsmen cannot be stumped and must be given LBW twice to be out.

Q.7 How can B1 fielders take a catch to get a batsman out?

Ans B1 fielders take a one-bounce catch to get the batsman out.

Q.8 How are B1, B2, and B3 players identified on the field?

Ans
- B1: White wristband or one white stripe
- B2: Red wristband or two white stripes
- B3: Blue wristband or three white stripes

Q.9 Name the countries that have won the Blind Cricket World Cup till 2018.

Ans South Africa, Pakistan and India have won the Blind Cricket World cup till 2018.

Game 8

Goalball

History

Goalball was originally developed in 1946 by Austrian Hans Lorenzen and German Sepp Reindle as a rehabilitative sport for veterans who lost their sight during World War II. The sport gradually evolved into a competitive game during the 1950s and 1960s. It was first introduced to the global stage as a demonstration sport at the 1972 Summer Paralympics in Heidelberg, West Germany.

Recognition and Growth

Goalball gained full recognition as a Paralympic sport at the 1976 Summer Paralympics in Toronto. The first World Goalball Championship was held in Austria in 1978. In 2011, the IBSA Goalball sub-committee aimed to become an independent international body, leading to the formation of the World Goalball Association.

Goalball Court Specifications

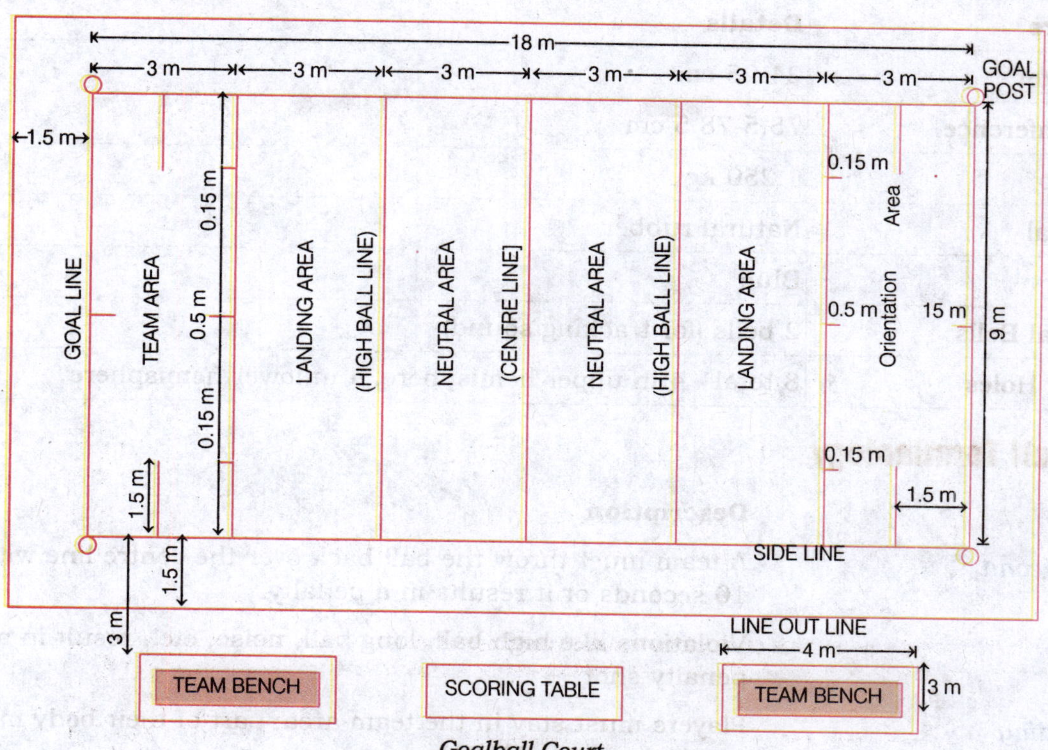

Goalball Court

Component	Details
Court Dimensions	18 meters long × 9 meters wide (standard volleyball court size)
Team Area (Each End)	9 meters wide × 3 meters long
Landing Area (Each Team)	9 meters wide × 3 meters long (beyond the team area)
Neutral Zone	9 meters wide × 6 meters long (centre two sections of the court)
Court Sections	6 sections total, each measuring 3 meters × 9 meters
Orientation Lines (Per Team Area)	2 wing lines (1.5 m) and 1 centre line (0.5 m)
Goals	9 meters wide (entire width of court) × 1.3 meters high
Tactile Markings	All essential lines are tactile (using duct tape layers for player guidance)
Tape Thickness	Two layers for player lines; one layer for referee-used lines

Goalball (Ball) Specifications

Feature	Details
Diameter	24-25 cm
Circumference	75.5-78.5 cm
Weight	1.250 kg
Material	Natural rubber
Colour	Blue
Internal Bells	2 bells (for tracking sound)
Sound Holes	8 total - 4 in upper hemisphere, 4 in lower hemisphere

Goalball Terminology

Term	Description
Ten Second	A team must throw the ball back over the centre line within 10 seconds or it results in a penalty.
Penalty	Violations like high ball, long ball, noise, etc., result in a penalty shot.
Defending	Players must stay in the team area; part of their body must touch the area while blocking.
Play	Command called by the referee to start or restart the game.
Throwing	Ball must touch the floor before the over-throw line; else, it is a high ball (penalty).
Eyeshades	Worn by all players for equal visual disadvantage. Can be adjusted only with referee's permission.
Delay of Game	Includes late arrival, wrong substitutions, or too many/few players.
Illegal Defence	Contacting the ball while no body part touches the team area
Short ball	Ball doesn't reach opponent's team area.
High Ball	Ball doesn't touch own landing zone before crossing the court.
Long Ball	Ball doesn't touch the neutral zone.
Unsportsmanlike Conduct	Includes arguing, swearing, or aggressive behavior.
Noise	Unnecessary sound by offense hindering defense from hearing the ball.

Fundamental Skills and Game Format

- Game consists of two 12-minute halves.
- 3 players per team on the court, 1–3 substitutes allowed.
- Teams roll the ball to score while the defense blocks using their bodies.
- Ball has internal bells to help players track it.
- Crowd silence is required during play.

Player Positions

Position	Role
Centre	Main defensive player, centrally positioned.
Left and Right Wings	Main offensive players, assist in defense as well.

Losing Possession

Term	Explanation
Premature Throw	Ball is thrown before play resumes.
Ball Over	Ball crosses back over centre line after a defensive block.
Pass-out	Ball goes out of bounds during a pass to a teammate.

Types of Shots

- Quick Throw: When a defender stops a shot and quickly sends the ball back before other team sets up.
- Curve Ball/Off-Speed Ball: A defender can also use special shots with varied speed or curve.

Scoring and Rules

- The ball must bounce in the player's landing zone and the neutral zone.
- 1 point is awarded for each goal.
- If the score is tied, overtime and shootout are used.
- According to the 10-second rule, defenders must return the ball within 10 seconds otherwise it results a penalty.
- During penalty shots, one player defends the full goal alone.

Game Protocols

- Referee commands: 'Quiet Please', 'Centre', 'Play'.
- Game starts with a triple whistle and the command 'Play'.
- During stoppages, no touching of eyeshades unless permitted by the referee.
- After penalties or dead balls, officials return the ball to play.
- The situation when the ball comes to rest in team area without being touched is called dead ball.
- No player can re-enter the court once off, until the end of the half.

Offense and Defense Mechanics

- Offensive players roll/bounce the ball past defenders into the goal.
- The must touch the player's landing zone and neutral zone.
- Defensive stay in team area, using their bodies to block by laying out (sliding with arms and legs extended).

Viva-Voce

Q.1 Who developed Goalball and why?

Ans Hans Lorenzen and Sepp Reindle developed Goalball in 1946 to rehabilitate visually impaired World War II veterans.

Q.2 In which year and event was Goalball first demonstrated internationally?

Ans Goalball was first demonstrated in 1972 at the Summer Paralympic in Heidelberg West Germany.

Q.3 When did Goalball become an official Paralympic sport?

Ans In 1976 Toronto Paralympics, goalball become an official Paralympic sport.

Q.4 What are the dimensions of a standard Goalball court?

Ans The dimension of standard Goalball court are 18 m × 9m.

Q.5 What is the function of tactile markings in Goalball?

Ans Tactile markings guide players by touch, helping them orient themselves on the court.

Q.6 What is the size and weight of a Goalball?

Ans The size of goalball is 24-25 cm and its weight is 1.25 kg.

Q.7 How many bells and sound holes are inside a Goalball?

Ans A Goalball has 2 bells and 8 sound holes.

Q.8 What is the 10-Second rule in Goalball?

Ans The ball must be thrown over the centre line within 10 seconds otherwise it results in a penalty.

Q.9 What is considered illegal defence?

Ans Defending without any part of the body touching the team area is considered illegal defernce.

Q.10 Name the three player positions in Goalball.

Ans Centre, Left Wing, Right Wing are three positions in Goalball.

Q.11 What are the two types of shots commonly used in Goalball?

Ans Quick throw and curve ball are two types of shots used in goalball.

Q.12 What happens if a ball doesn't reach the opponent's team area?

Ans If a ball doesn't reach opponent's team area its is called a short ball and results in a penalty.

Q.13 What is a dead ball in Goalball?

Ans When ball comes to rest in team area without being touched, it is called a dead ball.

Q.14 What happens during a penalty shot in Goalball?

Ans Penalised player defends the entire 9-meter goal alone.

Q.15 What protocol must be followed before starting or resuming play?

Ans Referee says 'Quiet Please' then 'Centre' and finally calls 'Play'.

Q.16 When and where was the first World Goalball Championship held?

Ans The first World Goalball Championship was held in 1978 in Austria.

Q.17 What is the height of a standard Goalball goal?

Ans The height of a standard Goalball goal is 1.3 metres.

Q.18 What is the total length of a Neutral Zone in a Goalball court?

Ans The Neutral Zone is 6 metres long and 9 metres wide, making its total length 6 metres.

Q.19 In goalball, if the ball stops in the team area without being touched, what is this situation called?

Ans This situation is called a dead ball.

Q.20 What is the rule regarding the re-entry of a player who has left the court?

Ans No player can re-enter the court once they are off until the end of the half.

Game 9

Floorball

History

Floorball was invented in Sweden in the late 1960s. It is most popular in countries where it has been played the longest, such as the Czech Republic, Denmark, Estonia, Finland, Latvia, Norway, Sweden, and Switzerland. It continues to gain popularity in Australia, New Zealand, India, Canada, Germany, Ireland, Japan, Singapore, Malaysia, the United States, and the United Kingdom.

Organised Development and Governance

Floorball was formally organised as an international and more structured sport in the late 1970s in Gothenburg, Sweden. The basic rules were established in 1979, when the first floorball club in the world, Sala IBK from Sala, was founded in Sweden. Official match rules were first written down in 1981. Over the time, several countries developed national associations, and the International Floorball Federation (IFF) was founded in 1986 to govern the sport internationally.

Rink and Goal Dimensions

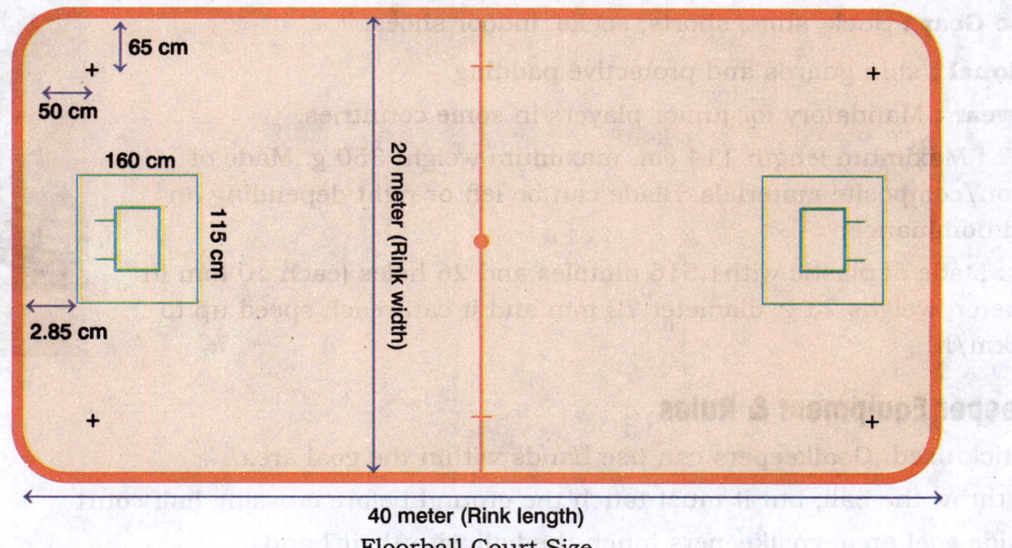

Floorball Court Size

Component	Measurement
Rink Length	36–40 m (118–131 ft)
Rink Width	18–20 m (59–66 ft)
Enclosure Height	50 cm (20 in) with rounded corners
Goal Width	160 cm (63 in)
Goal Height	115 cm (45 in)
Goal Depth	65 cm (26 in)
Distance from Boards to Goal	2.85 m (9 ft 4 in) from end boards

Face-off Dot Markings

Face-off Dot Location	Measurement
Centre Line	One face-off dot at the centre
Near Goal Lines	1.5 m (4 ft 11 in) from each side of the rink on the imaginary goal line extensions
Dot Size	Max diameter: 30 cm (12 in)
Dot Type	Can be circular dots or crosses

Equipment

- **Basic Gear :** Stick, shirt, shorts, socks, indoor shoes.

  Optional : shin guards and protective padding.
- **Eyewear :** Mandatory for junior players in some countries.
- **Stick :** Maximum length 114 cm, maximum weight 350 g. Made of carbon/composite materials. Blade can be left or right depending on hand dominance.
- **Ball :** Made of plastic with1,516 dimples and 26 holes (each 10 mm in diameter, weighs 23 g, diameter 72 mm and it can reach speed up to 200 km/h.

Goalkeeper Equipment & Rules

- No stick used. Goalkeepers can use hands within the goal area.
- May throw the ball, but it must touch the ground before crossing half court.
- Outside goal area, goalkeepers touch the ball with their hands.
- Must wear padded pants, chest protector, knee/elbow pads, jock strap, helmet.

Game Rules

- Team Composition: 6 players (5 field + 1 goalkeeper).
- Substitution: Unlimited, including entire line shifts.
- Game Duration: 3 × 20-minute periods (15 minutes for juniors) with clock stops for goals, penalties, time-outs.
- Breaks: 10–15 minutes between periods; teams switch ends.
- Timeouts: One 30-second timeout per team per match.

Major Competitions

Competition	Details
Floorball World Championship	Premier international event
Champions Cup	Top-4 ranked nations' club champions, started in 2011
Euro Floorball Cup	For clubs from 5th and lower ranked nations; annually since 1993
Asia Pacific Floorball Championship	Annual AOFC event hosted by New Zealand, Australia, Singapore or Japan
Canada Cup	Largest non-European club tournament, held in Toronto
Czech Open	World's largest club team event in Prague where more than 200 teams participates
North American Floorball League	Only semi-pro league outside Europe, US-based and not recognized by the IFF.
Special Olympics Floorball	3-on-3 with goalie, court size 20m × 12m and officially played since 2017.

Viva-Voce

Q.1 What is the country of origin of Floorball?
Ans Floorball originated in Sweden.

Q.2 In which decade was Floorball invented?
Ans Floorball was invented in 1960 s.

Q.3 Name any two countries where Floorball is most popular.
Ans Two countries where floorball is most popular are Sweden and Finland.

Q.4 When and where was the first Floorball club founded?
Ans The first floorball club was founded in Sala, Sweden in 1979.

Q.5 What is the name of the international governing body for Floorball?
Ans The international body governing for Floorball is the International Floorball Federation (IFF).

Q.6 When was the IFF founded?
Ans IFF was founded in 1986.

Q.7 What is the official length range of a Floorball rink?
Ans The official length range of a floorball rink is 36–40 meters.

Q.8 What is the height of the goal in Floorball?
Ans The height of floorball goal is 115 cm.

Q.9 What is the maximum length of a Floorball stick?
Ans The maximum length of floorball stick is114 cm.

Q.10 What is the weight of a Floorball ball?
Ans The weight of a floorball ball is 23 grams.

Q.11 How many players are on the court in a Floorball team?
Ans There are 6 players (5 field players + 1 goalkeeper) in floorball team.

Q.12 What is the duration of an official Floorball match for seniors?
Ans The duration of an official floorball match for seniors is 3 × 20-minute periods.

Q.13 Which country hosts the Canada Cup?
Ans Canada hosts Canada Cup.

Q.14 What is the court size used for Special Olympics Floorball?
Ans Court size used for Special Olympics Floorball is 20 m × 12 m.

Q.15 What is the unique feature of the Czech Open?
Ans The unique feature of Czech Open is that it is the world's largest club team tournament.

Game 10

Wheelchair Racing

History

Wheelchair racing originated after World War II as a way to rehabilitate soldiers suffering from spinal cord injuries. In 1944, Dr. Ludwig Guttmann, at the Spinal Injuries Center at Stoke Mandeville Hospital in England, began using sports as a form of therapy. Consequently, the first Stoke Mandeville Games were held in 1948, laying the foundation for competitive sports for the disabled. Wheelchair racing was soon included in these games, becoming one of the major events. In 1960, the sport became part of the first official Paralympic Games, held in Rome. Since then, wheelchair racing has become an internationally competitive sport.

International Expansion and New Federations

In 1952, the first international competition for athletes in wheelchairs was organised between Britain and the Netherlands. In 1960, the International Stoke Mandeville Wheelchair Sports Federation (ISMWSF) was formed to coordinate international competitions for individuals with spinal cord injuries. During the 1960s, sports competitions expanded to include other disability groups. In 1964, the International Sports Organisation for the Disabled (ISOD) was officially formed in Paris to provide sports opportunities for the blind, amputees, and persons with locomotor disabilities.

Equipment in Wheelchair Racing

- Wheelchair is an essential equipment for athletes in wheelchair racing and track and field events.
- Lightweight design with pneumatic tires is preferred.
- Dimensions and specifications are defined by IPC Athletics rules.

Key Equipment Specifications

Feature	Specification
Number of wheels	Minimum 2 large + 1 small
Max height (from ground to main body)	50 cm (1.6 ft)
Max. diameter of large wheels (incl. tyre)	70 cm (2.3 ft)
Max. diameter of small wheel (incl. tyre)	50 cm (1.6 ft)
Allowed hand rim	One plain, round rim per large wheel (exceptions allowed for single-arm drive)

Rules for Wheelchair Racing

1. No mechanical gears or levers are allowed for propulsion.
2. Only hand-operated mechanical steering is permitted.
3. In races of 800 m or more, the front wheel(s) must be manually turnable left and right.
4. No mirrors allowed in track or road races.
5. No part of the chair may protrude behind the vertical plane of the rear tyres.
6. Sprint distances include: 100 m, 200 m, 400 m.
7. Safety and conformity checks:
   - Wheelchairs must be inspected in the Marshalling Area.
   - No event will be delayed for adjustments.
   - Re-examinations may occur before or after the race.
   - Athlete's responsibility to ensure the chair meets all standards.
   - No part of the lower limbs should touch the ground or track during the event.
   - Officials may disqualify a chair based on safety violations.

Viva-Voce

Q.1 When and where was the Spinal Injuries Centre opened?

Ans The Spinal Injuries Centre was opened at Stoke Mandeville Hospital, Aylesbury, England 1994.

Q.2 Who introduced competitive sports for the disabled?

Ans Sir Ludwig Guttmann introduced competitive sports for disabled.

Q.3 What was the name of the first games held for paralysed athletes?

Ans The first games held for paralysed althletes was Stoke Mandeville Games.

Q.4 In which year was the first international wheelchair competition held?

Ans The first international wheelchair competition was held in 1952.

Q.5 Name the organisation formed in 1960 to govern wheelchair sports internationally.

Ans International Stoke Mandeville Wheelchair Sports Federation (ISMWSF) was formed in 1960 to govern wheelchair sport internationally.

Q.6 What is the minimum number of wheels required in a racing wheelchair?

Ans A racing wheelchair must have a minimum to two large wheels and one small wheel.

Q.7 What is the maximum height allowed from ground to the main body of the wheelchair?

Ans The maximum height allowed from ground to the main body of wheelchair is 50 cm (1.6 feet).

Q.8 Are mechanical gears allowed in wheelchair racing?

Ans No, only hand-operated mechanical steering is permitted.

Q.9 Name three sprint distances used in wheelchair racing.

Ans Three sprint distances used in wheelchair racing are 100 m, 200 m, and 400 m.

Q.10 Who is responsible for ensuring the wheelchair meets all regulations?

Ans The athlete is responsible for ensuring the wheelchair meets all regulations.

Game 11

Wheelchair Throws

Introduction

Wheelchair Throws form an important part of Paralympic Athletics, providing athletes with physical impairments an opportunity to showcase their strength, technique and balance. In these events, athletes perform their throws while seated on a specially designed throwing chair or wheelchair, allowing them to make the best use of their upper body strength and control.

The main wheelchair throwing events include Shot Put, Discus Throw, Club Throw and Javelin Throw. All these events are adapted to ensure fair competition and equal opportunities for all athletes, regardless of their physical condition.

This chapter specifically focuses on seated throwing athletes classified under F31-F34 and F51-F57, explaining their techniques, equipment and competition rules.

Equipment Needed for Wheelchair Throws

1. Throwing Chair

A specially designed chair used by seated athletes during throws. It must be securely tied down to prevent movement, as throwing involves significant force that could displace the chair.

2. Tie-downs

These include ratchet straps and metal stakes used to fasten the chair to the ground.

- A minimum of four tie-down points (one on each corner) shuld be used.
- Concrete stakes driven into the ground at an angle provide the best hold.
- Avoid aluminium stakes—they can form sharp edges after repeated use.

3. Sledge Hammer

Used to drive stakes into the ground at a 60° angle, angled away from the athlete to ensure safety and stability.

4. Alternative Setup

A portable ring made of angle irons with holes can be used to attach ratchet straps and secure the chair when staking into the ground is not possible.

Techniques and Rules for Seated Throws

1. Both legs must remain in contact seat from knees to buttocks.
2. Seated position must be maintained until throw is marked.
3. Use of leg and hip streps is encouraged.
4. Rules aim to reduce leg involvement.
5. Athlete must start from a stationary seated position.
6. Straps outside the ring must not be touched.
7. Any movement from seat before the throw is considered as foul.
8. Feet must not touch the ground.

Shot Dimensions in Wheelchair Throws

Paralympic shot puts vary in both weight and diameter, depending on the athlete's classification. These differences are designed to match the strength and physical condition of athletes in different classes. Larger diameter shots are generally preferred, especially for beginners, as they offer:

- Better grip and control
- A wider surface area to apply force
- Reduced chance of the shot rolling in the hand

Before purchasing a shot, especially for school-level competitions, athletes must ensure the size complies with school or event-specific regulations.

Below is the IPC-approved chart for different classes:

Classification	Weight	Diameter Range
Female – Classes 33, 34, 53, 54, 55, 56, 57	3 kg	85 mm – 110 mm
Male – Class 52	2 kg	85 mm – 100 mm
Male – Classes 33, 53	3 kg	85 mm – 100 mm
Male – Classes 34, 54, 55, 56, 57	4 kg	95 mm – 110 mm

These specifications are followed in national and international events for seated shot put events under wheelchair athletics.

Types of Wheelchair Throws

Club Throw

Club throw is a seated throwing event in which athletes throw a wooden or metal club as far as possible into a designated sector. It can be thrown forward, sideways, or backward.

Setup

- Thrown from a circle within a caged area or portable platform.
- Distance is measured from the first point of ground contact within the sector.

Key Techniques

Stage	Details
Start/Entry	Club held in palm or fingers, thrown forward or sideways from lap. Emphasis on tall and strong sitting posture.
Drawback	Club is swung back slowly to avoid premature release. Adhesive spray may help with grip.
Release	Club is swung and released either at the highest point or at max speed. Arm should stay straight to maximize throw length and speed.
Follow Through	After release, arm continues path. Athlete may rotate or lean forward; proper strapping is essential for support.
Safety	Ensure club is undamaged and securely weighted. Beginners should start slowly to avoid club bouncing back due to grip issues.

Shot Put (Wheelchair Athletics)

In seated shot put, athletes push the shot from the shoulder using one hand. The shot must remain in contact with or close to the neck or chin, and the hand must not drop below this level during the throw. It cannot be taken behind the line of the shoulders.

Technique of Shortput

- **Start**: Athlete sits upright. The shot is held above the head briefly, then positioned under the chin. Athletes with limited hand function may face the palm upward to prevent losing grip.
- **Grip and Support** : The non-throwing hand holds the pole, wrist turned slightly outward to assist in the forward pull.
- **Entry** : Leaning forward initiates movement, but over-leaning can limit backward extension. The elbow must remain stable to avoid imbalance.

- **Drawback** : Two styles exist—either moving straight back with square shoulders or rotating at the waist with the elbow and head leading. Choice depends on comfort and strength.
- **Release** : The non-throwing arm pulls on the pole while the throwing arm pushes explosively. The head rotates forward to ensure shot clearance. A wrist flick at the end adds force to the throw.
- **Follow-Through** : Natural body momentum causes the athlete to bend forward. Proper follow-through increases throw distance and ensures legal form.
- **Safety** : Ensure the shot is handed carefully, as athletes with limited grip may drop it unexpectedly.

Discus Throw (Wheelchair Athletics)

Athletes throw the discus as far as possible within a marked sector, using either a portable or permanent cage for safety.

Technique of Discus Throw

- **Start** : Athlete sits tall, holding the discus. If using a pole, the hand is placed at or above shoulder height to guide arm angle.
- **Entry** : The discus is moved in a circular motion while staying upright. Non-pole users may rotate at the waist; pole users bring the discus in front of the body.
- **Drawback** : The discus swings back with the palm down. Athletes lean away from the pole (if used), keeping a slight arm bend and turning the head for momentum.
- **Release** : Without a pole, the non-throwing arm swings to open the chest, generating rotation. With a pole, the non-throwing arm pulls the body upright and squares the shoulders. In both cases, the discus is released at the optimal angle with head rotation aiding separation.
- **Follow-Through** : The body finishes upright, the head continues turning, and the throwing arm ends high to complete the motion efficiently.

Javelin Throw (Wheelchair Athletics)

Athletes throw the javelin using one hand, over the shoulder. It must be held by the cord, land tip-first, and cannot be cartwheeled or spun.

Technique of Javelin Throw

- **Start** Athlete sits tall with javelin at shoulder or head height. The non-throwing hand holds the pole (shoulder height or above) with wrist turned slightly out. Elbow is kept at a 45°–90° angle from the body.
- **Entry** Some athletes move directly into the drawback to maintain the javelin's angle. Others bring the javelin forward while bending at the waist. Hand position on the pole remains steady.
- **Drawback** Javelin is brought back until the arm is fully extended. The athlete leans away from the pole, with the head typically facing forward toward the sector. Care must be taken to avoid the javelin hitting the back of the circle.
- **Release** The athlete pulls on the pole with the non-throwing arm, returning to an upright position. The javelin is then thrown with a whip-like motion, led by the elbow, followed by the forearm and a flick of the wrist.
- **Follow-Through** The arm continues along the javelin's path, ending with the thumb pointing downward. The body leans forward to maximize force, ensuring safe and complete follow-through.
- **Safety** Always carry javelins vertically when returning them, as seated athletes may not be able to move away from a horizontally held javelin.

Viva-Voce

Q.1 Name the four seated throwing events included in wheelchair athletics.

Ans The four seated throwing event in wheelchair athletics are shot put, discus throw, club throw, and javelin throw.

Q.2 Which classifications of athletes participate in seated throwing events?

Ans Athletes are classified under F31–F34 and F51–F57 participating in seated throwing events.

Q.3 What is a throwing chair used for in wheelchair athletics?

Ans It provides a stable, seated base for athletes to perform throws and must be securely tied down to prevent movement.

Q.4 What are tie-downs, and how many points of contact should they have?

Ans Tie downs are ratchet straps or stakes that secure the chair, they should have a minimum of four tie-down points.

Q.5 Why is a sledgehammer used in wheelchair throws?

Ans Sledgehammer is used to drive stakes into the ground at a safe angle for chair stability.

Q.6 What are two alternatives for securing the chair when staking is not possible?

Ans A portable ring made of angle irons or using ratchet straps through pre-drilled holes are two alternatives for securing the chair.

Q.7 Mention two key rules for seated throwing position.

Ans Legs must remain in contact with the seat from knees to buttocks, and feet must not touch the ground.

Q.8 What happens if the athlete moves from the seat before the throw is marked?

Ans If the athlete moves from seat before throw is marked, it is considered a foul and the throw is not counted.

Q.9 What is the purpose of using leg and hip strapping during throws?

Ans To reduce leg involvement and maintain stability during the throw.

Q.10 Which classification uses a 2 kg shot put, and what is its diameter range?

Ans Male – Class 52; weight 2 kg and diameter range is 85 mm – 100 mm.

Q.11 What is the club made of in club throw events?

Ans Club is made of wood or metal in club throw events.

Q.12 How is the club throw distance measured?

Ans Club throw distance is measured from the first point of ground contact within the designated sector.

Q.13 What is a critical safetyle measure when performing seated shot put?

Ans Ensuring the shot is handed carefully, especially for athletes with limited grip.

Q.14 What is the correct grip position for javelin throw in wheelchair athletics?

Ans Javelin is held by the cord with the arm at a 45°–90° angle and thrown over the shoulder.

Q.15 What is a key safety rule when carrying javelins back after a throw?

Ans Javelins must be carried vertically to prevent accidents.

Q.16 **What is the purpose of using a wider surface area to apply force for larger diameter shot puts?**

Ans A wider surface area allows for better grip and control, which is generally preferred, especially for beginners.

Q.17 **What are the dimensions for a female athlete (Classes 33, 34, 53, 54, 55, 56, 57) competing in the shot put event?**

Ans The shot put used by a female athlete in these classifications weighs 3 kg and has a diameter range of 85 mm – 110 mm.

Q.18 **What is the movement requirement for the discus in the "Entry" phase of the Discus Throw technique for non-pole users?**

Ans Non-pole users may rotate at the waist; pole users bring the discus in front of the body.

Q.19 **What is a key technique for the 'Follow Through' stage of the Club Throw?**

Ans Natural body momentum causes the athlete to bend forward. This follow-through increases throw distance and ensures a legal form.

Q.20 **What happens in a Shot Put (Wheelchair Athletics) throw if the shot drops below the shoulder level during the throw?**

Ans The shot must remain in contact with or close to the neck or chin, and the hand must not drop below the shoulder level during the throw.

Q.21 **How is distance measured in a Shot Put event?**

Ans Distance is measured from the first point of ground contact within the sector.

Q.22 **What is the specific role of the non-throwing hand during the 'Grip and Support' phase of the Shot Put technique?**

Ans The non-throwing hand holds the pole and is wrist-turned slightly outward to assist in the forward pull.

Q.23 **What is the recommended safety measure regarding javelins after they are carried back?**

Ans Javelins must be carried vertically to prevent accidents.

Q.24 **What does the 'Drawback' phase in the Javelin Throw technique involve?**

Ans The javelin is brought back until the arm is fully extended. The athlete leans away from the pole, with the head typically facing forward toward the sector.

Q.25 **What must athletes ensure about the shot before performing a shot put, especially for school-level competitions?**

Ans Athletes must ensure the size complies with school or event-specific regulations.

Yogic Practices

Yoga is an ancient and profound practice rooted in Indian philosophy. Originally a spiritual discipline, it has evolved into a way of life that promotes both physical and mental well-being. At its core, yoga means the union of the body, mind, and spirit. It connects the individual self with the universal self.

The word 'yoga' comes from the Sanskrit root 'yuj', which means to join, attach, or unite. According to the sage Patanjali, yoga is the process of steadying the mind to unite the soul (atma) with the divine (parmatma).

As stated in the Bhagavad Gita, "Through regular practice of yoga, one can overcome all challenges and eliminate weaknesses. Pain can turn into pleasure, sorrow into joy, failure into success, and illness into good health. With determination, patience, and persistence, one can move towards their highest goal."

Yoga also teaches the importance of balance—between effort and surrender, action and stillness. It helps harmonize the drive to control and lead with the wisdom to yield and accept.

Importance of Yoga

Yoga plays a vital role in enhancing overall health and well-being. Its regular practice offers a wide range of physical, mental and emotional benefits. For example

- It helps in reducing stress, promoting relaxation, and supporting mental balance and emotional stability.
- It encourages healthy lifestyle habits, improves sleep quality, and strengthens the immune system.

- Practicing yoga regularly helps relieve fatigue, back pain, neck pain, headaches, and symptoms of knee osteoarthritis.
- It also supports weight loss or maintenance by enhancing metabolism and promoting mindfulness in eating.

Asanas as Preventive Measures

Asana is a Sanskrit word meaning physical posture. It refers to the specific poses practiced in yoga, involving stretching, bending, and controlled breathing. These postures stimulate blood circulation, balance the nervous system, and support the healthy functioning of various organ systems. Asanas benefit not only the physical body but also the mind, energy centers (chakras), and emotional well-being, helping prevent and manage many lifestyle-related diseases.

Importance of Asanas

- Asanas provide exercise to every muscle in the body, stimulating both nerves and glands.
- They improve joint flexibility, reducing the risk of injury.
- Asanas ensure the smooth functioning of internal organs and body systems.
- Asanas are especially effective in preventing lifestyle diseases such as obesity, diabetes, asthma, hypertension, and back pain.

Obesity

Obesity is a condition where excess body fat accumulates to the extent that it negatively affects health. A person is considered obese when their Body Mass Index (BMI) exceeds 30. While not a disease itself, obesity increases the risk of several health problems such as diabetes, hypertension, cardiovascular diseases, osteoarthritis, and depression. This happens because excess fat disrupts the normal functioning of organs and body systems.

Asanas for Obesity

Certain yoga asanas help in preventing and managing obesity. These include Hastasana, Trikonasana, Halasana, Dhanurasana, and Ardha Matsyendrasana.

Hastasana

Procedure

- Stand with feet together, shoulders relaxed, and arms at the sides.
- Raise your arms overhead, keep arms shoulder-width apart and palms facing each other.
- Bring the arms in line with the ears and stretch upward without bending the elbows.
- Gaze at the thumbs if possible.
- Hold for a few breaths and slowly release.

Benefits

- Stretches the entire body and tones muscles.
- Improves posture and blood circulation.
- Enhances lung capacity and digestion.
- Builds focus and strengthens the spine and arms.

Contraindications

- Avoid in case of shoulder or neck injuries.
- Avoid if experiencing dizziness while looking upwards or if you have any other medical concerns.

Trikonasana (Triangle Pose)

Procedure

- Stand with feet 3 feet apart, arms extended parallel to the ground.
- Inhale and lift the right arm upward.
- Exhale and bend the torso to the left, touching the left foot with the left hand.
- Keep the right arm extended overhead, in line with the shoulder.
- Turn the head upward and hold the posture for a few seconds.
- Return to standing and repeat on the other side.

Benefits

- Strengthens legs, knees, ankles, arms, and chest.
- Stretches the spine, shoulders, hamstrings, calves, and groin.
- Improves digestion, blood circulation, and metabolism.
- Enhances focus, reduces stress, anxiety, and back pain.
- Helps in managing obesity.

Contraindications

- Avoid if suffering from migraine, diarrhea, neck, or back injury.
- People with high blood pressure should not raise the arm overhead.

Halasana (Plow Pose)

Procedure

- Lie on your back with arms by your side, palms facing down.

- Inhale and lift your legs to a 90° angle using abdominal muscles.
- Support your hips and back with your hands as you lift them off the ground.
- Sweep your legs over your head until toes touch the floor.
- Keep your back perpendicular to the floor; hold the pose and breathe steadily.
- After holding for a few seconds (or a minute), exhale and gently lower the legs.

Benefits

- Strengthens neck, shoulders, abdomen, and back muscles.
- Calms the nervous system, reduces stress and fatigue.
- Tones the legs and improves flexibility.
- Stimulates the thyroid gland and boosts immunity.
- Improves memory and digestion, reduces excess fat.

Contraindications

- Avoid if you have a neck injury, diarrhea, or high blood pressure.
- Not recommended during pregnancy or first two days of menstruation.
- Consult a doctor if you have spinal issues or chronic illness.

Dhanurasana (Bow Pose)

Procedure

- Lie on your stomach with feet hip-width apart and arms by your sides.
- Bend your knees and hold your ankles with your hands.
- Inhale, lift your chest off the ground and pull your legs upward and backward.
- Look forward and maintain the pose with steady breathing.
- Hold for 15–20 seconds; exhale and gently release the pose.

Benefits

- Strengthens back and abdominal muscles.
- Reduces stiffness in chest, neck, and shoulders.
- Tones legs and arms; improves back flexibility.
- Relieves stress and fatigue.
- Supports kidney health.

Contraindications

- Avoid if you have hernia, high/low blood pressure, back or neck pain, recent abdominal surgery, migraine, or headache.

Ardha Matsyendrasana (Half Spinal Twist Pose)

Procedure

- Sit with legs extended, feet together, spine straight.
- Bend the left leg and place the heel near the right hip (or keep it straight).
- Cross the right leg over the left knee.
- Place the left hand on the right knee and the right hand behind you.
- Twist your waist, shoulders, and neck to the right; gaze over the right shoulder.
- Keep the spine upright and breathe gently.
- Hold, then release step by step: right hand, waist, chest, neck.
- Repeat on the other side.

Benefits

- Aligns and strengthens the spine; increases spinal agility.
- Relieves lower back pain and tension.
- Improves digestion and regulates metabolism.
- Helps with sciatica and slipped disc.
- Calms the mind, aids sleep, and eases anxiety and depression.
- Strengthens shoulders, neck, and hips.

Contraindications

- Avoid during pregnancy and menstruation.
- Not recommended in case of hernia, peptic ulcers, severe spinal disorders, or recent injuries to the knees, hips, back, or shoulders.

Diabetes

Diabetes is a metabolic disorder in which the pancreas either fails to produce insulin or the body cannot effectively use the insulin it produces. Insulin is a hormone that helps glucose enter the body's cells to generate energy. When insulin is insufficient or ineffective, excess glucose remains in the bloodstream, leading to high blood sugar, which can damage internal organs.

Yoga asanas for Managing Diabetes

The following asanas help stimulate pancreatic function, improve digestion, and regulate metabolism:

- Bhujangasana (Cobra Pose)
- Pavanamuktasana (Wind Relieving Pose)
- Pascimottanasana (Seated Forward Bend)
- Mandukasana (Frog Pose)
- Salabhasana (Locust Pose)

1. Bhujangasana (Cobra Pose)

Procedure

- Lie on your stomach, feet together, forehead on the floor.

- Place palms under the shoulders, elbows close to the body.
- Inhale and lift your head, chest, and abdomen while keeping the navel on the floor.
- Straighten arms, arch back, and look up.
- Hold for a few breaths; exhale and return to rest.

Benefits

- Strengthens chest, shoulders, arms, and abdomen.
- Improves flexibility and blood circulation.
- Stimulates liver, pancreas, and kidneys, aiding in diabetes control.

Contraindications

- Avoid during pregnancy, hernia, ulcers, back pain, or heart issues.

2. Pavanamuktasana (Wind Relieving Pose)

Procedure

- Lie on your back, arms by the sides.
- Exhale and bring right knee to the chest, clasping hands around it.
- Exhale and lift head and chest, touching chin to knee.
- Hold while breathing deeply.
- Release and repeat with the left leg, then both legs together.

Benefits

- Relieves gastric and digestive issues.
- Strengthens back muscles and alleviates back pain.
- Helps in heart problems and arthritis.

Contraindications

- Avoid during pregnancy, high blood pressure, hernia, or ulcers.

3. Pascimottanasana (Seated Forward Bend Pose)

Procedure

- Sit with legs extended, spine straight.
- Inhale and raise arms, exhale and bend forward from hips, reaching toward the toes.
- Keep spine extended and focus on lengthening.
- Hold the position with deep breathing, then return to sitting.

Benefits

- Stretches hamstrings, back, and hips.
- Tones abdominal and pelvic organs.
- Aids digestion and reduces belly fat.

Contraindications

- Avoid if pregnant, or with slipped disc, ulcers, recent abdominal surgery, or severe back pain.

4. Mandukasana (Frog Pose)

Procedure

- Sit in Vajrasana (kneeling pose).
- Make fists and place them on either side of the navel.
- Exhale and bend forward, pressing fists into the abdomen.

- Hold the breath and pose briefly; return and relax.

Benefits

- Stimulates pancreas to produce insulin.
- Supports digestive and excretory health.
- Tones thighs, hips, and improves flexibility.
- Alleviates back, ankle, and knee pain.

Contraindications

- Avoid with knee, ankle, or lower back injuries.
- Not suitable for pregnant women, high BP, insomnia, or migraines.

5. Salabhasana (Locust Pose)

Procedure

- Lie on stomach, hands under thighs.
- Inhale and lift one leg; repeat with the other.
- Then, lift both legs together, keeping knees straight.
- Hold, breathe, and slowly release.

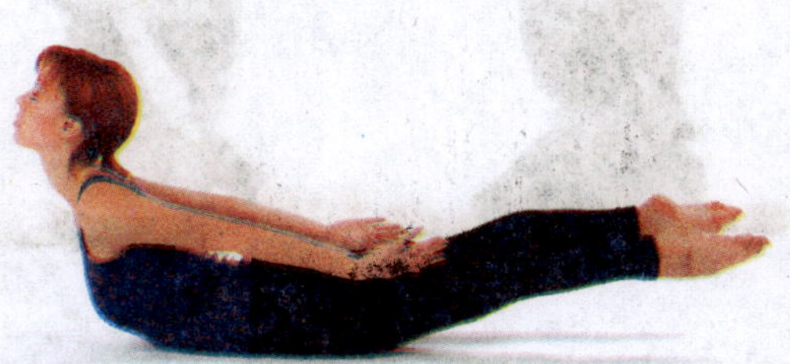

Benefits

- Strengthens back, hips, arms, and legs.
- Improves function of liver, kidneys, and abdominal organs.
- Relieves mild sciatica, slipped disc, and back pain.
- Enhances flexibility and stimulates digestion.

Contraindications

- Avoid during pregnancy, menstruation, hernia, high BP, or heart conditions.
- Not suitable for those with serious back issues.

Asthma

Asthma is a chronic condition where the airways in the lungs become inflamed and narrowed, making it difficult to breathe. It can last lifelong and may lead to breathing difficulties, wheezing, and chest tightness.

Asanas Beneficial for Asthma

The following yoga practices are known to support respiratory health and help in managing asthma symptoms

- Gomukhasana (Cow Face Pose)
- Anuloma-Viloma Pranayama
- Kapalbhati Pranayama
- Ushtrasana (Camel Pose)
- Matsyasana (Fish Pose)

1. Gomukhasana (Cow Face Pose)

Procedure

- Sit on the yoga mat with legs extended forward and back straight.
- Fold the right leg and place the right foot under the left buttock.
- Stack the left knee directly above the right.
- Raise the left arm, bend the elbow, and bring the right arm from behind the back to interlock the fingers.
- Hold the posture, breathing deeply.
- Exhale, release arms, uncross legs, and repeat on the other side.

Benefits

- Stretches ankles, hips, thighs, shoulders, and chest.
- Stimulates kidney function.
- Reduces stress and anxiety.
- Regulates blood pressure and helps in sciatica.
- Corrects posture and elongates the spine.

Contraindications

- Avoid in cases of knee, shoulder, or back injuries.

2. Anuloma-Viloma Pranayama (Alternate Nostril Breathing)

Procedure

- Sit in a meditative posture with the spine and neck straight.
- Rest hands on the knees; form a mudra with the right hand (fold index and middle finger).
- Close the right nostril with the thumb, inhale through the left.
- Close the left nostril with the ring finger, exhale through the right.
- Reverse the process and continue the cycle.

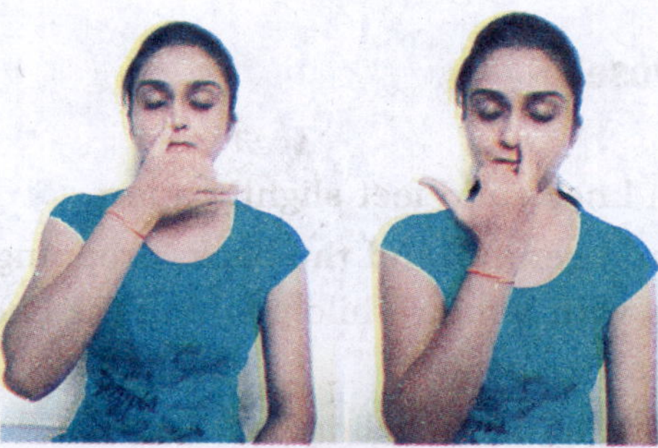

Benefits

- Reduces stress, anxiety, and depression.
- Effective in managing respiratory disorders like asthma and bronchitis.
- Improves lung capacity and oxygenation.
- Enhances focus, memory, and concentration.

Contraindications

- Should be practiced under expert guidance.
- Avoid if under acute asthma medication or unstable blood pressure.
- Beginners should not hold breath for too long.

3. Kapalbhati Pranayama

Procedure

- Sit comfortably with an erect spine and relaxed shoulders.
- Inhale deeply, and during exhalation, forcefully contract the abdominal muscles.
- Allow passive inhalation to follow.
- One round consists of 20 forceful exhalations. Do 2–3 rounds with rest.

Benefits

- Boosts lung function and respiratory health.
- Improves digestion and metabolism.
- Helps in detoxification and weight loss.
- Energizes the nervous system and brain cells.

Contraindications

- Not suitable for people with high/low BP, heart disease, hernia, ulcers, epilepsy, recent surgeries, or eye disorders like glaucoma.

4. Ushtrasana (Camel Pose)

Procedure

- Kneel on the mat with knees and feet slightly apart.
- Place hands on hips and gently bend the back, dropping the head backward.
- Slowly reach the heels with hands while pushing the chest upward.
- Hold the pose and breathe deeply.
- Inhale and slowly return to the kneeling position.

Benefits

- Improves spine flexibility and lung capacity.
- Strengthens back and shoulder muscles.
- Stimulates thyroid and thymus glands.
- Enhances digestion and posture correction.

Contraindications

- Avoid if suffering from neck pain or vertigo.
- Perform with support or trainer supervision if unsteady.

5. Matsyasana (Fish Pose)

Procedure

- Lie flat on the back with legs together and arms beside the body.
- Place hands under the hips, elbows close.
- Inhale and lift the chest and head slightly, then drop the crown of the head to the floor.
- Maintain the posture with support on elbows.

- Breathe gently, hold, and then release slowly.

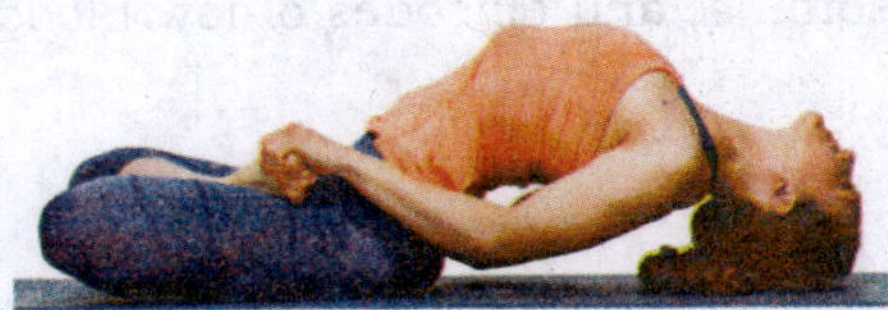

Benefits

- Opens the chest and enhances lung function.
- Relieves respiratory disorders.
- Stimulates the thyroid, parathyroid, and pituitary glands.
- Relieves tension in neck and shoulders.

Contraindications

- Avoid in cases of BP issues, migraine, insomnia, and serious neck/back injuries.

Hypertension

Hypertension is a condition in which the blood pressure in the arteries consistently remains higher than 140/90 mm/Hg.

- Systolic Pressure (140) – Pressure when the heart pumps blood.
- Diastolic Pressure (90) – Pressure when the heart relaxes and refills with blood. The normal blood pressure is considered to be 120/80 mm/Hg. High blood pressure can lead to serious health complications like heart disease, stroke, and kidney damage.

Asanas Beneficial for Hypertension

Yoga helps regulate blood pressure and reduces stress, a major contributor to hypertension. The following asanas are helpful:

- Tadasana (Mountain Pose)
- Vakrasana (Crocodile Pose)
- Makrasana
- Uttanpadasana
- Shaavasana

1. Tadasana (Mountain Pose)

Procedure

- Stand upright with feet slightly apart, distributing body weight evenly.
- Inhale and raise the arms above the head.
- Interlock fingers with palms facing upward.
- Stretch the body upward from the waist while maintaining balance.
- Lift shoulders toward ears, then roll them back and down while exhaling.
- Keep the face, eyes, and jaw relaxed.
- Hold the posture briefly, then exhale and return to normal standing position.

Benefits

- Improves posture and body alignment.
- Strengthens knees, thighs, ankles, buttocks, and abdomen.
- Makes the spine more agile.
- Enhances balance and may help in increasing height.
- Regulates the nervous, respiratory, and digestive systems.
- Reduces tension and stress.

Contraindications

- Avoid during headaches, insomnia, and episodes of low blood pressure.

2. Vakrasana (Twisted Pose)

Procedure

- Sit on the floor with legs extended forward.

- Bend the right knee and place the right foot on the outer side of the left knee.
- Inhale and lengthen the spine; exhale and twist the torso to the right.
- Place the left hand on the right knee and the right hand behind the back on the floor.
- Hold the pose for a few deep breaths.
- Release and repeat on the other side.

Benefits

- Improves spinal flexibility and tones the back muscles.
- Stretches shoulders, hips, and spine.
- Aids digestion and stimulates abdominal organs.
- Alleviates lower back pain and stiffness.

Contraindications

- Avoid deep twisting if suffering from spine or back injuries.
- Not recommended during pregnancy.

Makrasana (Crocodile Pose)

Procedure

- Lie down on the floor on your stomach with your hands folded under the head.
- Place the palms on your chin in a relaxed way and close your eyes.
- Stretch the legs as far as possible. The toes should point outwards.
- Relax the whole body. Breathe normally and slowly. Feel the whole body touching the ground and the deep relaxation in all your muscles.

Benefits

- Relaxes shoulders and spine to keep one rejuvenated.
- Treats asthma, any lung-related issues, hypertension, heart diseases and mental disorders.
- Cures slip disc, spondylitis and sciatica.
- Stretches the muscles of the hip, abdomen, chest and neck, relieving fatigue and aches in those areas.

Contraindications

- A practitioner with a recent serious neck conditions, back injury, sprains and strains, should consult a doctor before coming into this pose.
- Pregnant women should avoid practicing this asana.

Uttanpadasana (Leg Raised Pose)

Procedure

- First, come into a supine position with your back on the floor. Keep your both feet and knees together and breathe normally.
- Exhale and make a little arch from your back by raising your chin up and turn your head back until the crown of your head is touching the ground.
- Place your arms at your sides and take normal breathing.
- After that, extend (stretch) your back and take a deep breath.
- Next, lift your both legs at an angle of 50 degrees from the floor.
- After that, raise your both arms parallel to the floor and above to your torso.
- Maintain your bodyweight only the crown of your head and on your buttocks. Hold the position for few seconds.
- After that, lower down your both legs and arms along with breathing deeply.
- Rest in pose and follow the same procedure for five times.

Benefits

- Makes abdominal region stronger and strengthens hip, back and thigh muscles.
- Beneficial in arthritis pain, waist pain, and heart problems.
- Cures back pain.
- Reduces belly fats and tones your stomach muscles.
- It improves the digestive system.

Contraindications

- In case of high blood pressure, ulcer and slip disc or in any abdominal surgery strictly avoid this yoga Pose. Pregnant women avoid this Asana and don't practice this pose in days of periods. If you find any difficulties you can take the support of a wall.

Shavasana (Corpse Pose)

Procedure

- Lie flat on your back, preferably without any props or cushions. Use small pillow below your neck if absolutely required. Close your eyes.
- Keep your legs comfortable apart and let your feet and knees relax completely, toes facing to the sides.
- Place your arms alongside, yet a little spread apart from your body. Leave your palms open, facing upward.
- Taking your attention to different body parts one by one, slowly relax your entire body.
- Begin with bringing your awareness to the right foot, move on to the right knee (as you complete one leg, move your attention on to the other leg) and so on, and slowly move upwards to your head, relaxing each part of the body.
- Keep breathing slowly, gently, deeply and allow your breath to relax you more and more. The incoming breath energizes the body while the outgoing breath brings relaxation. Drop all sense of hurry or urgency or any need to attend to anything else. Just be with the body and the breath. Surrender the whole body to the floor and let go. Make sure you don't fall asleep!
- After some time, about 10-20 minutes when you feel fully relaxed, keeping your eyes closed, slowly roll onto your right side. Lie in that position for a minute or so. Then, taking the support of your right hand, gently sit up into a seated pose.
- Keep your eyes closed and take a few deep breaths in and out as you gradually become aware of your environment and the body. When you feel complete, slowly and gently open your eyes.

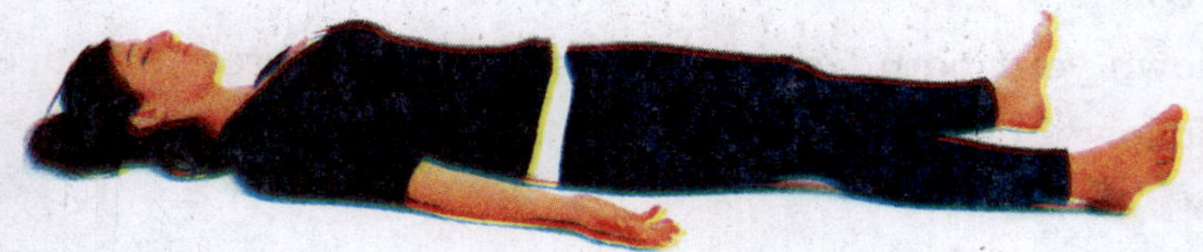

Benefits

- This posture brings a deep, meditative state of rest, which may help in the repair of tissues and cells and in releasing stress. It also gives time for the yoga workout to sink in at a deeper level.
- This posture leaves you in a state of rejuvenation.
- It helps reduce blood pressure, anxiety and insomnia.
- It boosts concentration and increases the energy levels.

Contradictions

- None (unless your doctor has advised you, for some medical reason, to avoid lying on your back).

Back Pain and Arthritis

Back pain, often caused by muscle strain or poor posture, and arthritis, an inflammatory joint condition, both lead to pain and limited mobility. Managing these conditions involves treatment and lifestyle adjustments to improve daily functioning and quality of life.

Asanas for Back Pain and Arthritis

Asanas like **Urdhwahastottiansana, Ardh-Chakrasana, Vakrasana, Bhadrasana, Nadi Shodhana Pranayama** among other asanas can prevent Back pain and Arthritis.

Urdhwahastottansana

Procedure

- Stand upright in the overhead-stretch pose with fingers interlocked.
- Breathing in, stretching the hands high, but keep the feet flat on the floor.
- Breathing out, slowly bend to the left/right. Pause for a few seconds at the limit of the bend.
- Straighten up slowly, breathing in.
- Slowly bend to the opposite side (left/right), breath out, hold for few seconds.
- Straighten up slowly, inhaling.

Benefits

- Stretches the entire body, including the shoulders, arms, and spine.
- Improves posture and balance.
- Relieves mild backache and reduces stress and anxiety.
- Regular practice of this Yogasana is helpful in overcoming back pain.

Contraindications

- This Asana should be avoided during pregnancy.
- Don't perform during headache.
- During insomnia, a yoga therapist should be consulted before practicing the yoga pose.

Ardha Chakrasana (Half Wheel Pose)

Procedure

- Stand upright with your hands clasped together in front of you.
- Lift your hands above your shoulders and rotate them upward.
- Gradually bend your upper body backward, extending your hands as far as possible.
- Hold this position for as long as is comfortable.
- To release, slowly return to a standing position with your hands by your sides.
- In a variation of Ardha Chakrasana, place your hands behind your hips before attempting the backbend.

Benefits

- Strengthens the back and abdominal muscles.
- Tones the abdominal organs, including those involved in digestion, excretion, and reproduction.
- Provides relief from back issues and improves posture.
- Opens the chest while strengthening the arms and shoulder muscles.

Contraindications

- Ardha Chakrasana should be avoided by individuals with neck, hip, or spinal injuries.
- Those with high blood pressure should refrain from practicing this pose.
- Pregnant women should avoid any poses that may strain the fetus.

Bhadrasana (Gracious Pose)

Procedure

- Sit with your legs extended in front of you.
- Bend your knees and bring the soles of your feet together, allowing your knees to drop to the sides.
- Hold your feet with your hands and bring your heels as close to your pelvis as possible.
- Inhale and lengthen your spine, sitting up tall.
- Hold the pose for a few breaths, then exhale and release.

Benefits

- Loosens joints by flexing and stretching the tendons, making the muscles of the pelvis, knees, and ankles more supple.
- Relieves tension in the spinal region.
- Provides relief from conditions like sciatica, varicose veins, and menstrual disorders.
- Helps prevent arthritis.
- Enhances posture.

Contraindications

- People with knee or groin injuries should practice with caution.
- Those with lower back problems should sit on a folded blanket for support.
- While this asana can be beneficial in preventing arthritis, those with severe arthritis should consult a yoga expert before attempting it.

Nadi Shodhana Pranayama (Alternate Nostril Breathing)

Procedure

- Sit in a comfortable meditation pose with your spine and neck straight.
- Close your eyes and rest your outer wrists on your knees.
- Using your right hand, fold your middle and index fingers toward your palm.
- Place your thumb on your right nostril and your ring finger on your left nostril.
- Close your right nostril with your thumb and inhale slowly and deeply through your left nostril.
- Release your thumb and close your left nostril with your ring finger, then exhale slowly through your right nostril.
- Inhale through your right nostril, then switch and exhale through your left nostril.
- Repeat for several breaths.

Benefits

- Balances the nervous system and calms the mind.
- Reduces stress, anxiety, and depression.
- Improves lung capacity and respiratory function.
- Enhances concentration and mental clarity.

Contraindications

- Should be practiced under the guidance of an experienced teacher.
- People with severe respiratory or heart conditions should practice with caution.
- Beginners should avoid holding their breath and practice with breaks.

Q.1 What is the meaning of the word Yoga?

Ans Yoga means union. It comes from the Sanskrit word 'yuj', which means to join or unite.

Q.2 Who defined yoga as the process of steadying the mind?

Ans Sage Patanjali defined yoga as the process of steadying the mind.

Q.3 According to the Bhagavad Gita, what can regular practice of yoga help achieve?

Ans It can help overcome challenges, turn sorrow into joy, and illness into good health.

Q.4 What is the normal range of Body Mass Index (BMI) for a healthy person?

Ans A BMI between 18.5 and 24.9 is considered normal for a healthy person.

Q.5 At what BMI is a person considered obese?

Ans A person is considered obese when BMI is above 30.

Q.6 Name any two lifestyle diseases that yoga can help prevent.

Ans Obesity and hypertension are two lifestyle diseases that yoga can help prevent.

Q.7 Which asana involves raising the arms overhead while standing straight?

Ans Hastasana involves raising the arms overhead while standing straight.

Q.8 Which asana is also called the Triangle Pose?

Ans Trikonasana is also called the Triangle Pose.

Q.9 What is the main benefit of Halasana?

Ans It improves digestion, strengthens back muscles, and reduces fat.

Q.10 Name one asana that should be avoided during pregnancy.

Ans Ardha Matsyendrasana should be avoided during pregnancy.

Q.11 What is the main precaution for people with high blood pressure while doing Trikonasana?

Ans People with hight blood pressure they should avoid raising the arm overhead.

Q.12 Which yoga pose looks like a bow and involves lifting both chest and legs?

Ans Dhanurasana looks like a bow and involves lifting both chest and legs.

Q.13 Which system of the body does yoga help to balance apart from muscular and skeletal systems?

Ans Yoga helps to balance the nervous system and digestive system.

Q.14 What is diabetes and which hormone is responsible for controlling blood sugar levels?

Ans Diabetes is a metabolic disorder and insulin hormone is responsible for controlling blood sugar levels.

Q.15 Which asana is also known as the Cobra Pose and is useful in stimulating pancreatic function?

Ans Bhujangasana is also known as the Cobra Pose and is useful in stimulating pancreatic function.

Q.16 Which yoga pose helps release gas and aids digestion, useful for diabetic patients?

Ans Pavanamuktasana helps release gas and aids digestion, useful for diabetic patients.

Q.17 What is the main benefit of Mandukasana in diabetes management?

Ans Mandukasana stimulates insulin secretion from the pancreas.

Q.18 Which asana is known as the Locust Pose?

Ans Shalabhasana is known as the Locust Pose.

Q.19 Name any two yoga practices that support respiratory health in asthma.

Ans Anuloma-Viloma, Gomukhasana support respiratory health in asthma.

Q.20 Which pranayama involves alternate nostril breathing and helps manage asthma?

Ans Anuloma-Viloma Pranayama involves alternate nostril breathing and helps manage asthma.

Q.21 Which pose is also known as the Camel Pose and helps expand the chest and lungs?

Ans Ushtrasana is also known as the Camel Pose and helps expand the chest and lungs.

Q.22 What is the function of Matsyasana (Fish Pose) in asthma management?

Ans Matsyasna Enhances lung capacity and relieves respiratory issues.

Q.23 What is hypertension and what is the normal range of blood pressure?

Ans Hypertension is high blood pressure and the normal range of blood pressure is 120/80 mm Hg.

Q.24 Name two yoga poses helpful in managing hypertension.

Ans Tadasana and Vakrasana are helpful in managing hypertension.

Q.25 Which yoga pose improves posture and reduces tension, useful in hypertension?

Ans Tadasana improves posture and reduces tension, useful in hypertension.

Q.26 Which asana involves a gentle spine twist and helps stimulate digestion in hypertensive patients?

Ans Vakrasana involves a gentle spine twist and helps stimulate digestion in hypertensive patients.

Q.27 Which asana does not have any contraindication?

Ans Shavasana does not have any contraindication.

Q.28 How does the leg raised pose help the digestive system?

Ans The leg raised pose reduces belly fat and tones your stomach muscles to improve your digestive system.

Q.29 What condition can be helped by practicing UrdhvaHastottanasana?

Ans Back pain and arthritis can be helped by practicing UrdhvaHastottanasana.

Q.30 What is one benefit of NadiShodhana Pranayama?

Ans NadiShodhana Pranayama balances the nervous system and calms the mind.

Experiment No.________ Date ________ Page No. ________

Teacher Signature________________

Experiment No.________ Date ________ Page No. ________

Teacher Signature________________

Experiment No.________ Date ________ Page No. ________

Teacher Signature________________

Experiment No.________ Date ________ Page No. ________

Teacher Signature________________

Experiment No.________ Date ________ Page No. ________

Teacher Signature ________________

Experiment No.________ Date ________ Page No. ________

Teacher Signature________________

Experiment No.________ Date ________ Page No. ________

Teacher Signature ________________

Experiment No.________ Date ________ Page No. ________

Teacher Signature________________

Experiment No.________ Date ________ Page No. ________

Teacher Signature________________

Experiment No.________ Date ________ Page No. ________

Teacher Signature ________________

Experiment No.________ Date ________ Page No. ________

Teacher Signature________________

Experiment No.________ Date ________ Page No. ________

Teacher Signature ________________

Experiment No.________ Date ________ Page No. ________

Teacher Signature________________

Experiment No.________ Date ________ Page No. ________

Teacher Signature________________

Experiment No.________ Date ________ Page No. ________

Teacher Signature________________

Experiment No.________ Date ________ Page No. ________

Teacher Signature ________________

Experiment No.________ Date ________ Page No. ________

Teacher Signature________________

Experiment No.________ Date ________ Page No. ________

Teacher Signature________________

Experiment No.________ Date ________ Page No. ________

Teacher Signature ________________

Experiment No.________ Date ________ Page No. ________

Teacher Signature________________

Experiment No.________ Date ________ Page No. ________

Teacher Signature____________________

Experiment No.________ Date ________ Page No. ________

Teacher Signature________________

Experiment No.________ Date ________ Page No. ________

Teacher Signature________________

Experiment No.________ Date ________ Page No. ________

Teacher Signature________________

Experiment No.________ Date ________ Page No. ________

Teacher Signature________________

Experiment No.________ Date ________ Page No. ________

Teacher Signature________________

Experiment No.________ Date ________ Page No. ________

Teacher Signature________________

Experiment No.________ Date ________ Page No. ________

Teacher Signature________________

Experiment No.________ Date ________ Page No. ________

Teacher Signature________________

Experiment No.________ Date ________ Page No. ________

Teacher Signature ________________

Experiment No.________ Date ________ Page No. ________

Teacher Signature ________________

Experiment No.________ Date ________ Page No. ________

Teacher Signature________________

Experiment No.________ Date ________ Page No. ________

Teacher Signature________________

Experiment No.________ Date ________ Page No. ________

Teacher Signature________________

Experiment No.________ Date ________ Page No. ________

Teacher Signature ________________

Experiment No.________ Date ________ Page No. ________

Teacher Signature________________

Experiment No.________ Date ________ Page No. ________

Teacher Signature________________

Experiment No.________ Date ________ Page No. ________

Teacher Signature________________

Experiment No.________ Date ________ Page No. ________

Teacher Signature________________

Experiment No.________ Date ________ Page No. ________

Teacher Signature________________

Experiment No.________ Date ________ Page No. ________

Teacher Signature________________

Experiment No.________ Date ________ Page No. ________

Teacher Signature________________

Experiment No.________ Date ________ Page No. ________

Teacher Signature________________

Experiment No.________ Date ________ Page No. ________

Teacher Signature________________

Experiment No.________ Date ________ Page No. ________

Teacher Signature________________

Experiment No.________ Date ________ Page No. ________

Teacher Signature ________________

Experiment No.________ Date ________ Page No. ________

Teacher Signature________________

Experiment No.________ Date ________ Page No. ________

Teacher Signature ________________